THE BOOK OF EQUANIMITY

THE BOOK OF EQUANIMITY

Illuminating Classic Zen Koans

Gerry Shishin Wick

FOREWORD BY BERNIE GLASSMAN

 Wisdom Publication • Boston

Wisdom Publications, Inc.
199 Elm Street
Somerville MA 02144 USA
www.wisdompubs.org

Library of Congress Cataloging-in-Publication Data
Wick, Gerry Shishin.
  The book of equanimity : illuminating classic Zen koans / Gerry Shishin Wick ;
foreword by Bernie Glassman.
      p. cm.
  Item consists of English translation and commentaries of Zhengjue's Tiantong Jue he
shang song gu.
  Includes bibliographical references.
  ISBN 0-86171-387-7 (pbk. : alk. paper)
  1. Zhengjue, 1091–1157. Tiantong Jue he shang song gu. 2. Koan. I. Zhengjue,
1091–1157. Tiantong Jue he shang song gu. II. Title.
  BQ9289.Z543W53 2005
  294.3'444—dc20
                                            2004028142
ISBN 0-86171-387-7

First Edition
09 08 07 06 05
5   4   3   2   1

Cover design by Rick Snizik.
Interior design by Gopa&Ted2, Inc. Set in Weiss 10.5/14 pt.

Printed in the United States of America.

dedicated to Hakuyu Taizan Maezumi
(1931–1995)

Table of Contents

Attention! Master Jizo asked Hogen, "Where have you come from?" "I pilgrimage aimlessly," replied Hogen. "What is the matter of your pilgrimage?" asked Jizo. "I don't know," replied Hogen. "Not knowing is the most intimate," remarked Jizo. At that, Hogen experienced great enlightenment.

—Case 20 of the *Book of Equanimity*

I met Gerry Wick at the Zen Center of Los Angeles in the early 1970s, during the time when I was studying with Taizan Maezumi Roshi. He had just arrived in California from London, England, where he had worked as a physicist and science editor for a magazine while studying Zen with Sochu Suzuki Roshi, a disciple of Soen Nakagawa Roshi. He had received a Ph.D. in physics from the University of California-Berkeley in the 1960s and soon began to work at the Scripps Institution of Oceanography. At ZCLA, Maezumi Roshi gave him the Buddhist name Shishin, which means "lion heart."

This was the early 1970s, and hippies were far more common than scientists at the Zen center. Shishin stood out. Eventually, Maezumi Roshi put him in charge of the administration of both the Zen Center of Los Angeles and the Kuroda Institute for the Study of Buddhism and Human Values. In 1990, Shishin Wick succeeded Maezumi Roshi in his lineage, becoming full heir to his Dharma.

I recall during that time that Shishin wrote a scientific paper on tornadoes—not those born of the meeting of warm, moist Gulf air with cold Canadian air or the dry air from the Rockies, but rather tornadoes created by cars going speedily in different directions on the Los Angeles freeways, seeding dramatic swings in wind patterns, which were, in fact, small tornadoes. You might say that at that time tornadoes were also coming out of the vortex of the Zen Center of Los Angeles, not due to freeway traffic but the traffic going back and forth across the Pacific. Japanese and American teachers and practitioners were bringing their Zen from Asia to America and back to Asia again. The impact of Japanese Zen on America is clear. Important Japanese teachers introduced the Dharma to thousands of new students in this country. And even in those days America was beginning to have some perceptible impact on Japan. American practitioners were seen by certain Japanese teachers largely as more sincere, energetic, and committed to realizing the Buddha Way than their Japanese counterparts. Americans like Shishin were invigorating the practice with fresh ideas and inquisitiveness and exploring the very essence of Buddhism. And that caused turbulence.

This American Zen master who as a Zen student once wrote so cleanly and scientifically about tornadoes on Los Angeles freeways now turns his scientific eye to what lies at the center of the twisters of our minds, the twisters of our lives. In the present book, Shishin provides an incisive Western commentary on a collection of koans, poems, and thoughts developed in China many centuries ago. Known as the *Book of Equanimity*, this twister has equanimity at its core—the equanimity that arises out of the state of not knowing, which is, as Master Jizo says in the epigraph, the most intimate.

Shishin Wick brings to this important work the depth, precision, and the true vision of the scientist who always stands ready to question everything, never satisfied with platitudes or old standards. He exemplifies the relentless clarity of the teacher challenging us to start afresh in each moment and unabashedly explore in these koans the essence of Zen—and the essence of our lives—in our own words, in the time, culture, and places where we find ourselves.

After receiving Dharma transmission, Shishin moved to Colorado where he started his own Zen center in an area known for its thunderstorms and violent weather. He is now a *roshi*, which is the highest designation a teacher can receive in our lineage. Yet even now, Roshi Shishin Wick never stops questioning, never stops learning, never stops not knowing. And with great clarity and elegance in this valuable and highly enjoyable commentary, he invites us to do the same.

Bernie Glassman

Montague, Massachusetts

Fall 2004

Acknowledgments

About ten years ago when he was a student at Zen Mountain Monastery, Josh Bartok asked me about writing a book on Zen—and I promptly put his suggestion into the "I should do that some day" file. A couple of years ago when Josh, now an editor at Wisdom Publications, made the same suggestion, I had just finished giving talks on all one hundred cases of the *Book of Equanimity*. Josh suggested they would make a good book and helped me grind away the rough edges of those talks and shape them into short commentaries. Without his efforts and persistence, this book would continue to exist only in my "I should do that some day" file.

I especially want to thank and acknowledge my teaching partner and successor, Ilia Shinko Perez. She carefully read all one hundred commentaries and offered suggestions for improvement. We had some lively dialogues about some of the cases. Due to her efforts, many of the commentaries now read better, are more incisive, and contain more of the feminine aspects of Zen. Of course, all errors and omissions within these pages are solely my responsibility.

Some of my students assisted. I particularly want to thank Paul Gyodo Agostinelli who helped me proofread all of the translations and a number of the commentaries, and John Fugetsu Rueppel who did the bulk of the transcriptions among others.

My warm appreciation to Bernie Glassman for sharing his teachings with me over many years and for writing the foreword. I also want to acknowledge Sochu Suzuki Roshi for starting me on my practice of the Zen Way, and offer my boundless thanks to my core teacher, Taizan

Maezumi Roshi. If he had not put me through the Dharma fires, I could not have written this book.

Deep bows of gratitude to all my teachers.

In Zen training, koans are used to liberate students from their rigid, restrictive ways of viewing themselves and the world around them and to open their eye of wisdom. One literary wag facetiously said that koans are stories that Zen masters use "to blow their students' minds!" *Koan* literally means "public case." In Zen, koans are usually a record of dialogues between a Zen master and his student, a section from a sutra (Buddhist scripture) or piece of Zen liturgy, or a statement by a Zen master. In the field of law, prior legal cases and decisions set precedents for how to evaluate current cases. In a somewhat analogous way, we can use koans to test our understanding against the expressions and actions of the ancient masters. When we see eye to eye with these ancient worthies the subtle meanings of the koans become revealed to us.

Formal koan study can be traced to the tenth century in China. Over the centuries the study of koans had deteriorated as a practice, becoming essentially formulaic and heavily stylized, but was revivified by Master Hakuin in eighteenth-century Japan. By Hakuin's time, traditional "answers" were recorded and even sold. Contrary to some views, there is no fixed response to each koan, and the idea of koans having "answers" as such is absurd. In fact, some teachers have even changed their interpretation to maintain freshness or to respond to the needs of a particular student. I express that view in some of my commentaries in this collection. Koans require a whole-body response. "Correct words" without the corresponding inner experience will cause the teacher to immediately ring the bell dismissing the student.

I spent over twenty years studying with Taizan Maezumi Roshi. Much of that time was devoted to examination and appreciation of about seven hundred koans during our face-to-face encounters in the private interview (*dokusan*) room. In the system of koans presented by Maezumi Roshi, we start with two hundred "miscellaneous" koans designed to bring the student to experiential realization of oneness of all things. These koans are drawn from various sources including traditional collections and more obscure sources. (For my students I have decreased the number of miscellaneous koans to one hundred.) Next we study the *Gateless Gate* which contains forty-eight koans. Then there are the hundred koans of the *Blue Cliff Record* followed by the hundred koans of the *Book of Equanimity*. In the present book I present these hundred koans of the *Book of Equanimity* with my commentaries. Next we study the fifty-three koans of *The Transmission of Light,* which detail the enlightenment experiences of the Zen Ancestors from Shakyamuni Buddha to Master Dogen. Next we appreciate the Five Ranks of Master Tozan with about fifty koans and testing points. The final collection is a series of one hundred koans based on detailed examination of the sixteen bodhisattva precepts which are transmitted during ceremonies for both laypeople and monks when they commit to the Way of the Buddha.

I cannot overestimate the importance of doing koan study with a qualified teacher. Some Zen students pride themselves on their understanding of koans, but unless they have been thoroughly examined by their teacher in the dokusan room, that understanding can remain superficial.

The hundred cases in the *Book of Equanimity* were compiled in the twelfth century by Master Wanshi Shokaku. He presented each koan and wrote a verse for each one. Wanshi was a brilliant scholar who entered a monastery at the age of eleven. Wanshi succeeded the Dharma from Tanka Shijun in the main Soto school lineage. This collection of koans is highly revered in the Soto School although they are not approached in the same way as koans are in the Rinzai School, which requires face-to-face presentation with one's teacher. In the Soto School, the koans are approached more as liturgy to be studied and discussed. A parallel koan collection, the *Blue Cliff Record,* was compiled by Setcho Juken in the eleventh century. He compiled one hundred koans and presented verses for each one. A contemporary of Wanshi's named Engo Kokugon, who is in the Rinzai lineage, wrote a preface to each of the cases in the *Blue Cliff Record* and also wrote commentaries on the main case and on Setcho's verses. Since Engo is in the Rinzai lineage, the *Blue Cliff Record* is highly esteemed in the Rinzai School, although about one-third of the koans overlap between the two collections.

Here I'd like to quote extensively from what my grandfather in the

Dharma, Hakuun Yasutani Roshi, wrote in the last century regarding the relationship of the *Blue Cliff Record* and the *Book of Equanimity*:

Master Engo, who gave the preface and commentary to each case of the *Blue Cliff Record*, and Master Wanshi were of approximately the same generation. Both men were close Dharma friends, but whether we speak of their views regarding Zen or of their teaching policies, each had his own distinctive characteristics, and each took a position from which he did not yield an inch. Right from them the special characteristics of Soto and Rinzai Zen oozed out. I think it is most desirable that Zen students become intimately familiar with both the *Blue Cliff Record* and the *Book of Equanimity*, and make the strong points of both Rinzai Zen and Soto Zen their own.

Rinzai and Soto Zen have their respective strong points and weak points, but since strong points are liable to change into weak points, by correctly learning each kind of Zen the strong points of both are taken in, and one is saved from the easily engendered shortcomings and ill effects of both. I believe this is important. To become attached to one-sided sectarian pride and for one sect to exclude the other are things with which I find it difficult to concur.

In stating, "I put *samadhi* [single-pointed meditative concentration] foremost and wisdom afterwards," Master Wanshi promoted the cultivation of samadhi power (*joriki*) through energetic sitting, but of course he also stressed seeing one's nature, attaining enlightenment, as is clear when we consider the appreciatory verses in the *Book of Equanimity*.

As a contrast to this, in stating, "I put wisdom foremost and samadhi afterwards," Master Engo settles beforehand the problem of seeing one's nature and attaining enlightenment, and follows up with the cultivation of samadhi power as his method. In such fashion the policies and emphases regarding Zen were utterly different. But it seems that their Dharma relationship was always warm-hearted. Wanshi on the eve of his death left his affairs entirely in Engo's hands, and Engo on his part responded by discharging his trust well. It is my hope that we too, having such wise men as our mirror, in utter freedom may work at guiding others, by discarding sectarian pride and leaving one-sided views, and by learning the strong points of both Soto and Rinzai. Then, each may devise his own characteristic methods of guidance without imitating anyone, in accord with the times and adapting to the country.

Almost one hundred years after Wanshi compiled the koans and the verses for the *Book of Equanimity*, Master Bansho Gyoshu added a preface to each case, as well as "capping phrases" (*jakugo*) for each line of the koan and the verse. A capping phrase is a one-line verse that comments on the line of the koan or the verse. He also wrote longer commentaries on both the case and the verse. Since Bansho lived at Equanimity Monastery at the time, the entire collection became known as the *Book of Equanimity*.

In this book I present Master Wanshi's main case (the koan) and his verse, as well as the preface by Master Bansho. These translations come primarily from Taizan Maezumi Roshi working with Dana Fraser. The commentaries in this volume are entirely mine and I take full responsibility for them. You can find Bansho's capping phrases and commentaries in the *Book of Serenity* translated by Thomas Cleary.

When I studied these koans with Maezumi Roshi we used the Japanese translations of all the Zen masters' names. There is a trend in present-day Zen books to use the proper Chinese transliterations of these names. For example Master Joshu in Japanese is called Master Zhaozhou in Chinese and Ummon (Japanese) is Yunmen (Chinese). I spent many years becoming intimately familiar with Master Joshu. Quite frankly, I do not know Zhaozhou—even though Joshu's Chinese contemporaries probably addressed him this way. Therefore I have used the Japanese romanization in this volume. I am just too stubborn and too old to learn and integrate the Chinese names. For those who expect and prefer the Chinese names, I apologize and I have provided an appendix that cross-references the Japanese names and Chinese ones. The appendix also contains the Sanskrit names of some of the earlier Buddhas, bodhisattvas, and Ancestors from India as well as reference to modern teachers mentioned in the commentaries.

ON THE STUDY OF KOANS
A koan is a public case in the sense that it is brought forward as an example of a dialogue to help us elevate our practice and understanding. The more we

can understand the content, the meaning, the purpose of that dialogue the more we can deepen our realization of our own practice. Koan study with a koan teacher is a skillful means that is unique to Zen. Like any skillful means, one should not become attached to it as a device, but use it and let it go.

In order to penetrate a koan, the student must drop away attachments to images, beliefs, and projections. As Dogen Zenji said, "To study the Buddha Way is to study the self and to study the self is to forget the self." He is talking about the small ego-grasping self that hinders our free functioning in life. In order to drop that away, we have to see the fundamental nature of our mind and our self.

The dialogue between Bodhidharma and Eka, who would become the second Zen Ancestor, illustrates the nature of mind. This koan appears as Case 41 in the *Gateless Gate*. Eka sat out in the cold waiting for instruction and one night after it had snowed, in order to show his determination he cut off his arm. At that point Bodhidharma asked him what it was he wanted. Eka said, "My mind is not at rest, please pacify it." Bodhidharma said, "Bring me your mind and I will pacify it for you." And Eka said, "After searching exhaustively, I find the mind is ungraspable." Bodhidharma said finally, "Then I have pacified it for you."

One essential point about koan study is to reflect on the dialogue and determine exactly what is being said. If you are assigned a koan to study, the first thing you should do is memorize it and think about it. Just don't imagine deep realization will immediately come to you in a flash of light. Think about the koan. What are the people in it saying? What is motivating them? What is motivating you? Which line in the koan is most important? In the example above, Master Eka says, "Mind is ungraspable." He is not saying, "I cannot grasp the mind" but that the very nature of mind is that it is ungraspable. He is not saying, "I looked exhaustively and I can't find it." What he is saying is, "I have looked exhaustively and it is unfindable." This is a crucial difference. He is not saying, "Boy, I don't think I will ever find this thing"— rather, he is saying, "I am telling you, this thing can't be found!"

So, what is the purpose of koans? Why do we study them? Our practice is to examine the very nature of the ignorance that causes us to grab onto the self—not only the self as we perceive it but also the self in relation to everything else.

There is a notion among Zen students that they should not use their reasoning faculties when practicing meditation. That is true when you are focusing on the breath or "just sitting" (a practice called *shikantaza*). When I first started doing koan study I imagined, "When I sit, I shouldn't be thinking." I am telling you from my experience if you don't think about your koans, whether you are sitting or not sitting, you are not going to penetrate them. Of course, thinking alone will not reveal a koan's subtle meaning. You need to empty your mind of thoughts in order to do that, but thinking will help you set the proper course. I believe thinking in meditative disciplines has been given a bum rap. But be very clear: I am not referring to egocentric or self-grasping thinking—that kind of thinking will *not* help you.

With each koan, you have to know what the problem is you are trying to solve. If you don't know what the problem is, you don't know what target you are shooting at. So what are you aiming at? What's your purpose? What's your goal? Ultimately the goal of Zen is "no goal"—but you have to have a goal first in order to realize no-goal. And in koan study, the goal is to penetrate each koan as thoroughly as possible.

Even though the function of the brain is to think, there are moments when you *don't* think, or at least you are unaware of your thinking. My favorite example is downhill skiers. They go eighty–ninety miles per hour down a slope of snow with these two little pieces of wood or plastic on their feet. What happens if they think, "I am supposed to lift my right leg and bend my ankle this way and lean into the hill"? By the time they think it, they will be rolling down the hill! How about a gymnast or platform-diver? If they are thinking during their maneuvers, they will make a mistake and possibly even come to great harm! In Zen practice as in these other disciplines, you just have to train and train and train so that you are not thinking at certain times. You can be aware without thinking and without being self-conscious. Beyond the realm of thought, I am fascinated by how one comes to a realization of the meaning of a koan and how one integrates it or embodies it.

In trying to solve problems of physics, Albert Einstein didn't just always think about the problem at hand. He would feel bodily sensations and would move these sensory patterns around with his body and see how they fit together. And once he saw some patterns that fell into place, he would test them. He would try and devise mathematical equations that explained these patterns.

Another scientist named August Kekule discovered the structure of benzene, one of the most important structures in organic chemistry, through a dream. The structure is in the form of a ring, a circle of six carbon atoms. This organic structure had puzzled scientists for a long time. Kekule wrote, "I turned my chair to the fire [after having worked on the problem for some time] and dozed. Again the atoms were gamboling before my eyes. This time the smaller groups kept modestly to the background. My mental eye, rendered more acute by repeated vision of this kind, could not distinguish larger structures, of manifold conformation; long rows, sometimes more closely fitted together; all twining and twisting in snakelike motion. But look! What was that? One of the snakes had seized hold of its own tail, and the form whirled mockingly before my eyes. As if by a flash of lighting I awoke.... Let us learn to dream, gentlemen."* Then he had to go back to his lab and he had to prove that the ring structure was it.

In Case 39 in this collection and in Case 7 of the *Gateless Gate*, a monk asks Joshu in all earnestness, "I have just entered the monastery, I beg you master, please give me instruction." It doesn't say a monk *"casually"* asked Joshu. "In all earnestness" is important. And Joshu asked, "Have you eaten your gruel yet?" The monk said, "Yes, I have." Then Joshu said, "Then wash the bowls." And the monk attains some realization. Now I ask you, are they talking about eating rice gruel and washing bowls? On one level they certainly are—but there is more there as well. You must open your Dharma eye to realize your Buddha mind. In every one of these koans realization of your true self is the topic on some level.

Einstein was once asked about his creativity and he touched upon the subject of patience. He said the search may take years of groping in the dark; hence the ability to hold on to a problem for a long time and not be destroyed by repeated failure is necessary for any serious researcher. The same sentiment applies aptly to koan study.

The best koans are those that come from your own life experience. The koans in this collection should not be approached as a conversation between two men or women taking place a thousand years ago. Every one of these koans, if you take it correctly, is part of your life experience right now—otherwise they are just dead pieces of literature. Make each your own experience. This is your life.

*Arthur Koestler in *The Act of Creation*

When I was working at the Scripps Institution of Oceanography, we were developing an apparatus that would allow a deep-sea diver to remain warm. We were testing it in a tank that was about forty feet deep containing deep cold ocean water that was continually circulating. I was a subject in the tests. With probes all over my body, I went to the bottom of the tank while my core body temperature, blood pressure, and other variables were measured. While I was floating near the bottom of the tank, I thought of Case 43 in the *Blue Cliff Record*, "Tozan's Hot and Cold":

> A monk in all earnestness asked Master Tozan, "How do you avoid the discomfort of hot and cold?" And Master Tozan said, "Go to that place where there is no hot and cold." And the monk said, "Where is that place?" And the Master said, "When you are hot, be hot and when you are cold, be cold."

"When you are cold, be cold." Since I was not wearing a wet suit, it was very cold. I asked myself, "What's cold?" I totally experienced the cold. With each breath my whole universe was a feeling of cold penetrating my whole body.

Most of the subjects had to leave the water after twenty minutes because their body temperature dropped too low. I sat there concentrating on the cold and after an hour they finally told me to come up. My body temperature had barely dropped. The naval officer who was running the tests said, "What were you doing down there?" I replied, "Nothing." But after that experience I didn't get cold for the longest time. I really understood "Tozan's Hot and Cold."

So when you sit and you feel that you understand the content of the koan and you have examined each line of dialogue carefully, a response pops up. Test it. Sometimes a response will pop up and you know that that's it. *Aha! That's it!* Most of the time, you have to think about it.

Consider the way Gandhi formed his political strategy in India. All of his lieutenants would express their opinions to Gandhi. He would then retire and do his meditation. While he was meditating, a strategy integrating the important information would come up. By emptying himself of thoughts, it arose.

You can take this approach to koan study and apply it to your life in general. When you have a problem, think about it. Then think about it some more. And then think about it and after you've thought all you can think about it, then just think "non-thinking." In *"Bendowa"* ("The Wholehearted Way") Master Dogen, referring to a dialogue from Yakusan Igen, wrote, "Think not-thinking. How do you think not-thinking? Non-thinking! This in itself is the essential art of zazen." When you touch the origin of thinking, this is not-thinking. Our practice is neither about thinking nor non-thinking. As Case 20 in the *Book of Equanimity* says, "Not knowing is the most intimate thing." Let go of your cherished opinions and cultivate the mind of "not-knowing" and the True Dharma will appear.

Make sure that your insight agrees with the Dharma. Dharma means the teachings of the Buddhas and the patriarchs and the Zen masters. The Dharma also is the reality of our life itself. The Dharma means the grass is green and the sky is blue. Mountains are high and valleys are low. The Dharma is the words exclaimed by the Buddha upon attaining enlightenment: "I and all sentient beings and the great earth simultaneously attained enlightenment." Having a conceptual understanding is not sufficient. You need to experience it. Experiencing your Buddha Nature eliminates attachments to self-grasping ignorance.

If your insight does not agree with the Dharma, start over again. That's what Einstein would do. When he worked out the mathematical equations based on his bodily patterns, he would check them against details of reality. If according to his new theory there would be, for instance, no gravity created by massive objects, he would have to reject it. Reality says when you release something it falls down. So he would have to start over again.

Penetrate each of the koans in this collection—and in your life itself— with every fiber in your body. And allow each koan to penetrate into you. Take each one as personally as possible. Using nonjudgmental awareness developed in your meditation, never stop examining your insights and understanding.

My own study of koans is not finished. Life is a continuous koan.

Gerry Shishin Wick
Great Mountain Zen Center
Lafayette, Colorado
September 2004

CASE 1

The World-Honored One Ascends the Platform

PREFACE TO THE ASSEMBLY

Close the gate and snooze—that's how to treat a superior person. Reflection, abbreviation, and elaboration are used for middling and inferior ones. How can you stand for someone to ascend the high seat and scowl? If anyone around here doesn't agree, step forward. I have no doubts about him.

MAIN CASE

Attention! One day the World-Honored One ascended the platform and took his seat. Manjushri struck the sounding post and said: "When you realize the Dharma-King's Dharma, the Dharma-King's Dharma is just as is." At that, the World-Honored One descended from the platform.

APPRECIATORY VERSE

Do you see the true manner of the primal stage?
Mother Nature goes on weaving warp and woof;
the woven old brocade contains the images of spring—
nothing can be done about the Spring God's (Manjushri) outflowing.

Attention! When the Buddha, also known as the World-Honored One, ascends the platform it means he's ready to give a discourse on the Dharma. In this koan, Manjushri, the bodhisattva of wisdom who is renowned for cutting delusion with Dharma words, announces the beginning of the talk with the statement: "When you realize the Dharma-King's Dharma, the Dharma-King's Dharma is just as is." And then, the Buddha descends the platform; his discourse is over. What more could he say? Even Manjushri's announcement is unnecessary. He's saying too much; he's "leaking" or as the verse says he is "outflowing."

When you truly understand the Dharma, it's just *thus*, just this; it's *as is*. All kinds of words and phrases have been invented in Zen to express *thusness* or *"as-is"-ness*, but none are needed. Don't add anything extra. Just let everything be as it is. That's liberation. But letting everything be as is, is difficult for us because we're always trying to fiddle around with things, always adding something, wishing something were taken away. We're always putting another head atop our own.

I know people who want to be a lion but feel just like a frightened kitten—and not only that, they feel like a frightened kitten frightened about feeling like a frightened kitten! But the Dharma-King's Dharma is as is; if you're frightened, be frightened, leave it at that and don't add anything extra.

What does it mean to let it all be and let it all go? And what about when you can't let it go, what then? Well, if you're holding on, hold on. That's liberation too. Let the Dharma-King's Dharma be as is.

This seems straightforward, but the subtlety comes in each moment: Each moment, how do you practice the Dharma-King's Dharma? And let me ask you this: Why do you practice Zen? If you think you're going to become something else, you're fooling yourself. If you think that you don't need to practice zazen because everything is perfect as it is, that is an erroneous view.

The first line of the verse says, "Do you see the true manner of the primal stage?" This is inviting us to realize the truth of ultimate reality. Is that ultimate reality the World-Honored One ascending the platform, or is it the World-Honored One descending the platform? If you let the light of ultimate reality blind your eye, it's hard to see. If it does not blind your eye, then it's hard to let go. If you see it, don't dwell there.

The Dharma-King's Dharma is *as is*. If you continue to be frightened and to maintain your judgments about being frightened, then you are not truly feeling fright. You are holding on to your opinions. By accepting your experience without judgments, you allow transformation to take place. I cannot count the times I heard Maezumi Roshi say, "Appreciate your life." Appreciating your life means that the Dharma-King's Dharma is just as is. From that place you can embrace yourself and appreciate yourself. It is not a matter of being a superior or inferior person. It is not a matter of Manjushri's outflowing. Just let everything be as is and appreciate every moment of this life *as* the life of the Dharma-King.

CASE 2

Bodhidharma's Vast Emptiness

PREFACE TO THE ASSEMBLY

Benka's three offerings did not prevent his being punished: If a luminous jewel were thrown at them, few are the men who would not draw their swords. For an impromptu guest, there is not an impromptu host; he's provisionally acceptable but not absolutely acceptable. If you can't grasp rare, valuable treasure, let's toss in a dead cat's head and see.

MAIN CASE

Attention! Emperor Wu of Ryo asked the great master Bodhidharma, "What is the ultimate meaning of the holy truth of Buddhism?" Bodhidharma replied, "Vast emptiness. No holiness." The Emperor asked, "Who stands here before me?" Bodhidharma replied, "I don't know." The Emperor was baffled. Thereafter, Bodhidharma crossed the river, arrived at Shorin and faced the wall for nine years.

APPRECIATORY VERSE

Emptiness, no holiness—
the questioner's far off.
Gain is to swing the axe and not harm the nose;
loss is to drop the pot and not look back.
In solitude he sits cool at Shorin;
in silence the Right Decree's fully revealed.
The autumn's lucid and the moon's a turning frosty wheel;
the Milky Way's pale, and the Big Dipper's handle hangs low.
In line the robe and bowl handed on to descendents
henceforth are medicine to men and devas.

Emperor Wu had heard about Bodhidharma, the Indian monk who brought Zen to China in the sixth century, and summoned him to his court. In preparation for meeting with this great bodhisattva, the emperor must have asked his advisors what was the single most important question to ask a great monk. When he meets Bodhidharma, he presents that question. Yet Bodhidharma's answer to him—"Vast emptiness. No holiness."—surprises and confuses the emperor so utterly that he wonders if the man before him is the great and learned monk he had expected and not an imposter—hence his second question. And Bodhidharma's thunderous reply is, simply, "I don't know."

What is this vast emptiness? What is this "I don't know"? What does *empty* mean? It doesn't mean blackness or nihilism or nothingness, and it isn't the emptiness we complain about when we say "I feel empty." Everything is impermanent; nothing is fixed. One's own form is empty of any fixed thing. Realizing this emptiness, experiencing it directly, is one of the most important aspects of our practice. There is no fixed thing that is the self—nothing to grasp onto, no firm ground upon which to stand, no right understanding to attain. As soon as you think you've grabbed "it," you have lost "it." Realizing "it" directly, tremendous freedom is manifest.

When self-aggrandizing thoughts arise—or even negative thoughts that affirm the illusion of an independent self—we grab onto them instead of just letting them go. Why do we grab onto them? If we didn't reinforce the illusion of a fixed self, what would we be? What would be left?

There is an old Zen expression that is appropriate here: "Even the water melting from the snow-capped peaks finds its way to the ocean." It finds its way without even knowing the direction and against all obstacles! We think that we need to control everything. Out of ignorance we keep affirming this false self to feel secure and to feel that we are in control of our life.

We believe that we are the content of our thoughts (and our opinions, beliefs, feelings, and reactions). We resist seeing that we ourselves are "vast emptiness" and thus are denying our deep unlimited nature. The Buddha realized that there is no gap between ourselves and others. We are all one body. And by not recognizing who we are, we're creating a chasm between ourselves and others that is greater than the Grand Canyon, and being unable to cross this chasm makes us miserable. But even so, we feel secure in our own misery because it is familiar to us, it makes us feel in control.

Commenting on this case, one ancient Zen master said, "Leaving aside the ultimate meaning for the moment, what do you want with the holy truth?" What are you going to do with it? Another master said, "If you just end attachments, there's no holy understanding." The Third Ancestor said, "Don't seek after the truth, just don't cherish your opinions." Just let the clouds of delusion disperse. If you don't cherish your delusions, then wisdom will shine through naturally. One of the scriptures says, "If you create an understanding of holiness, you will succumb to all errors." How many wars have been fought in the name of an understanding of what is holy? What kind of holiness is that? If you create an understanding of holiness, if you *know*—right there, you're stuck in the mud. As soon as you *know*, that knowing becomes dualistic, and as soon as it becomes dualistic it no longer corresponds to reality.

Yasutani Roshi said, "When you make Bodhidharma's 'I don't know' your *own*, it does not break into consciousness. If you know it, at a single stroke it's gone." When you make it your own, it's a part of your flesh, bones, and blood. But if you describe it, it becomes something else.

Relating to this case, Yasutani Roshi wrote this poem:

> Holy reality, emptiness.
> The man, unknowing.
> Spring breeze and autumn moon speak heavenly truth.
> Reverent monks building temples to no merit.
> Emperor Wu, how could you know the willows' new green?

How could you know the willows' new green? You're so busy trying to figure it out, you're missing the buds under your own nose.

So what is this not knowing? There are all kinds of "I don't know." In this case, this "I don't know" snatches everything away. We can point at it, but how can we really express it? It is like a mute serving as a messenger to us. But if we really open ourselves up, we can receive the message nonetheless. But what is given? What is received? What is maintained?

When Bodhidharma left the emperor, he spent nine years facing a wall. What was he doing for those nine years? If you understand this koan, you can answer without hesitation.

CASE 3

An Invitation for the Patriarch

By the activity existing before even a hint of this kalpa, a blind turtle faces the fire. By the phrase that's transmitted outside the scriptures, a mortar's rim spouts a flower. Tell me: is there something to receive, maintain, read, and recite?

MAIN CASE

Attention! The ruler of a country in Eastern India invited the Twenty-Seventh Ancestor, Hannyatara, for a midmorning meal. The ruler asked him, "Why don't you read the sutras?" The Ancestor replied, "This poor follower of the Way, when breathing in does not dwell in the realm of *skandhas*, and when breathing out is not caught up in the many externals. Always do I thus turn a hundred thousand million billion rolls of sutras."

APPRECIATORY VERSE

Cloud rhino sports with the moon and glows embracing its beams;
wooden horse plays in the spring, unfettered and fleet.
Beneath his brows, two chill blue eyes—
what need to read sutras as though piercing oxhide!
Bright white mind transcends vast kalpas,
a hero's strength tears through nested enclosures.
The subtle round hub-hole turns marvelous activities.
When Kanzan forgets the road whence he came,
Jittoku will lead him by hand to return.

Hannyatara, Bodhidharma's teacher and the twenty-seventh Ancestor in our lineage, doesn't dwell in the realm of form, sensation, perception, conception, and consciousness—the *skandhas*—and so he doesn't get caught in a notion of a fixed separate self. Inhaling and exhaling, there is no inside or outside. Each breath reveals the sutra.

Sutra usually refers to the teachings of the Buddha, but a sutra could be anything that is undeniably true. With each breath Hannyatara revolves the sutras. Breathing in, breathing out, the fundamental holy truth of the primary principle is revealed.

Hannyatara turns a nice phrase: "This poor follower of the Way." To be poor is to have nothing and to hold onto nothing. Being poor in that way gives us the richness of not being constrained by external conditions.

This is a prescription for all of our dis-ease: Breathe in without attaching to internals, breathe out without attaching to externals. When we do that, we manifest clear, unclouded vision. But if we add anything to that simple practice, it becomes something else entirely. To learn simple breathing in and breathing out takes steady years of meditation. Breathe in and do not create a false self; breathe out and don't perturb the world or be perturbed by the world—the ultimate meaning of the holy truth is revealed.

The verse says "A hero's strength tears through nested enclosures." Breathing in, you're a minister. Breathing out, you're a general. These "nested enclosures" are all of the cloaks that we wear. "I am a teacher." "I am a Buddhist." "I am an artist." Breathe in and you see past the teacher. Breathe out and you see beyond the artist. The hero's strength tears through these wrappers that we put around ourselves. Each time we breathe it is a new sutra.

In this way whatever you're doing, you're revolving the sutras. Picking the weeds, changing a diaper, and making a flower arrangement are a hundred thousand million billion rolls of sutras. Completely *become* breathing in and breathing out and that's all there is. In that moment, where's Hannyatara? If you realize "this poor follower of the Way" you are free to come and go. But if you don't, you're using counterfeit money to buy stock in a corrupt corporation.

CASE 4

The World-Honored One Points to the Earth

PREFACE TO THE ASSEMBLY

When a speck of dust is raised, the great earth is fully contained in it. It's very well to open new territory and extend your lands with horse and spear. Who is this person who can be master in any place and meet the source in everything?

MAIN CASE

Attention! When the World-Honored One was walking with his disciples he pointed to the ground and said, "It would be good to erect a temple here." The god Indra took a blade of grass and stuck it in the ground and said, "The temple has been erected." The World-Honored One smiled faintly.

APPRECIATORY VERSE

On the hundred grass-tips, boundless spring—
taking what's at hand, use it freely.
Buddha's sixteen foot golden body of manifold merit
spontaneously extending a hand, enters the red dust—
within the dust he can be host
coming from another world, naturally he's a guest.
Wherever you are be content with your role—
dislike not those more adept than you.

Part of experiencing growth in our life requires developing a larger vision unconstrained by our usual, limited mind, like Indra and Buddha. Doing so requires great awareness. We all have blind spots, and we project our world view from those dark places. That projection inevitably distorts our relations with others, with the world, and with ourselves. We need to practice awareness in order to develop clarity and to perceive the difference between reality and distortions. We also need perseverance because without it we will not generate the heat necessary to melt our self-grasping ignorance.

Suppose you saw a black raven flying by, and everybody in the room said, "That's not a black raven. That's a white snowy egret." You'd say, "No it's not. It's a black raven!" "No, everybody here except you says it's a snowy egret." You might see certain things with the clarity developed from your Zen practice, and yet everyone is telling you something else. This often happens when you visit close relatives. Someone might say, "This Zen stuff, sitting on the cushion all these hours—it's a total waste of time!" What do you say? Whenever visitors would say something argumentative to him, Maezumi Roshi would give them space for their opinions. He would respond, "It could be so."

The verse says, "Taking what's at hand, use it freely." Just put aside all of your ideas, standards, and judgments, then look at the world with your larger vision and see what arises. How can you manifest the sixteen foot golden body of the Buddha? How can you erect a temple from a blade of grass? The Bible says that your body is your temple. A piece of grass is your temple too. All dharmas in the ten directions are your body and your temple. But, as Master Bansho says in commenting on this case, "Repairs won't be easy."

The verse also says: "Wherever you are, be contented with your role. Don't dislike those that are more adept than you." No matter how good you are there is always somebody better. No matter how bad you are there is always somebody worse. How can we be everything that we want to be? Everywhere life is sufficient. Just be who you are, and don't restrict it.

CASE 5

Seigan's Cost of Rice

PREFACE TO THE ASSEMBLY

Though you cut your flesh like Shatai did to feed his parents, you won't have your biography entered with those noted for filial piety; though you try to crush Buddha like Devadatta did when he started a landslide, you won't be afraid of being struck by lightning. Having passed through bramble thickets and walked through the fragrant forest, you'd better wait until the very end of the year. As of old, the beginning of spring is cold. Where is the dharma-kaya of Buddha?

MAIN CASE

Attention! A monk asked Seigan, "What is the ultimate meaning of the Buddhadharma?" Seigan replied, "What does rice cost in Roryo?"

APPRECIATORY VERSE

Peaceful governing has no special form;
rustic styles are utterly plain:
they just drink together and sing folk songs.
Why should they care about Shun's merits or Gyo's benevolence?

This question—"What is the ultimate meaning of the Buddhadharma?"—is the kind of question that appears in many dialogues between students and teachers. In this case, Seigan replies, "What does rice cost in Roryo?"

Seigan is considered the brightest of the successors of the Sixth Ancestor in China, Huineng. Seigan had only one successor, Sekito Kisen, but through their lineage, three of the five schools of Zen arose, including the

Soto School, the Ummon School, and the Hogen School. Only the Soto School still exists today.

When the monk questions Seigan, he's looking for some kind of truth that's constant, that can guide his life and give him security. But Seigan won't give it to him because truth has no special form; truth is not constant. Seigan's answer is unique. Let's examine what it means.

Perhaps Roryo is a place where rice is so abundant that it's completely free. Perhaps trying to sell rice in Roryo is like selling water by the river—who would buy it? Is the Buddhadharma like that? Everywhere you look, the land is full of golden beings, Buddhas.

Or perhaps rice is so rare as to be priceless. Even with all the money in the world, it can't be purchased. Is the Buddhadharma like that? So is it expensive or inexpensive? If I ask you Seigan's question and you say, "The price of rice cannot be assessed,"—at that moment you've assessed it! You've already entered into the business of bushels and pecks, and furthermore you've set up a shop and started selling.

Commenting on this case Master Bansho said, "The price of rice in Roryo is indeed mysterious and profound. But how does it compare to festive dancing and singing?"

So what can we rely on prior to thinking good and evil, prior to self-evident truths and obvious lies, what is the price of rice in Roryo? Keep letting go of your cherished opinions and there will surely be an unexpected realization that you can't get anywhere else.

CASE 6

Baso's White and Black

When the mouth cannot be opened, the tongueless person knows how to talk. When a foot cannot be lifted, the legless person knows how to walk. If you fall for someone's words and are burdened by them, how can freedom be yours? When the four mountains close in, how can you pass free of them?

MAIN CASE

Attention! A monk once asked Baso, "Your reverence, abandoning the four propositions and wiping out the hundred negations, please point out to me directly the meaning of Bodhidharma's coming from the West." Baso said, "I don't feel like explaining to you today. Go ask Chizo." The monk then went to ask Chizo, and Chizo said, "Why don't you ask the master?" The monk said, "The master told me to ask you." Rubbing his head with his hand, Chizo said, "I've got a headache today. Go and ask Brother Kai." The monk asked Kai, and Kai said, "Ever since I have been here, I don't know." The monk returned and told Baso what had happened, and Baso said, "Chizo's head is white, Kai's head is black."

APPRECIATORY VERSE

Medicine becomes a sickness—reflecting on saints of old;
sickness becomes a doctor—who would he be?
White head, black head—sons of a good family
having phrases or being phraseless—the activity of cutting
    off the streams of thinking
magnificently cuts off the path of the tongue-tip.
You should laugh—Vaisali's venerable old awl.

When you read koans such as this one, it's natural to want to know what these "four propositions" and "hundred negations" are, but this knowledge will not reveal the ultimate meaning of Zen and is not necessary to penetrate this koan. The monk is essentially saying, "Leaving aside Buddhist philosophy and cosmology, show me ultimate reality."

How can you describe the ultimate reality? Baso said, "I don't feel like explaining it today." Baso gave a perfect demonstration, but the monk doesn't get it. And so he goes to Chizo who says, "Why don't you ask the master?"—again a perfect demonstration and the monk misses it. So Chizo goes further and adds to his demonstration: "Ah, I've got a headache. Why don't you go ask Brother Kai?" The monk still misses it, and brings his question to Kai who says, "Ever since I have been here, I don't know."—yet another demonstration for the benefit of the monk! But nonetheless he returns confused to Baso. Baso cuts through it all with the statement, "Chizo's head is white, and Kai's head is black."

Baso's teaching was so powerful that he helped many people enlighten themselves; he had 133 successors. Chizo and Kai are Seido Chizo and Hyakujo Ekai, respectively, and both are successors and students of Master Baso.

The preface says: "When the mouth cannot be opened, the tongueless person knows how to talk. When a foot cannot be lifted, the legless person knows how to walk." How do you walk? How do you speak? You can look in a physiology book, and read certain explanations about how to walk, but does it really tell it all to you? When you watch a child learn how to walk, it's like they have an inner force compelling them to do it, and they do it over and over and over. I've never seen a child say, "This is too hard!"—and then give it up once and for all.

But how many times do discouraging thoughts come to you when you're doing zazen? How strong is your aspiration to drop away the four propositions and the hundred negations? When you walk, just walk, when you talk, just talk, when you sit, just sit—without carrying extra baggage around.

Can you see what Baso is describing? To see it, you must look with your Dharma eye, the eye that's not attached to any form or color. Then you must learn to walk without lifting a leg and to talk without moving your tongue.

"Chizo's head is white, Kai's head is black." I was crying then, I'm laughing now. The sky is blue, the grass is green. Dogs bark, cats purr. Ducks have ducklings, geese have goslings. Why do we make it so complicated? The fundamental truth is always expressing itself perfectly; we just need to see it.

CASE 7

Yakusan Takes the High Seat

PREFACE TO THE ASSEMBLY

Eyes, ears, nose, and tongue are each unique. The eyebrows are above the eyes. In soldering, farming, crafts, and trades each performs a service. Such a one is always at ease. How does a true Zen teacher proceed?

MAIN CASE

Attention! For a long time, Yakusan had not ascended the high seat. The administrator monk spoke to him, saying, "The monks have been wondering about some guidance for a long time. Your reverence, for the sake of the assembly, will you please give us a talk?" Yakusan had the gong struck, and the monks then assembled. Yakusan ascended the high seat, remained silent for a while, then got down and went back to his quarters. Later on, the administrator monk said to him, "Master, a little while ago you agreed to give us a talk on behalf of the assembly. Why didn't you give us even a single word?" Yakusan replied, "There are sutra teachers for the sutras, and instructors for the commentaries. Why do you come and bother this old monk?"

APPRECIATORY VERSE

Catering to an idiot's whim with bogus bills,
Ryoshi and Tsuifu both look back at the whip's shadow.
A cloud sweeps the endless sky; a crane nests in the moon.
Pure cold penetrates the bones—he sleeps no more.

Yakusan Igen was the Dharma great-grandson of the Sixth Ancestor, and the Dharma heir to Sekito Kisen.

This case is reminiscent of the first case in this collection, the World-Honored One Ascends the Platform, in which the Buddha ascends the high seat and then concludes his discourse without speaking a word. Uchiyama Roshi, a modern Soto teacher would conduct *sesshins*, meditation retreats, "without toys"—no interviews with the teacher, no Dharma talks, nothing to amuse your mind with…just zazen.

In this koan, the monks want guidance, want toys. Providing this is what Wanshi calls in the verse, "catering to an idiot's whim with bogus bills." Even the most eloquent talk is no better than fool's gold. All words aside, each of you must take care of this Great Matter by yourself. Yakusan has been steadfastly refusing to offer toys to his monks, to pay them with bogus bills, to temporarily satisfy them with clever words. But, here at the urging of the administrator monk, the old softy takes the high seat. But he doesn't just recite sutras, as do the sutra teachers, or expound shastras, like the commentarial teachers. Nonetheless, his Dharma arrow goes deep.

When I gave Dharma talks at Centro Zen de Mexico, I learned a few phrases that I would use over and over again. One of them is, *"A buen hambre no hay pan duro,"* which means, "If you are really hungry, there is no stale, hard bread." Yakusan expressed this point when he said, "Why do you bother this old monk?" He's saying, "What is it you want? If you were really hungry for the Dharma, you would have heard my Dharma talk." The hungry will eat anything, and the thirsty will drink anything. Yakusan was expressing the Dharma marvelously for those with eyes to see.

The *Daodejing* says, "The Tao abides in non-doing yet nothing is left undone." There's no limit to what you can accomplish if you just get out of the way. Forget the self and let the Dharma flow freely. That's non-doing. That's what Yakusan was doing. One ancient commented, "One must be like a farmer, who lets the fields, from time to time, dry. Parched and thirsty after that, when water is poured, the crops sprout."

When Yakusan met Sekito, Yakusan was sitting in meditation, and Sekito asked him, "What are you doing?" and Yakusan said, "I'm doing nothing at all," and Sekito said, "Then you're sitting idly," and Yakusan said, "If I were sitting idly, then I would be doing something." Checking him further, Sekito said, "You say you're doing nothing. What is it you're not doing?" And Yakusan said, "Even thousands of old Buddhas do not know." Sekito wrote a verse to express his approval of Yakusan: "Living long together and not knowing his name, naturally you have worked along with him, but even the ancient Buddhas do not know. How can an ordinary soul know him?"

When he was eighty-four years old, Yakusan went running around the monastery, saying, "The halls are falling down, the halls are falling down!" The monks went out and started grabbing the pillars, trying to hold them up. Then Yakusan said, "You didn't understand a word I said." Then he sat down and quietly died. During his whole life, Yakusan was hitting his monks with Dharma arrows and most of them did not feel a thing.

CASE 8

Hyakujo's Fox

PREFACE TO THE ASSEMBLY

If you put this One in mind, you'll enter hell like a flying arrow. If you swallow a drop of wild fox's drool, you can't vomit it for thirty years. It is not that the decree of the Western Heaven is strict, just that rascals' karma is heavy. Are there any such offenders here?

MAIN CASE

Attention! Every time Hyakujo ascended the high seat, an old man was present, listening to the Dharma. He would leave with the monks, and one day he didn't leave, and Hyakujo asked, "Who's this standing there?" The old man replied, "Once in the time of Kashyapa Buddha, I lived on this mountain. There is a student who asked me, 'Does a person who has accomplished his practice fall into cause and effect?' I replied to him, 'He does not fall into cause and effect.' Thereupon, I fell into having a wild fox's body for five hundred lives. I beg you Osho, give me a turning word now." Hyakujo said, "He does not evade cause and effect." At these words, the old man attained great enlightenment.

APPRECIATORY VERSE

A foot of water, a fathom of wave—
for five hundred lives he couldn't do a thing.
"Not falling, not evading" was their exchange;
as before they're bound in a tangle.
Ah, ha, ha! Understand?
If as to this you're unattached
my baby-talk won't disturb you.

Shrine-songs and dance of themselves harmonize—
hands clap the intervals and melodies are hummed.

This koan is classified by the great Master Hakuin as one of the *nanto* koans, or koans difficult to pass through. This case also appears, in a longer form, in the *Gateless Gate* as Case 2. This is a very important koan, and if you understand Hyakujo's koan, you understand Zen.

Hyakujo was born in China in 720 and died in 814, at the age of ninety-four. He was a successor of Baso and Hyakujo's successor, Obaku, was the teacher of the great Master Rinzai. Hyakujo is remembered as being exceptionally articulate and incisive, but one of his greatest accomplishments was developing the monastic rules and regulations for Buddhism in China. The importance of that feat was not the rules and the monastic order in themselves, but that he modified the monastic rules from India to make them relevant to his own time and place. He developed Zen Buddhism so that it could conform to the Chinese mind and the Chinese way of doing things. If we just parrot what the Buddha taught without bringing our own understanding, our own awakening, our own insight to it, then our practice will become dead. In this koan, Hyakujo demands that we bring our understanding of karma to life.

The traditional Buddhist understanding of karma teaches that upon attaining enlightenment, a person is no longer subject to transmigrations based upon past karma, having transcended the law of cause and effect—but be careful talking that way or you too may be reborn as a fox or become a ghost! But once we open our Zen eye and see clearly what karma is, then this ghost story doesn't really have any significance. Once we penetrate into this koan we can experience our own liberation.

Whenever I've had the opportunity, I've asked the Zen masters I've encountered about rebirth. My first teacher, Sochu Roshi, said, "It's a nice story." I asked another teacher, Eido Roshi, about the same thing and he thought for a moment then he said, "It's better to say, 'Could be' than to say, 'No.'" When I asked Maezumi Roshi about it, he never answered me except with thunderous silence. Nonetheless, I overheard heard him telling others, "Yes, definitely, there's rebirth!" Rather than talk about it, they wanted me to find out for myself.

Dogen Zenji says, "We students of Zen should not forget for even a moment that our life is in a constant state of birth and decay." Our life is constant birth and decay, with each breath—and even faster than with each breath. How we are born and how we die is subject to cause and effect.

The fact of cause and effect is clear and undeniable; nothing in the universe exists, if not for the actions of cause and effect. Every moment, every breath, every life is causation itself.

How are we born? How do we manifest? We are born and manifest according to karma, but the karma is not just *our* karma, it's the karma of everyone and everything. There are myriad causes and conditions, all interdependent, so how can we know exactly what they are?

One ancient master wrote, "When fish swim, the water becomes cloudy. When birds fly, they lose their feathers. For nothing can escape from the perfect mirror of causality, which is as vast and universal as the sky. For five hundred lives, the monk became a wild fox, because he failed to understand Buddhist causality, which is as strong as a bolt of lightning or a raging typhoon, as unchangeable as gold which has been purified many times over."

The Bible (Hosea 8:7) says, "Whosoever sows the wind will reap the whirlwind." If we commit bad actions, we reap the results of them, and if we sow good actions, we reap those rewards. But how can we know what will be "good" and what will be "bad"?

It's said that doing zazen wholeheartedly purifies years of bad karma. Yet so does suffering. When we feel pain and experience suffering and we stay with it rather than attaching to our stories about it or pushing it away, that purifies karma as well. Our faith, our prayers, our offerings, can also purify bad karma, as can repentance and atonement.

Commenting on this koan, Master Mumon said, "Not falling into causation, he was turned into a fox. The first mistake. Not ignoring causation, he was released from a fox body. The second mistake."

When falling and ignoring, and not falling and not ignoring, are transcended and wiped away, then you will see yourself as Hyakujo and as the fox, and you will experience directly the truth of this koan. If you are born as a fox, be a fox. Then it is not a matter of heavy karma or liberating karma.

We're all subject to karma, to cause and effect, birth and decay. But how can we be peaceful no matter what conditions our karma brings? That's the challenge of our practice. To liberate ourselves from our karma we must become karma itself.

CASE 9

Nansen Cuts a Cat

PREFACE TO THE ASSEMBLY

Kick up the blue ocean and the whole earth flies like dust. Shout apart the white clouds and the vast sky is crushed like powder. Though you strictly perform the right decree, that is still only half enough. With the great function fully manifested, how can it be applied?

MAIN CASE

Attention! At Nansen's place one day the monks of the east and west halls were arguing about a cat. Seeing this, Nansen held it up before him saying, "If you can say a word, I won't cut it." The assembly made no response. Nansen cut the cat in two. Nansen later told Joshu what happened. Joshu took off his straw sandals and, placing them on his head, went out. Nansen remarked, "If you had been here, you could have saved the cat."

APPRECIATORY VERSE

All monks of both halls were arguing.
Old Teacher King could put right and wrong to the test.
By his sharp knife cutting, the shapes were both forgotten.
A thousand ages love an adept man.
The Way is still not overthrown.
The good listener's indeed appreciative.
For cleaving the mountain to free the river only Laiu is honored.
For smelting stone and mending heaven only Joka is capable.
Old Joshu has his own style—
putting sandals on the head is worth a little.

Coming upon differences, he's still a luminous mirror;
true gold does not mix with sand.

Master Nansen lived in the eighth and ninth centuries and was a successor of Baso. Joshu studied with Nansen and stayed with him for forty years. They were both outstanding masters of the Golden Age of Zen in China.

This case is both famous and controversial. Since this koan has such a cruel appearance when understood only from the surface of our mind, it's important to address the purpose of koans in general. Koans are records of the sayings and doings of our Zen Ancestors presented in a specific form meant to break through the hardened layers of our discriminating, deluded minds. Koans as such do not ignore the rules of moral and ethical behavior, nor do they promote them. The purpose of a koan is to liberate us from the suffering caused by the rules with which we bind ourselves. Koans teach us to be free, and to make lively use of all rules. Until we understand this, no koan can be understood.

In this koan, Master Nansen, with his fearless challenge of life and death, is trying to bring his disciples to the reality of the moment. Nansen is begging his disciples to say one word to save the cat—but they're paralyzed, dumbfounded. If you were confronted with this challenge, how would you save the cat?

As long as there's a trace of self-grasping ignorance, you would not be able to do it. Hundreds and thousands of animals are killed every day, but none of these deaths is a sacrifice for our liberation. Nansen sacrificed the life of one cat for the liberation of hundreds of millions of beings. He also was willing to sacrifice himself and accept whatever karma might have come from that act. Contrary to the opinions of some modern Zen teachers, that knife did cut the fur, the skin, the muscle, and the viscera. His hands and the whole universe cry out tears of blood. We don't have to apologize for Nansen. Master Setcho, commenting on this case said, "Fortunately, Nansen took a correct action. Sword straight away cuts it in two. Criticize as you like." All of our gratitude to Nansen, and to that cat.

Master Dogen commented on this case, "A sword straight away cuts it. No cut!" In order to understand "no cut" you first have to understand "cut."

In the second part of the koan, Joshu hears of the incident and puts his sandals on his head and walks out. That very day, blood and guts were spilt. Is this mere stoicism on Joshu's part? Does Joshu's response mean we should close our hearts to the suffering of other beings? If you would think that Joshu was divorcing himself from the screeching and scratching and splattering of the dying cat, you don't understand Joshu's action, nor what it means to save the cat. Is he just playing the jester, implying Nansen made a mess of things and got everything all upside-down?

It's said that in China putting the shoes on top of one's head is a sign of mourning. Is that what Joshu is doing? How could that have saved the cat? This koan is about life and death, and Joshu was no stranger to questions about life and death. Once Joshu asked Nansen, "Where did the worthies of old go when they died?" Nansen replied, "How badly do you want to know?" When you die, just die! When you die thoroughly and completely you will transcend life and death and become a living Buddha. But if you show no feeling for the cat, then you'll be no different than a stone Buddha in the garden.

Zen practice is not about killing your compassionate heartfelt responses to life and its events. When things get uncomfortable, most people divert their attention by withdrawing, getting angry or depressed, or numbing themselves to their own feelings. That's not the Zen Way. Unless you open your heart, you cannot say a word to save the cat.

CASE 10

Joshu Sees Through the Old Woman

PREFACE TO THE ASSEMBLY

There is grasping and releasing; a wooden pole accompanies the body. Able to kill or vivify, the scale's handle is held in hand. Dust, toil, demons, and heretics are utterly disposed of with a finger. The great earth, mountains, and rivers all become playthings. Tell me: What state of mind is this?

MAIN CASE

Attention! There was an old woman on the road to Great Mountain (Taizan). Sometimes a monk would ask which way it was to Taizan, and she would reply, "Straight ahead." The monk would proceed a little, and the old woman would say, "A fine priest, going on like that again!" A monk related this to Joshu, and Joshu said, "Wait, I'll examine her for you." Joshu went and also asked the same question, and the old woman gave the same answer. The next day, Joshu ascended the high seat and said, "For your sakes, I've seen that old woman through and through."

APPRECIATORY VERSE

He's gotten old—become the essence—doesn't transmit
   in error;
Old Buddha Joshu succeeded Nansen.
By a design on its shell the withered turtle lost his life.
Even the steeds "Chariot" and "Wind-chaser" are encumbered
   by halter and bridle.
Grandma Zen seen through and through—
told to people it's not worth a cent.

It's not too often that women appear in Zen literature, and when they do, they're usually old, nameless women. All we know about this particular woman is what it says in this koan. At our Zen center, we honor this old woman and other forgotten women by offering the merits of our services to "all women, honored ones, whose names have been forgotten or left unsaid." Obviously, she has clear understanding, and furthermore she responded to Joshu, himself a great master of Zen, exactly as she did to the other monks she encountered.

You might ask why didn't she recognize Joshu and say something different to him. But if you do, I'll bring up the case of Master Gutei (see Case 84), who would just raise a finger in response to any question he was ever asked. "Why did Bodhidharma come from the west?" "What's the meaning of Zen?" "What's Buddha Nature?" One finger. Gutei learned that finger from his teacher and he never exhausted it. Similarly, this old woman has never exhausted "Straight ahead," and "A fine monk you are, going on like that."

In this koan, we are required to see the differences in the sameness, and see the sameness in differences. We all have Buddha Nature, and it is the same in each of us. Yet, our Buddha Nature is different, because each one of us is different. How do we see the differences in the sameness, and appreciate them? How do we see the sameness in the differences?

But we might get caught up in speculation about this point and miss the main teaching of this koan: "Go straight ahead!"

Where is this Taizan, this Great Mountain? Let me tell you a story I once heard: A ship was sailing off the coast of South America and running low on drinking water. It happened to wander into the mouth of the Amazon River, which is so wide that you can't see the banks from the middle of it, and so they thought they were still in the ocean. At one point, they saw another ship in the distance, and asked in semaphore where they could find fresh water. The other ship responded, "Lower your buckets." Fine sailors, going on like that! They were on the Great River and did not realize it.

We're so busy trying to figure out how Joshu saw through the old woman, that we don't see that the old woman saw through Joshu and that they both saw through us. What motivated the monk? What motivated Joshu? Perhaps the monk related this tale to Joshu because he felt swindled by the old woman—but if that's the case, Joshu was an even bigger swindler. The monk was trapped in some emotional game of loss or gain, victory or defeat, caught on the old woman's hook. Was Joshu hooked, too? Why did he hide himself as one of the monks and put on an act in front of the old woman? Why couldn't he act naturally as himself? Joshu just went, saw, acted the same as the other monks, and returned. So was Joshu caught or did he wriggle free?

The old woman sees through Joshu, Joshu sees through the old woman. How did Joshu see through the old woman? That is one checking question for this koan. How does the old woman see through Joshu? That is another checking question.

Master Bansho had a capping phrase for the last line of this koan: "If you don't understand, it's like gold, but if you see through it, it's like manure." If you don't understand, you think it's something precious: "Where's the road to Taizan?" But if you see through it, it's like manure—although even manure has value!

So tell me: Where is the road to Great Mountain? What is this Great Mountain? Where do you find it? Where are you looking for it? Just keep going, straight ahead.

CASE 11

Ummon's Two Sicknesses

PREFACE TO THE ASSEMBLY

A bodiless person suffers illness. A handless person compounds medicine. A mouthless person takes meals. A nonreceiving person has ease and comfort. Tell me: for incurable disease, what's the prognosis and the treatment?

MAIN CASE

Attention! The great master Ummon said: "When the light doesn't penetrate completely, there are two kinds of sicknesses. When you're not quite clear, and there are things in front of you, that's one sickness. Even though you thoroughly penetrate the emptiness of all Dharmas, there still somehow seems to be something. In this also, the light has not penetrated completely. Again, there are two kinds of sicknesses in the dharmakaya. Though you reach the dharmakaya, because Dharma attachment is not forgotten, and a view of self still persists, you plummet into the dharmakaya side—this is one sickness. Though you penetrate through this, if you are negligent, it's still no good. Even after a minute examination, when however you look at it, the question arises, 'What inadequacy can there be?'—this is also a sickness."

APPRECIATORY VERSE

Multitudes of shapes allowed to be as is—
boundless, thorough liberation still obstructs the eye.
To sweep out this garden, who has the strength?
Concealed in one's heart, it of itself gives rise to thoughts;
steeped in gathering autumn lies a boat upon the blue;
illumined by snowy reed-flowers stands a pole with light suffused.

An old fisherman with skewered perch thinks of going to market;
carefree, a leaf sails over the waves.

Ummon lived in the ninth and tenth centuries, and was one of the greatest masters who ever lived, and he is the teacher most quoted in the ancient collections of koans. Ummon's teachings penetrate heaven and earth, emptiness and form. They follow the waves and adapt to the currents according to each situation—and they cut quickly through all streams of delusion.

In this koan we can see how the *Book of Equanimity* differs from the *Blue Cliff Record*. The *Blue Cliff Record* is primarily a Rinzai-School collection, and the koans in it are like large boulders which can be moved only by vigorous effort. But koans like this one, more typical of the Soto School, challenge us to practice more subtly, to find the dust within the dust within the dust, and sweep even that away.

Penetrating this kind of koan requires deep understanding and concentration, and it can only be plumbed after an initial opening—because it is only after some insight that the "two sicknesses" occur.

An ancient Ancestor said, "Searching for an ox while riding on an ox is an illness." That's an illness that comes before the illnesses that Ummon is talking about. The Ancestor goes on to say, "After mounting the ox, not being willing to dismount is also an illness." *That's* what Ummon is talking about here. If you think you're enlightened, that's a grave illness indeed.

Here, Ummon talks about two kinds of sicknesses we encounter in Zen practice. He speaks of each sickness in two ways.

Even though you may be in a state of samadhi, having dropped away body and mind, you may subtly think that there is still something there. You can have an awakening experience, but you still have to continue to practice. In vast, empty space if there's still a single hair, the light hasn't "penetrated completely" and there is sickness. Don't rest anywhere; just keep letting it all go. The *Identity of Relative and Absolute* says: "Encountering the absolute is not yet enlightenment." In the first of Ummon's two sicknesses, there is a belief that there is something outside of oneself. Attachment to one's uniqueness has not dropped away.

This sickness is articulated in the verse: "Boundless, thorough liberation still obstructs the eye." It is so hard to cover all of the tracks—even the most accomplished criminal leaves a clue. The tiniest mote obstructs the eye. "Concealed in one's heart, it of itself gives rise to thoughts." Those thoughts make one think that there still seems somehow to be something that can be called self and something that can be called other.

Ummon explains the second type of sicknesses using the dharmakaya, which literally means "Dharma body," and is another word for our true self. Once you have an insight into the nature of the dharmakaya, your true self, you form a fixed belief that the dharmakaya is your true self. Any fixed belief about the true self is limited and false and thus is an illness. There's a tendency to think the dharmakaya is some fixed thing, something that persists. Sticking in the absolute is sickness. But as soon as you say, "This is the true self," it is no longer your true self. Even though you have reached the dharmakaya, if there is any separate awareness of dharmakaya, dharmakaya is not forgotten and a view of self still persists. It's not the view of self you had before awakening but it's still a sense of self, and so there is still sickness.

This sickness is also articulated in the verse: "Illumined by snowy reed-flowers stands a pole with light suffused." You plummet into the reed-flowers since you are blinded by the bright light and get bogged down by clarity.

Even as you continue to deepen your awareness and understanding, stop subtly looking for a place to hang your hat. Don't stand still; don't rest anywhere. As soon as you rest, you're stuck. Ultimately there's not even a square inch of ground on which to stand. As soon as you say, "This is it!" you've fallen into illness.

The verse points to the cure—acting freely, without any thought or attachment to mind: "An old fisherman with skewered perch thinks of going to market. Carefree, a leaf sails over the waves." We often think that our survival depends upon certain beliefs and ways of behaving. As we are able to let go of some of our conditioned behavior, even more subtle conditioning appears. Our practice is to clarify and let go of this conditioning—endlessly.

CASE 12

Jizo Plants the Field

PREFACE TO THE ASSEMBLY

Scholars cultivate the pen. Orators cultivate speech. Zen students tire of seeing the white ox on the bare ground, and we don't even turn to look at the rootless, splendid herb. How do we pass our days?

MAIN CASE

Attention! Priest Jizo asked Priest Shuzan, "Where did you come from?" Shuzan replied, "I came from the South." Jizo replied, "How is the Buddhadharma down South these days?" Shuzan answered, "There's a lot of debate going on." Jizo said, "Here, it is better for me to plant the fields, make rice balls, and eat." Shuzan asked, "What about the three worlds?" Jizo replied, "What is it that you call the three worlds?"

APPRECIATORY VERSE

Zen discussions numerous, altogether artificial;
flowing between mouth and ear they cause separation.
Planting the field, making rice-balls—an everyday affair:
unless replete with his inquiry, a person can't know it.
Replete with his inquiry, he knows for sure there is nothing to seek;
General Shiho after all didn't value awards of rank.
Activity forgotten, having returned, he's like the fish and birds;
washing his feet in the smoky Soro waters of autumn.

Master Jizo, who is not to be confused with Jizo Bodhisattva, is also known as Rakan Keichin. He lived in the tenth century and succeeded Master Gensha. A student named Priest Shuzan visits him, and the first thing Jizo asks him is, "Where do you come from?" In the past, when a Zen master asked a question that seemed simple, there's usually something hidden, a probe into the student's understanding. When Shuzan replies that he comes from the South, he has stuck his foot in Jizo's trap. Jizo then asks how the Buddhadharma is in the South, and with Shuzan's answer the trap springs shut. Buddhadharma is the reality of all things; how can it be any different in the South than it is in the North?

When the Sixth Ancestor first met the Fifth Ancestor, the Fifth Ancestor asked where he was from. When the Sixth Ancestor said he was from Reinan, the Fifth Ancestor challenged him by saying that barbarians from Reinan do not have Buddha Nature so how can he expect to be a Buddha. The Sixth Ancestor replied, "Although there are northern men and southern men, north and south make no difference to their Buddha Nature."

But Shuzan misses the opportunity, so Jizo expresses for him the very essence of Zen: "Here, it is better for me to plant the fields, make rice balls, and eat." You get up in the morning, clean your teeth, eat your breakfast, and go to work. That's an expression of the Buddhadharma. Somehow, we want to make something much more out of it, we want Zen to conform to some image that satisfies our ego—and that's the very cause of all the problems.

Still, Shuzan doesn't quite understand this simple point and wants to make it more complicated by asking about the three worlds—the world of desires, the world of form, and the world of formlessness. In daily life, each one of us transmigrates through these three worlds, moment by moment. In our practice, the three worlds correlate with raising the mind that seeks enlightenment (desire), cultivating the concentration of samadhi (form), and experiencing the illumination of wisdom (formlessness).

The Zen path begins with the world of desire, the desire to exhaust your inquiry. Unless you exhaust your attachments, you can't reveal wisdom. In the world of form you exhaust the attachments of your mind. In the world of formlessness there's not one thing to exhaust or hold onto.

An important teaching of the Buddha is impermanence; everything changes. Our minds are changing, our bodies are changing, and our environment is changing. Nothing is fixed. This is formlessness, emptiness.

Because the nature of reality is formless, it can arise in myriad forms according to whatever the conditions are at hand. But trying to limit the formless into just one fixed form is like trying to nail Jell-O to a wall.

So what is it that you call the three worlds? As long as you create a separation, you're creating something outside yourself. But in reality, there's no gap, no separation. You plant the fields, make the rice balls, and eat. Right here, experience the three worlds.

CASE 13

Rinzai's Blind Donkey

PREFACE TO THE ASSEMBLY

Devoted entirely to others, oneself is unknown. Straightaway eliminating Dharmas, you shouldn't be bothered by there being no one. Mean treatment, like breaking a wooden pillow, should be used. What about when it's time to depart?

MAIN CASE

Attention! When Rinzai was about to pass away, he charged Sansho: "After I depart, do not let my True Dharma Eye be extinguished." Sansho said, "How could I let your True Dharma Eye be extinguished?" Rinzai countered, "If someone suddenly asks you about it, how will you reply?" Sansho gave a shout, and Rinzai remarked, "Who would have thought that my True Dharma Eye would be extinguished on reaching this blind donkey?"

APPRECIATORY VERSE

At midnight the robe of faith's transmitted to No of Ro (Huineng):
seven hundred upset monks on Yellow Plum Mountain (Huineng's
    monastery)!
The True Dharma Eye of Rinzai's limb;
the blind ass extinguished it and people despised him.
Mind and mind together sealed—
Ancestor to Ancestor transmitting the lamp.
Seas and mountains being leveled,
a giant fish becomes a phoenix.
It's just that such splendid words are hard to compare with;
any time as a device he can metamorphose.

In the Zen tradition, it's said that the first instance of Dharma transmission was when Shakyamuni Buddha said, "I have the all-pervading True Dharma Eye. Now I give it to Mahakashyapa."—and thereby acknowledged Mahakashyapa as his successor. The True Dharma Eye is the reality of what is— but as soon as you think about it, it's something else. In this sense, the True Dharma Eye is unborn and undying, and cannot be extinguished.

Yasutani Roshi says the True Dharma Eye sees absolute equality and absolute difference in the Dharma, in all phenomena. This is the identity of Relative and Absolute. It's freely expressed, and functions under all circumstances. Formless form is the true form of reality, and this formless form takes shape only when there's absolute differentiation. Seeing this clearly is not letting the True Dharma Eye be extinguished.

Master Rinzai died quite young, at the age of fifty-five, but the school he founded continues to thrive; his Dharma has been transmitted through the generations to this day. This is another sense in which the True Dharma Eye has not been extinguished. Transmission in Zen does not rely on letters but is transmitted outside the scriptures, from teacher to student, because the experiential fact of the truth does not belong to the realm of logic and intellect (though it does not exclude it either). Because the transmission is always from teacher to student, there can be no self-proclaimed masters in Zen. The teachings arise in each generation out of one's own experience, unrestricted by scriptures, and each generation vows to his or her teacher to not let his or her True Dharma Eye be extinguished.

In this koan, you might think that Rinzai is criticizing Sansho by calling him a blind ass, but in fact this is very high praise indeed. Here, to be "blind" means to manifest the state of "no eye"—the state the Heart Sutra describes as "no eye, no ear, no nose, no tongue, no body, no mind." When you manifest that state, there is no separation between you, the act of seeing, and the object being seen—like an artist who does not know she is holding her brushes, just putting the paint onto the canvas.

Many people think of Rinzai as a brash, shouting master who beat up his students, but in fact his teaching was creative and subtle in many ways. In this case, it was his student who was shouting, and Master Rinzai who was pointing out some of the finer points. Have you seen this blind donkey? Look! Smell! Hear! Taste! Feel! Be like a blind donkey. Not deceived by intellectual conundrums, delusions, knowledge, preconceptions, and attachments the blind donkey is a liberated person who maintains the heart of not-knowing, not-seeing. Sansho says, "How could I let it be extinguished?" But tell me: How could you extinguish something that's unborn and undying?

CASE 14

Attendant Kaku Serves Tea

PREFACE TO THE ASSEMBLY

A searching-stick is in hand and a grass cape hugs the body. Sometimes one wraps a cotton ball in iron, sometimes one wraps a large pebble in brocade. It has always been that hardness overcomes softness. What happens when something soft encounters strength?

MAIN CASE

Attention! Attendant Kaku asked Tokusan, "Where did the holy ones of the past go?" Tokusan answered, "What? What?" Kaku said, "Give an imperial order for a fleet horse, and out comes a lame tortoise." At that, Tokusan desisted. The next day, Tokusan left his bath, and Kaku brought over tea and served it to Tokusan. Tokusan patted him once on the shoulder. Kaku said, "Old man, at last you're beginning to see." Tokusan once again desisted.

APPRECIATORY VERSE

When you come face to face, the adept knows;
that moment is quicker than flint sparks or lightning flash.
The master strategist seeming to lose has profound intent;
the militarist who underestimates his enemy lacks deep reflection.
Every shot hits—how could this be slighted!
He whose jawbones can be seen from behind is hard to touch;
with eyes set deep beneath his brows, he is a *nouveau riche*.

Tokusan lived at the end of the eighth century and beginning of the ninth century in China, and was a scholar of the Diamond Sutra, writing many commentaries on it. After Tokusan became a successor of Ryutan, he burned all his commentaries and said that they were not even like a hair in a vast chasm. From various cases involving Tokusan, we can see that when he was young, he was a rough and vigorous teacher, often beating his students with his stick, but his style evolved over the course of his life and by the end, he was considerably gentler. The case at hand occurred when Tokusan was quite old, so he doesn't respond to Kaku simply by striking him as he might have in his younger days.

Here, Tokusan desists; he refrains from saying or doing anything. You might imagine he is just too old and tired to respond, or that he's senile and doesn't know what to say. When Tokusan was a young teacher, he used the stick freely. If his students moved to the right, he struck them; if they moved to the left, he struck them; if they stood still, he struck them. He hollered at the Ancestors (see *Blue Cliff Record*, Case 4) and beat the wind. Kaku's error reached to the sky, why did Tokusan let him go?

But I ask you: What is the best way for a teacher to teach? How we react to a situation always depends upon conditions: the time, the place, the people involved, and the intensity of the relationships and the situation. There isn't some kind of absolute response that we can apply identically in every situation. Sometimes you wield the stick; sometimes you back off. Sometimes you retreat; sometimes you go forward. But we must understand that whatever we do affects everyone else. So how can we respond appropriately to each situation, how can we react in a way that's most effective? That's part of what this koan is about.

Kaku was not one to accept the stick easily. Tokusan knew that and desisted right away. Sometimes a tough word from the teacher that drives a rigid student away is the correct action. Each student is different, so the teacher tries to meet each student in the place where he or she can benefit most from the teaching. That's only one side though; the student must meet the teacher where he or she is also. When you go in to see your teacher, drop your ideas, opinions, and beliefs, and then, being empty, meet the teacher in "no place."

When the attendant asks where the holy ones went, he's basically saying, "Wherever the holy ones went, that is where I am going! That's where I am!" There's a case about the seven sisters who were going to go to a party, and one sister says, "Instead of having a party, let's go to the charnel ground." The charnel ground was full of corpses, and one of the sisters said, "With all of these corpses, where did the people go?" Another sister said, "What? What?"—and at those words, all seven sisters became enlightened. Nonetheless Tokusan's answer—"What? What?"—should give Kaku a clue. But instead Kaku insults Tokusan, and Tokusan desists.

Then, when attendant Kaku brings Tokusan tea the next day, Tokusan pats him once on the shoulder. He's showing Kaku the answer to his question. Kaku says, "Old man, at last you're beginning to see," and once again, Tokusan lets it pass. Every time this attendant Kaku tries to grab onto something to aggrandize himself, Tokusan gives him nothing to hold onto.

Tokusan was like a grandfather who lets his grandchild be just as he is, even if the child is playing in the mud. Eventually the child will want to get out of the mud and be clean. How about you? When will you want to clean the muddy mind? If not now, when? If not here, where?

CASE 15

Kyozan Plants His Mattock

PREFACE TO THE ASSEMBLY

To know before a word is spoken is called "the silent utterance." To not be bright but reveal itself is called "the dark activity." Place the palms together in front of the three gates and in both hallways they promenade. Such empathy there is! Dance in the middle garden and at the back gate a head is moved. How about that!

MAIN CASE

Attention! Isan asked Kyozan, "Where did you come from?" Kyozan replied, "I came from the fields." Isan asked, "How many were in the fields?" Kyozan stuck his mattock in the ground, and stood with hands folded on his chest. Isan said, "In the southern mountains, lots of people reap thatch." Kyozan pulled up the mattock and left.

APPRECIATORY VERSE

The old awakened one with deep feeling considers his descendents.
But now he's spurred on to uphold his household.
Keep in mind the part about the southern mountains:
with it inlaid in bone, engraved on the skin, let's show our
    gratitude together.

The two people in this case are the founders of one of the five schools of Zen that arose in ancient China, called the Igyo School. One of the distinguishing features of this school was that it carefully considered both sudden enlightenment and the gradual cultivation of it, not getting caught up in the "sudden versus gradual" dispute that was popular at the time. Seeing clearly is one thing, the Igyo School teaches, but integrating it into your life is something else. Insight is sudden, integration is gradual.

In this case, Isan is the teacher and Kyozan is the student. Isan probes with his first question, to see where Kyozan is coming from, both literally and to test his Zen understanding. Then Isan asks Kyozan how many were there with him in the fields. Is that question a Zen question or an ordinary question? Kyozan sticks his mattock in the ground, demonstrating "Just this!" Kyozan got the point of the question. When he planted his pick in the ground, everything disappeared including Buddhas and Ancestors.

According to the sutras, the Buddha was born fully formed out of the side of his mother, took three steps, and pointed one finger up to the heavens and one finger to the earth saying, "Above heaven and earth, I alone am the World-Honored One." The whole world is my self. Planted firmly in the ground, Kyozan's mattock removed every square inch of soil.

But Kyozan has only partially expressed it, so Isan pushes further: Who are the other people, then, the ones reaping thatch? What about them? What about all the people who are suffering? What about all the people who are getting old, getting sick, dying? What about all the people who are going to work every day to support their families instead of sitting zazen like a solitary monk?

There are two sides here, and this koan requires that you see both of them. Do you comprehend?

Relating to this case, an ancient Zen poem says, "From the top of the solitary peak, I gaze at the clouds. Close by the old ferry landing, I am splashed with mire."

When we practice and penetrate into our concentration, we see that there's no self and no other. That is the view from the solitary peak. Expressing this state, Kyozan plants the mattock. Realizing that there are innumerable sentient beings who are suffering, the whole body is splashed with mire. Pull up that mattock and go take care of them!

CASE 16

Mayoku Thumps His Staff

PREFACE TO THE ASSEMBLY

Pointing to a deer, it becomes a horse. Grubbing the soil, it becomes gold. On the tongue, wind and thunder are raised. Between the eyebrows, a bloody blade is stored. While sitting, success or failure is perceived. While standing, life and death are examined. Tell me: what kind of samadhi is this?

MAIN CASE

Attention! Mayoku arrived at Shokei's place holding his staff. He walked three times around the meditation seat of Shokei and thumped his staff once. Shokei said, "Right! Right!" Mayoku afterward went to Nansen's, walked three times around the meditation seat of Nansen, and thumped his staff once. Nansen remarked, "Wrong! Wrong!" Mayoku said, "Shokei said, 'Right!' Why do you say, 'Wrong'?" Nansen said, "For Shokei, it is right. For you, it is wrong. What comes from the power of wind in the end becomes broken and crumbled."

APPRECIATORY VERSE

"Right" and "Wrong"—watch out for the trap;
it seems to be putting down, seems to be approving.
Who's the elder is difficult to tell; who's the younger is difficult to tell.
He knows to release when it's time.
What's special about my snatching away?
Thumping the golden staff, standing all alone;
circling the rope mat thrice he plays at leisure.
Being agitated a Sangha spawns right and wrong.
I reflect that a demon's seen in a withered skull.

Can you imagine going to another Zen center and instead of greeting the teacher, you just walk around her three times and bang the ground, and then walk out? Shokei says, "Right! Right!" and Mayoku says to himself, "Oh, I've been approved! I'm going to go do the same thing again!" So he goes to Nansen, and Nansen says, "Wrong! Wrong!" Why does one say he's right, and one say he's wrong? Is this an elaborate play that Shokei and Nansen are putting on? Shokei and Nansen are both successors of Baso who lived in the eighth century. Mayoku eventually succeeded Baso, but in this case he is on a pilgrimage to visit other teachers.

If we carefully look at this right and wrong, we see that it is the basis of our motivation. We always want to be right, to be approved in some way. When the Buddha sat under the Bodhi tree and vowed that he wouldn't rise until he realized this Great Matter, he was visited by the fiend Mara who would try all kinds of devices to distract him. Mara also visits each one of us while we are sitting and trying to quiet our mind. When he was not able to distract the Buddha, Mara finally said, "Even if you do realize your True Nature, who's going to witness it for you? Who's going to approve you?" Who's going to say, "Right! Right!"? The Buddha struck the ground, and said, "The great earth is my witness!" My own life is my witness! What good is approval from someone else, if you don't approve of yourself?

When we're children and as we grow up, we're reinforced in certain ways through approval. We hear, "You're a good boy, you're a good girl." We can't get in touch with our own basic feelings, because we always have to be a good boy or a good girl, and we hear, "Good boys don't do that, good girls don't do that." We're taught what's right in order to fulfill the American dream of wealth and fame.

What do wealth and fame give us? Other than the comforts and privileges they bring, they also bring approval. Judging from the number of unhappy celebrities, even approval is not sufficient. I read an interesting psychological study that was done on Nobel laureates, which showed that the amount of stress they're under when they're trying to win the Nobel Prize is not much compared to the amount of stress they're under after they win it. After they win it, everybody expects them to be brilliant all the time. What are they going to do for an encore? How are they going to get even more approval? It's never enough for them, because the great earth is not their witness.

The appreciatory verse says, "Being agitated, the Sangha spawns right and wrong." Some people who used to sit with us have left because they didn't like the form. They learned in another tradition or another lineage where they do things differently, and they didn't want to do it our way. The best form is to be grounded in no form.

Soto Zen students in this country often think there's one right way to do things. The two main temples in the Japanese Soto School, Eiheiji and Sojiji, have different styles. In Eiheiji, the monks wear their *kesa* tucked into their robe. At Sojiji, they wear it out. When you approach the altar during chanting service, after offering incense, at Eiheiji they turn to the right, at Sojiji they turn to the left.

It's not a question of right or wrong, it's a question of letting go of your fixed positions. The appreciatory verse also says, "Right and wrong. Watch out for the trap." It's a trap! If we stop and reflect on our life, we'll see that we all want approval. There's nothing wrong with acknowledging people, and it can be important. When it becomes addictive, then it is a sickness. Then one can't have enough fame, enough money, enough recognition. That is why Nansen says, "What comes from the power of the wind, in the end becomes broken and crumbled." It's addictive because somehow, we're holding very firmly to this notion of self. Watch how good you feel when someone approves of you, and how bad you feel when someone disapproves of you. What is it?

"Right and wrong, watch out for the trap. It seems to be putting down, seems to be approving." When Shokei said, "Right! Right!," was he approving, and when Nansen said, "Wrong! Wrong!," was he disapproving? Some of you know the story of a spiritual community where two members were arguing, and they went to the guru. The first one presented his case, and the guru said, "You're right!" Then the second one presented his case, and the guru said, "You're right!" The guru's attendant was there and heard the exchange, and said, "Wait, this person presented his case, and you said he was right, and the other presented the opposite case, and you said he's right." The guru looked at him and said, "You're right!" You're right too!

"I reflect that a demon is seen in a withered skull." We create all kinds of things that aren't there, in order to reaffirm our life, not as the life of the Buddha, but as the ego-centered life. That's the withered skull. See the demon clearly and it will vanish. With the earth as your witness, affirm your life as the life of the Buddha.

CASE 17

Hogen's Hair's-Breadth

PREFACE TO THE ASSEMBLY

Paired geese beating the ground with their wing tips fly up high. A pair of wood ducks stands alone at the edge of a pond. Leaving aside the matter of arrow points meeting head on, what about sawing on a steel counterweight?

MAIN CASE

Attention! Hogen asked Administrator Monk Shuzan, "If there's even a hair's breadth of difference, heaven and earth are clearly separated. How do you understand this?" Shuzan replied, "If there's even a hair's breadth of difference, heaven and earth are clearly separated." Hogen said, "If that's so, how could you understand it?" Shuzan answered, "I am just this. How about you, Osho?" Hogen remarked, "If there's even a hair's breadth of difference, heaven and earth are clearly separated." At that, Shuzan bowed low.

APPRECIATORY VERSE

A fly settles on a balance pan and it tilts.
The ten-thousand-generation scale illuminates unevenness.
Pounds, ounces, pennyweights, grains—measure exactly as you will.
In the end you'll lose to my fixed indicator.

If there's even a hair's breadth of difference, heaven and earth are clearly separated. This line comes from the "Xinxinming" or "Faith in Mind," a verse that was composed by the Third Ancestor in China. This is the third line in the verse which begins, "The Great Way is not difficult for those who are not attached to their preferences."

As you know everything depends upon conditions. This is also true of being rich or poor, happy or unhappy, being in heaven or hell. When we attach to our preferences we create heaven and hell. So, if there's a hair's breadth of difference, heaven and earth are set infinitely apart. How do you understand it? How could Shuzan, who's an administrator monk, a senior student of Hogen's, express it without falling into one side or the other? In Case 43 of the *Gateless Gate* Shuzan Shonen (a different Shuzan) holds up his staff and asks the same question: "If you call this a staff, you are committed to the name. If you say it's not a staff, you negate the fact. What will you call it?" How do you avoid falling into one side or the other?

This Shuzan understands it by just repeating it. "If there's even a hair's breadth of difference, heaven and earth are clearly separated." Hogen said, "If that's so, how could you understand it?" If there's no separation, how could you understand it? Understanding relies upon the subject that's understanding and the object that's being understood. Hogen is testing him further, and Shuzan answers, "I am just this. How about you, Osho?" That's the way I am, whether I understand it or not. How about you?

And Hogen replies, "If there's even a hair's breadth of difference, heaven and earth are clearly separated." Here it comes back again, the same statement. Is there any difference between Shuzan stating it and Hogen stating it? How do we take it into our life? It's not just a game they're playing. Hogen is testing Shuzan, to see how many hooks he can grab onto. Most of us walk around with these big hooks sticking out of our bodies. Anyone can come by, jerk them and upset us.

How do we create this gap, this hair's-breadth of difference—this smallest distinction between oneself and others, between ourselves and ourselves? This breadth could become a huge chasm. We should pay close attention to it. In the *Blue Cliff Record*, Case 57, a monk asks Master Joshu, "The Supreme Way is not difficult, it simply dislikes choosing. What is choosing?" This is another translation of the first line of "Faith in Mind." Joshu said, "Above the earth and beneath the heavens, I alone am the World-Honored One." That expression comes from one of the sutras, and supposedly is what the Buddha said when he was born. The student said to Joshu, "Isn't that still choosing?" Joshu said, "You country bumpkin. Where is the choosing?"

It always comes down to the question, what is this "I"? I alone. What is that "I"? If it is the "I" that has no boundaries, then "I alone" includes everything.

For this "I" that includes everything, how can there be even a hair's breadth of difference?

How do you avoid setting heaven and earth infinitely apart? One of our koans asks, "How do you walk straight on the mountain road that has a thousand curves?" How do you walk straight in your life, which has ten thousand twists and turns, ups and downs? If you try to walk straight on a mountain curve, where do you end up? In a ravine. So how do you walk straight? How do you maintain a fixed indicator? If the mountain road curves to the right, you curve to the right. If the mountain road curves to the left, you curve to the left. If upset comes into your life, you're upset. If joy comes into your life, you're joyful. If confusion comes in, you're confused. If fear comes in, you're afraid.

As soon as you recognize, "I am afraid," the quality of the fear shifts. No matter how you try to measure it, it changes. If you think you've grasped it, it's gone. If there's even a hair's breadth of difference, as long as there is a subject and an object, heaven and earth are clearly separated.

CASE 18

Joshu's Dog

PREFACE TO THE ASSEMBLY

Poke a floating gourd on the water and it turns. A diamond in the sun has no fixed shade of color. No-mindedness cannot understand. Yes-mindedness cannot perceive. Even an immeasurably great person can be turned about by words. Is there any way to escape that?

MAIN CASE

Attention! A monk asked Master Joshu, "Does a dog have Buddha Nature?" Joshu replied, "Yes." And then the monk said, "Since it has, how did it get into that bag of skin?" Joshu said, "Because knowingly, he purposefully offends." On another occasion a monk asked Joshu, "Does a dog have Buddha Nature?" Joshu said, "No!" Then the monk said, "All beings have Buddha Nature. Why doesn't the dog have it?" Joshu said, "It is because of his having karmic consciousness."

APPRECIATORY VERSE

A dog's Buddha Nature, yes;
a dog's Buddha Nature, no.
From the first a straight hook seeks fish with abandon.
Chasing the spirit, seeking the fragrance—a cloud and water guest.
Pattering and chattering to make debates and excuses,
it is evenly revealed, grandly displayed;
don't worry that he is not careful at the start.
Pointing to the fault, he snatched the jewel away;
King Shin did not know Shojo Rin.

An abbreviated version of this case appears as Case 1 in the *Gateless Gate*. In all earnestness a monk asked Joshu, "Does a dog have Buddha Nature or not?" Joshu answered, "Mu!" which literally means "No!" This koan has traditionally been used as the first barrier for a Zen student to pass through. You need to see eye to eye with Joshu and embody his "Mu." There is not even a toe-hold or a fingerhold to grab onto. You have to let go of all of your ideas and conceptions in order for Joshu's intent to be revealed. With weak concentration, Mu will be as elusive as a star at dawn.

Before Joshu said, "Mu" to that question, he said, "Wu" which means "Yes!" Then the monk said, "If that's so, why does the dog exist in that flea-bitten bag of skin?" There was a belief that one had to be in the human realm in order to realize Buddhahood. The dog is in the animal realm, so how can it have Buddha Nature? Joshu says, "Because knowingly, he purposefully offends." What kind of dog is it that offends on purpose with full knowledge? In Zen, the most offensive thing is to be deluded. All suffering arises from our ignorance and delusion. The point of our practice is to shine light in all of our ignorant dark places in order to see them clearly and dispel delusion in order to liberate all sentient beings.

We chant the four great bodhisattva vows at the end of every sitting. The first is, "Sentient beings are numberless; I vow to save them." You can look at this chant in two ways. In one way, it's an amazingly humble thing since we are serving all beings everywhere. In another way, it's an amazingly futile thing to say. It's like carrying snow to the well, to fill it. If we dump snow into the well, it melts in the water in the well and is swept away in the underground aquifer. You can never fill the well with snow no matter how hard you try. That is why knowingly it purposely offends.

Purposely offending can also be called "delusion within delusion." Since from the Buddha Nature perspective, there is no one to save and no one to do the saving, we delude ourselves twice when we vow to save all beings everywhere. So, the monk could be asking, "What's so wise about a person who's trying to save people who don't need to be saved? Since each one of us is the Buddha, what are we saving?" Master Dogen says, "To raise the bodhi mind is to vow and endeavor to help all sentient beings to cross to the other shore of enlightenment." That is your job description as a Zen student and bodhisattva.

Dogen also says in "Raising the Bodhi Mind," "Without the discriminating mind, we cannot awaken to bodhi mind." That discriminating mind is the very vehicle that allows us to raise the bodhi mind, to elevate, to awaken to the bodhi mind, and to realize the enlightened mind. So, if we don't reject that, but just accept it, that is elevating the bodhi mind.

That bodhi mind is always present. It just needs to be revealed. When we realize who we are, everything is as it is! The dog is the dog, and Buddha Nature is Buddha Nature.

Master Joshu said, "Yes, the dog has Buddha Nature." The monk said, "Since it has, how did it get in that bag of skin?" Joshu said, "Because knowingly, he purposefully offends." If we see the dog clearly, he is the great bodhisattva coming to liberate each one of us.

Later the monk said, "Does a dog have Buddha Nature?" and Joshu said, "No!" "All beings have Buddha Nature. Why doesn't the dog?" "Because of having karmic consciousness."

With one hand Joshu is releasing his grip: the dog has Buddha Nature. And with the other hand, he's snatching it back: no Buddha Nature. That "no" wipes away everything. So what does it have to do with karmic consciousness? When Buddha Nature is Buddha Nature, there is no self, no other, and no karma. When the dog is the dog, we can see its karma in action.

So first he says, yes. Then he says, no. "From the beginning, a straight hook seeks fish with abandon." When Zen masters go fishing with a straight hook, they only catch the best students. When Dogen's teacher, Tendo Nyojo said, "Drop off body and mind!," he caught Dogen with his straight hook. The straight hook will catch those students who drop off body and mind, but as long as we are attached to them, we're caught by a different kind of hook.

If you say it's *Mu*, I say it's *Wu*. If you say it's *Wu*, I say it's *Mu*. If you say nothing, then you defy the fact. If you say something, then you don't perceive it. So, does a dog have Buddha Nature or not?

CASE 19

Ummon's Mount Sumeru

PREFACE TO THE ASSEMBLY

I always admire the novel activity of Ummon. All his life he pulled out nails and wedges for people. Why did he sometimes open his gate and set out a tray of glue, or dig a pitfall in the middle of the road? Try to examine it and see.

MAIN CASE

Attention! A monk asked Ummon, "When not producing a single thought, is there any fault, or not?" Ummon said, "Mount Sumeru."

APPRECIATORY VERSE

Not raising a single thought—Mount Sumeru!
Ummon's Dharma giving is not meant to be stingy.
Come to accept it and you'll get a double handful.
Go doubt it and you'll never scale that thousand-yard height.
Blue oceans vast, white clouds at ease.
Between them there's not a hair's breadth.
A false cock's crow never deceives one;
be unsure and you'll not pass through the barrier.

In Sanskrit, *sumeru* means "wonderfully high," and Mount Sumeru is the center of the universe in Buddhist cosmology. It's the dwelling place of the gods. It is surrounded by seas and continents, and under it is the realm of hell, and above it is the realm of heaven.

The monk asked, "When not producing a single thought, is there any fault, or not?" It reminds me of the joke: If a man is all alone in the woods without his wife, is he still wrong?

If you say, "I don't produce a single thought!" then the fault is right there. Ummon says, "Mount Sumeru." In the preface, it says he's always pulling out nails for people, and sometimes he puts a bowl of glue down for them to step into. It is said that Ummon always had a very pithy expression for any question.

In the Vimalakirti Sutra, when the Buddha was referring to an accomplished bodhisattva, he said, "Like Mount Sumeru, you are unmoved by honor or scorn. You love moral beings and immoral beings equally. Poised in equanimity, your mind is like the sky. Who would not honor such a precious jewel of a being?" Like Mount Sumeru, you are unmoved by honor or scorn, and you love moral and immoral beings equally. Like Mount Sumeru, not being moved by praise or criticism. How many of us can say that? Somehow, somebody praises you and you get a fat head. Is that Mount Sumeru? Somebody criticizes you and you get upset. Is that Mount Sumeru?

In a small village in Japan a young unmarried woman got pregnant. Her parents were enraged and she didn't want to incriminate her boyfriend, so she said, "That monk did it." That monk was the famous Master Hakuin. The parents went to him, and told him that he had to take care of the baby. He just said, "Is that so?" When the baby was born, he took care of it, and took the baby with him on begging rounds in order to get milk for the baby. Of course, everybody thought, "You dirty monk!" Eventually, he couldn't get anything. He had to go to other villages where his reputation hadn't preceded him. Finally the girl felt remorse, and admitted that it wasn't the monk. The parents went and apologized, and wanted the baby back. Hakuin said, "Is that so?" That's Mount Sumeru, unmoved by honor or scorn. We honor Master Hakuin now because of that!

Mount Sumeru is the universe. Even the ten thousand arms of Avalokiteshvara, the Great Compassionate One, cannot hold it. Wherever you look, whatever you see, whatever you feel, whatever you think: Mount Sumeru. So, when not producing a single thought, Mount Sumeru. Is there fault? Mount Sumeru. No fault? Mount Sumeru. And yet, you can't see through it. Why not? Because you are IT!

There's another Chinese monk in the seventh century who wrote a commentary on Mount Sumeru and its relation to bowing. He said, "Is this not wonderful? Before, your body was just a speck on Mount Sumeru, and Mount Sumeru was the size of a dust mote in the Dharma realm. But when you reach the point of the true appearance which has no appearance, Mount Sumeru is contained within your Dharma body. You now contain Mount Sumeru. Is this not wonderful? You contain absolutely everything. Everything in the universe is contained within your nature, and you understand everything. The true mark of impartial bowing is an inconceivable state. You can reach this state when bowing to Buddha. Can you then explain all of its wonderful aspects? No. They are ineffable, indescribable."

If you really truly learn how to bow, then your body itself is Mount Sumeru. People who come to Buddhist practice in this country are not used to bowing, because bowing generally means "putting somebody above us." In a democracy, we don't do that. But there are examples of when Americans do bow. One is when people almost lose their life in an airplane that's disabled. When it finally lands, the first thing people do when they get on the ground is prostrate all the way down, put their head to the earth, and kiss it! It takes a near-death experience for Americans to naturally bow.

The Buddhist practice of bowing to the Buddha diminishes one's habits of self-importance, pride, and arrogance. It is a misconception though, to think that the worshipper is bowing to a statue of a Buddha, to a wooden, or stone, or clay image. The Buddha we bow to is the Buddha of our true minds. Mount Sumeru is bowing to Mount Sumeru.

The verse says, "Be unsure and you'll not pass through the barrier." Maezumi Roshi used to say, "I want you to be confident in yourself." That confidence is nothing but Mount Sumeru.

CASE 20

Jizo's "Not Knowing Is the Most Intimate"

PREFACE TO THE ASSEMBLY

A profound talk of entering the Principle derides the three and rends the four. The broad way of Choan runs seven vertically and eight horizontally. Suddenly opening your mouth to speak decisively, and lifting your foot to tread firmly, you should hang up your traveling bag and bowl and break your staff. Tell me: who is such a person?

MAIN CASE

Attention! Master Jizo asked Hogen, "Where have you come from?" "I pilgrimage aimlessly," replied Hogen. "What is the matter of your pilgrimage?" asked Jizo. "I don't know," replied Hogen. "Not knowing is the most intimate," remarked Jizo. At that, Hogen experienced great enlightenment.

APPRECIATORY VERSE

Right now, investigation replete, it's the same as before.
Utterly free from minute obstacles, one comes to not know.
Short's short, long's long. Cease pruning and grafting.
According with high, according with low, each is even and content.
A family's manner of abundance or thrift is used freely according
    to circumstances.
Fields and lands excellent, sportive; one's feet go where they will.
The matter of thirty years' pilgrimage—
a clear transgression against one's pair of eyebrows.

"I don't know" could also be translated, "Not knowing." Not knowing is most intimate. As soon as we know something, it becomes separate. It becomes a piece of knowledge or understanding that we can manipulate. That doesn't mean it's not useful; but it's just not very intimate.

Jizo (who we met in Case 12) was a teacher in China in the Golden Age of Zen. The student, Hogen, was founder of one of the five schools of Zen in China. Bodhidharma predicted there would be five schools before he died, one flower with five petals. Hogen was the founder of the Hogen School, and one of the characteristics of the Hogen School was to find realization not just in yourself, but in all things, in your environment. When all things in the universe manifest as Absolute, it leads to realization.

Typical of this school is this exchange: When asked by a young monk, "What is Buddha?" Hogen said, "First I want to ask you to practice it. Second, I want to ask you to practice it." Similarly when a contemporary Zen abbot retired, his final words were, "First, I want you to practice for ten years. Second, I want you to practice for ten more years. Third, I want you to practice for ten more years." Whatever ails you, get on a zafu and sit on it, and call me in thirty years.

But how to practice it? Not knowing is most intimate, yet we've developed all kinds of patterns and habits that prevent us from being intimate with ourselves and with others. It's so hard to see them because they're in our blind spots. We just do these things without even thinking or reflecting on them. They are so much our habitual way of behaving that we don't even recognize them.

We have certain twisted patterns of behavior, but we don't see them, because we're too comfortable with them. In order to be free of them, we have to begin to see them, to cultivate awareness that transcends thoughts and knowledge. To expand the context of your life, you must experience your own discomfort and misery. Just notice how protective you are of whatever it is you think you are.

By honoring this "not knowing" instead of fighting it, we can discover new possibilities in the midst of our problems. When we think we know all the answers, we feel safe. But life is not safe. We're all going to die. Life is a journey into the unknown.

When you hear how Hogen was enlightened, you can get fixated with "not knowing is the Way." "Not knowing" can become just another principle.

In Case 19 of the *Gateless Gate*, Nansen says, "The Way is not in knowing or in not knowing. Knowing is false consciousness, not knowing is indifference."

When Jizo said, "Not knowing is most intimate," it covered all possibilities and supports everything everywhere. This "not knowing is most intimate" contains knowing and not knowing. It contains both and neither, all together. So when you affirm, totally affirm, but don't settle down in affirmation. When you deny, totally deny, but don't settle down in denial.

Master Jizo said, "In walking and sitting, just hold to the moment before thoughts arise. Look into it, and you'll see not seeing. Then, put it to one side." In other words, if you see not seeing, or hear not hearing, put it to one side. Don't attach to that. "When you direct your efforts like this, rest does not interfere with meditation, and meditation does not interfere with rest." Before thinking, what is it? That's most intimate. When we think, we immediately form images and ideas and concepts.

So how can each one of us take care of the minute obstacles? If you think there are no obstacles there, you're just kidding yourself. Really see those obstacles, and be willing to look at your patterns of behavior. Look at how you defend yourself, then you can get out of your comfort zone. You can do it on your cushion, you can do it during work, you can do it during eating, you can do it during chanting, and you can do it during dokusan. Each of us should strive to awaken. Take heed! Do not squander your life.

CASE 21

Ungan Sweeps the Ground

PREFACE TO THE ASSEMBLY

Although you are freed of delusion and enlightenment, and have exhausted holiness and ordinariness, a particular capability is still needed to establish who is host and guest and distinguish between noble and base. It is not that there is no measuring of character or assigning of work. How do you understand the kindred spirit of the same branch?

MAIN CASE

Attention! As Ungan was sweeping the ground, Dogo said, "You're hard at it!" Ungan replied, "You should know there's one who isn't hard at it!" Dogo said, "So, is there a second moon?" Ungan held up the broom saying, "Which moon is this?" Dogo desisted. Regarding this, Gensha remarked, "Indeed, this is the second moon." Ummon also said, "The butler watches the maid politely."

APPRECIATORY VERSE

Using what's at hand he finished up the yard.
He could use it and know when to desist.
Before Elephant Bone Crag, a hand fiddles with a snake.
What you did as a youngster, now aren't you ashamed?

Both Ungan and Dogo were students of Hyakujo. They later went to study with Yakusan Igen, and became his successors. These two Dharma brothers were almost inseparable. They used to take every opportunity to engage each other in Dharma dialogue. They were constantly prodding each other. Nothing was said innocently between them.

Ungan was sweeping the ground. Right there, you can take that as a koan—sweeping the ground. In our practice, cleaning is greatly emphasized: What is the best way to clean? How do we sweep? What are we sweeping away? There's a koan: Empty handed yet holding a hoe. Why not: Empty handed yet holding a broom? How do you sweep empty-handed?

When we practice we are continually sweeping the ground of our mind. We sweep it clean, and then the dust settles again, and then we sweep again. Sometimes we're like kids. You tell your kid, "Clean your room." He'll say, "What for? It's just going to get dirty again!" Keep sweeping your mind clean.

Since all is emptiness, who is the one who's hard at it? "You should know there's one who isn't hard at it." It's not a question of hard or easy. It's just a question of totally putting yourself into it, so that the self completely disappears, and all there is, is "hard at it."

When there's no place to rest, you will know there's one who isn't hard at it. Dogo said, "So, is there a second moon?" Who are you—the one hard at it or the one not hard at it? If you say one, then there's two. So, is there a second moon?

The one who's hard at it and the one who isn't hard at it: Are they the same or are they different? To see the one who's not hard at it, we have to penetrate through the barriers set up by the Zen teachers. How about the one who's not bothered by anything? As long as there's a gap, a separation, a judgment, then there's upset. Then we're like that puppet on the shelf. Somebody's pulling our strings. To be the puppet master, you have to see that one who's not hard at it. But we don't see it because we are fascinated and attached to two moons: good and bad; man and woman; the one hard at it and the one not hard at it. It's true. If you're okay, everything's okay, because when you're the one who's not hard at it, there's no separation between you and everything. If that's the case, what do you have to complain about?

So all of our complaints are relative, relative to something. Maybe it's wanting to be better than somebody else, or wanting to protect our self from something or to not be bothered. So Dogo said, "Is there a second moon?" He's asking, "Haven't you fallen into duality? Aren't you adding something extra?" Being stuck in the absolute state is as useless as a second moon. So Ungan holds up his broom and says, "Which moon is this?" Is he coming from the absolute or the relative? Is he snatching everything away: absolute, relative, moon, broom, sweeping? When we look into our own mind there's all kinds of places where we stick, like Velcro. There's even places we stick that we don't see. Don't think that Dogo didn't know what to say when he desisted, when he was silent. That was the way he answered Ungan. It's just a second moon as soon as he says something. It's "which moon is this" as soon as he says something. He's splitting it into two again.

This case includes comments by Gensha and Ummon, who studied together under Seppo. They made their comments about eighty years after the main dialogue in the case took place. Gensha and Ummon's comments were appended to this case by Master Wanshi, the compiler of the *Book of Equanimity*. Gensha remarks, "Indeed, this is the second moon!" He's saying that instead of just sweeping, Ungan and Dogo are throwing dust in our eyes. What's all this chattering about? But at the same time, if it is the second moon, what's wrong with that? Ummon says, "The butler watches the maid politely." He's calling Ungan and Dogo the "butler" and "maid." He's saying something similar to what Gensha is saying but in a subtler way. Servants are kind of crude and unrefined compared to the aristocrats who employ them. So Ummon, in one sense, is saying Ungan and Dogo are like two uneducated servants; almost like children, just making noise to disturb people. But if they really disturb us, it is to help us to see directly into that one who isn't hard at it.

The verse has the line, "What you did as a youngster, now aren't you ashamed?" Each moment is new and fresh. As soon as I write these words, they become stale. It's a shame.

The one who isn't hard at it, that's the same as not-knowing. If you come from that place, if you tap into that place, each one of us is not-knowing. Each one of us is the one who isn't hard at it. But the one who's hard at it is obscuring that view. We work so hard trying to be something else other than just being who we are. If you're nervous, just be nervous. There is no second moon in that.

CASE 22

Ganto's Bow and Shout

PREFACE TO THE ASSEMBLY

People are probed with words. Water is sounded with a stick. Pushing away weeds and seeing the true manner is an everyday affair. When suddenly a burnt-tail tiger is transformed, then what?

MAIN CASE

Attention! Ganto arrived at Tokusan's place. He straddled the entrance gate and asked, "Is this common or holy?" Tokusan gave a shout, and Ganto bowed low. Tozan heard of this and said, "Had that not been Ganto, it would have been most difficult to take." Regarding this, Ganto remarked, "Old man Tozan doesn't know good from bad. At the time my one hand upheld, and the other hand put down."

APPRECIATORY VERSE

Crushing the visitor, wielding a scepter.
Affairs have a way of appropriate dispatch;
countries have their own inviolable laws.
If the guest serves reverently, the host is haughty;
if the king resents admonition, the people flatter.
Ganto's asking Tokusan—what did he mean?
One upheld, one put down—see the movement of mind!

In this case Ganto came to study with Tokusan. Ganto was still a little green, but he later became a famous successor of Tokusan, whom we met in Case 14. Ganto straddles the gate, not coming in or going out. And he says, "Is this place holy or ordinary?" He's checking to see if it's a place he wants to study. Some of you do that too, you check this place out, and ask, "Is this place ordinary, or is it sacred? Am I going to have a great time here, or is it just going to be like the rest of my life?" Do I really want to be here or not?

Tokusan gave a shout, and Ganto bowed. Ganto was checking out Tokusan, but then he bows. So is the bow genuine, or is it just flattery? What's his intention?

Tozan, one of the founders of the Soto School in China, was a contemporary of Ganto and Tokusan. When he heard about this, he said, "Had that not been Ganto, it would have been most difficult to take." Is he genuinely praising Ganto, or is he just probing Ganto to see how he would react? It got back to Ganto, and he said, "Old man Tozan doesn't know good from bad. At the time my one hand upheld, and the other hand put down."

In this case, Ganto thinks he's better than Tozan, and he's explaining what he was doing. The commentaries on this koan say there's a stench of Zen on Ganto, a kind of arrogance.

In olden times, the Buddha straddled a gate, and he said, "Tell me: Am I about to leave, or about to enter?" There's a song lyric that says, "If you're not busy living, you're busy dying." If you are born when the sun is on the horizon, how would you know if it is a sunrise or a sunset?

The question asked by Ganto, "Is this common or holy?" is the same kind of principle. It's a trap. What can you say? As soon as you say one or the other, you're stuck in that position. How can you express it?

You can't fully describe it, yet it exists. If you don't experience it, your understanding is just a projection. When you finally get down to what you're really experiencing, you will know how to express yourself.

In the verse, "If the guest serves irreverently, the host is haughty" refers to Ganto's bow to Tokusan. Is it a genuine bow? "The king resents admonition, the people flatter" is Tozan's comment about Ganto, when he said, "Had that not been Ganto, it would have been most difficult to take." The king resents admonition. We are all like that as well. When we criticize someone who resents admonition and hates to be criticized, it shuts off all possibilities of interaction.

But Ganto got even more arrogant, saying, "Old man Tozan doesn't know good from bad. At the time my one hand upheld, and the other hand put down." The verse says, "One upheld, one put down, see the movement of mind." When someone praises you, how do you respond? When someone criticizes you, how do you respond? See the movement of the mind. Who is it that's feeling pride? Who is it that's feeling remorse?

Where are you stuck? How do you respond in these situations? Entering could be good or it could be bad. Leaving could be good or it could be bad. Or they could both be good. You never know whether something is going to turn out to be good or bad. It's all grist for the mill, as long as we're aware of it. Just do the best you can.

CASE 23

Roso Faces the Wall

Bodhidharma's nine years are known as wall gazing. Shinko's three prostrations are outflowings of heavenly activity. How can the traces be swept away, the footprints be eliminated?

MAIN CASE
Attention! Whenever Roso saw a monk coming, he would face the wall. Hearing of this, Nansen remarked, "I always tell others to receive directly, even before the empty *kalpa*, and to realize themselves even before the Buddha came into the world. But still, I haven't found half a man, let alone a whole man. If he is thus, he will be stuck in the year of the donkey."

APPRECIATORY VERSE
Plain water has flavor, subtly transcending the senses.
It precedes forms, though seeming endlessly to exist.
The Way is precious, though seeming massively to be foolish.
Inscribe designs on a jewel and its glory is lost;
a pearl even from an abyss naturally beckons.
Plenty of bracing air purely burnishes autumn's swelter;
far away a single tranquil cloud divides sky and water.

When Bodhidharma came from India to China, no one understood his teaching and so he went to Shorin and spent nine years facing the wall (see Case 2). What was Bodhidharma doing for those nine years? Some of you have spent nine years facing the wall, too. Is your nine years the same as Bodhidharma's nine years? Was he waiting for something? Do you think he thought that if he sat there something would happen?

"Whenever Roso saw a monk coming, he would face the wall." Roso and Nansen, who comments here, are brother monks, both are successors of Baso. They studied together and knew each other well. A monk would come and ask Roso, "Does a dog have Buddha Nature?" and Roso would face the wall. A monk would ask him, "What is the meaning of Bodhidharma coming from the west?" and he would face the wall. What was he doing?

You could say he's demonstrating the first principle of life, everything is as it is. We could say that facing the wall is symbolic of something. What is the wall each one of us is facing? Or at another level of sophistication, can you face the wall without facing the wall?

If you can directly face the pain of your life, that's the joy in life. If you don't face the pain in your life, that's the pain in your life. So what is facing the wall? How can you really face the wall without adding anything else, thinking something, projecting something, rationalizing something?

Even though you intellectually understand it and can explain it thoroughly, it does not compare to personally experiencing it once. Nansen remarked, "I always tell others to receive directly, even before the empty kalpa." A *kalpa* is a really long period of time. My teacher used to describe a kalpa this way: There is as a huge solid granite mountain, a mile on each side and a mile high. An angel comes down every thousand years and brushes her wing against it, and when the mountain is worn away, that's one kalpa.

The kalpas are endless, but there are four of them: The empty kalpa, the kalpa of growth, the kalpa of dwelling, and the kalpa of decay. Buddhist philosophy describes the nature of thoughts in the same way. They arise, or grow, they persist, or dwell, and then they decay. Then there's the empty kalpa. So Nansen is talking about seeing directly, even before the empty kalpa. Even before a thought arises, see directly.

Then Nansen says "to realize yourself even before the Buddha comes into the world." When the Buddha came into the world, suddenly there was enlightenment and delusion. Prior to the Buddha, we didn't have thoughts of enlightenment and delusion. We didn't think, "If he's enlightened, I must be deluded." So how can we realize, even before the Buddha appears? It's before the appearance of duality, dichotomy, separation.

Nansen goes on to say, "But still, I haven't found half a man, let alone a whole man. If he is thus, he will be stuck in the year of the donkey." The Chinese zodiac has no year of the donkey. The Chinese zodiac goes in twelve-year cycles, and each year has a different animal, but if you're stuck in the year of the donkey, there's no end to your spinning.

From another perspective, the year of the donkey is beyond time. All the various meditation practices have their own unique advantages and disadvantages. Contemplating your breath is often used as a beginning practice, but it is not only for beginners. With deep conviction, continue to practice without end, and you might encounter the year of the donkey beyond time.

When we're facing the wall, we transmigrate through the six realms. These are the realms of hell, hungry ghosts, animals, humans, fighting spirits, and gods. When we're angry we're in the realm of fighting spirits, and when we're feeling greedy or desperate we're in the realm of hungry ghosts. When we have no sense of the consequences of our actions, we are in the animal realm. And we create our own heaven and hell. But in the human realm, we have the potential to see clearly and recognize our True Nature. It's the only realm where we can be conscious and aware.

The verse says, "Plain water has flavor, subtly transcending the senses." Water always takes the shape of its vessel and it also takes the flavor of whatever is added, salt or sugar or lemon. True Nature has no flavor other than the categories you create to describe it. If you talk about delusion and enlightenment, then ordinary and holy come into existence.

Those of you who have gone on hot, tiring hikes through the mountains know how wonderful clean, pure water can taste. That plain water transcends expressions. So does Roso facing the wall. When you thoroughly exhaust reason, you transcend thoughts and expressions. How can there be any comparison?

Roso seems like an idiot, facing the wall when people come to see him, but in fact he's transcending all the dualities. It seems foolish, but it's precious. My late teacher, Maezumi Roshi, used to say, "It's easy to sit facing the wall—but it's not easy to sit facing the wall."

CASE 24

Seppo's Poison Snake

The carp of the Eastern Sea, the poison snake of South Mountain; the donkey's bray of Fuke, the dog's bark of Shiko—these do not fall into the commonplace. They do not behave like animals. Tell me: what is the conduct of such persons?

MAIN CASE

Attention! Seppo addressed the assembly, saying, "There's a poison snake on South Mountain. All of you had better look out!" Chokei said, "Today in the hall there are many who have lost their lives." A monk related this to Gensha, and Gensha remarked, "Only Dharma brother Chokei could say that, but be that as it may, I am not like that." The monk asked, "What about you, Osho?" Gensha said, "Why bother using South Mountain?" Ummon threw down his staff before Seppo and gave the appearance of being afraid.

APPRECIATORY VERSE

Gensha's great vigor; Chokei's small bravery.
South Mountain's poison snake died uselessly;
where wind and clouds gather the head sprouts horns.
As expected, we see Joyo (Ummon) take a hand and fiddle around.
Among brilliant lightning flashes see the change!
When it's mine I can let go or call back.
When it's with him he grabs and releases.
What's that! Right now can you give it to someone?
Its chill mouth rends them, but men don't feel the pain.

Seppo was a teacher who took many years to awaken and see clearly. He succeeded Tokusan and had many successors of his own. Three of them appear in this case: Chokei, Gensha, and Ummon (who was also known as Joyo). Each one of them is commenting on Seppo's expression, "There's a poison snake on South Mountain. All of you had better look out."

The donkey's bray of Fuke mentioned in the preface is a reference to Master Fuke, a Chinese Zen master who lived in the ninth century and was a contemporary of Master Rinzai. Whenever Master Fuke was asked an intellectual question about Buddhism, he would get down on all fours and bray like a donkey while kicking over anything his feet could reach. Whenever he was scolded for such coarse behavior he would say, "What does Buddha-dharma have to do with coarse or fine?" Whatever you think you've accomplished, Master Fuke kicks it over.

This koan centers on the poison snake of South Mountain, which, like the carp of the Eastern Sea mentioned in the preface, is a way of referring to the Original Self, the True Dharma. If you don't know what it is, you had better look out.

Chokei says, "Today in the hall there are many who have lost their lives." He's expressing that absolute sameness, that absolute equality, that intrinsic state of oneness. You have to realize it, and through that realization you will see and appreciate that world of absolute equality. This is what it means to lose your life in Zen.

Gensha says, "Why bother using South Mountain?" He's pointing to the world of absolute difference. Everybody and everything is equal in the True Dharma, yet there is South Mountain and North Mountain, old women and young men, good and evil. Gensha's absolute difference is not ordinary difference; it covers everything and swallows heaven and earth—and swallows itself too!

Chokei is expressing that form is emptiness and Gensha is expressing that emptiness is form. What about Ummon? He throws down his staff in front of Seppo and makes the appearance of being afraid. It is beyond words and thoughts. Is he expressing equality or difference, emptiness or form?

Seeing the differences in the sameness is not two. When we realize that one truth is both truths, that both eyes are one eye, altogether it is the True Dharma. That's the eye of Shakyamuni Buddha, where nothing is lacking and nothing is extra. That wisdom of Shakyamuni Buddha is never exhausted, just like Gutei's finger (see Case 84), Fuke's donkey, and Seppo's poison snake. Wherever you sit, wherever you walk, that's where it is. However you see, however you hear, that's what it is. So how do you see?

Sometimes you see the difference, sometimes the sameness. If it changes as fast as a lightning flash, as it says in the verse, what is it? Same or different?

Putting aside same and different: There's a poison snake on South Mountain. All of you had better look out!

CASE 25

Enkan's Rhinoceros-Horn Fan

PREFACE TO THE ASSEMBLY

Lands and seas are boundless, yet they are not apart from right here. Things and previous kalpas, numerous as the dust, all exist right now. As when one is asked to show it face to face, being caught unprepared, one cannot present it. Tell me: Where is the fault?

MAIN CASE

Attention! One day Enkan summoned his attendant and told him, "Go out and fetch the rhinoceros-horn fan." The attendant replied, "The fan is broken." Enkan said, "If the fan is broken, bring me back the rhinoceros." The attendant made no reply.

Later, commenting on this case, Shifuku drew a circle and wrote within it the character for "ox."

APPRECIATORY VERSE

Break the fan and look for the rhinoceros.
The word within the circle has prior significance.
Who knows the thousand years' darkness of the new moon?
It subtly turns into autumn's harvest moon.

In Case 24, True Nature took the form of the poisonous snake on South Mountain. In this case, it's a rhinoceros-horn fan. In the east, the rhinoceros is regarded as a kind of ox, which is a frequent representation of True Nature—as in the famous ox-herding pictures.

Enkan lived at the end of the eighth and beginning of the ninth centuries, and was a Dharma heir of Baso—though he is less well-known than his Dharma brothers Nansen and Hyakujo. Enkan trained for over thirty years with Baso, and then when Baso died, he wandered around from place to place for thirty more years. When he was over seventy, he finally settled down and began to teach, until he died at the age of ninety-two.

We know very little about Shifuku, who later added his comments to the case, except that he is in the lineage of Isan and Kyozan, who founded the Igyo School, which died out in China. Teachers in the Igyo School often use objects and gestures in their teachings, particularly circles, and here Shifuku draws a circle. What is that?

When Enkan asks for the rhinoceros-horn fan, he's asking the attendant to bring him the mind that abides in no place. But the attendant was no slouch! He replies, "I can't bring it to you. It's broken." It wasn't broken until you brought it up and started talking about it; now it is broken.

Enkan then says, "In that case, bring me the rhinoceros." This is similar to another koan: A monk once asked Joshu, "If everything returns to the one, what does the one return to?" (Case 45 of the *Blue Cliff Record*). If the one is destroyed, what can you bring up?

When we practice zazen, both pleasure and pain come up, and we can get stuck in either one. But when we are able to let them both pass, something new arises. If we take care of one thing, something else comes up. How can we keep taking care of each thing as it comes up?

If we face our attachments, these negative ways of behaving, without really delving into our true self, we won't find peace or reach nirvana. In order to grow and develop, we have to face all of life's realities, which means to face ourselves as we are, with all of our so-called imperfections. If we don't look at our "imperfections," we'll continue to be a slave to them. Often in meditative practices like Zen, people think they've eliminated negative feelings if they ignore them. We think we can just act good and the negative part will go away. But that's not so: Even if you avoid the feelings, they are still there. Using zazen to cover them over and ignore them is sitting in an ice cave. It's a form of denial. Zazen is not about denial. True peace comes at a price, and the price is no self-pity and no self-delusion; the price is letting go of the small grasping self and putting in the time, effort, and perseverance to really see clearly; the price is patience and courage.

The verse says, "Who knows the thousand years' darkness of the new moon? It subtly turns into autumn's harvest moon." In other words, who knows a thousand years in the darkness of the new moon? A thousand years of darkness! Who knows that? It's really going into that dark place, the dark night of the soul. Yet a thousand years of darkness can suddenly turn into autumn's harvest moon. Going into the darkness, the light is revealed. A thousand-mile-deep root yields a sprout after a thousand years. The preface says, "Things and previous kalpas, numerous as the dust, all exist right now." So, how do you manifest a thousand years of darkness right now?

When Shifuku draws the circle, he is manifesting an empty state. When he draws the character for "ox," he is creating diversity arising from the emptiness. Emptiness and diversity: Are they one, or are they two?

The fan is broken, so look for the rhinoceros. When you find the rhinoceros, it is broken also. Whatever you bring, it just keeps breaking. The preface says, "Being caught unprepared, one cannot present it." Being prepared, how can you present it?

CASE 26

Kyozan Points to Snow

PREFACE TO THE ASSEMBLY

Ice and frost are one color. Snow and moon merge their light. Freeze the dharma-kaya to death, and ruin Gyoho with purity. Is this worthwhile to appreciate?

MAIN CASE

Attention! Kyozan pointed to a snow lion and said, "Can anyone go beyond this color?" Regarding this, Ummon said, "Right then, I'd push it down for him." And Setcho later added, "He only knows how to push it down, not how to raise it up."

APPRECIATORY VERSE

A pushing down, a raising up—the lion in the snowy garden.
Restraining offenses, embrace virtue; acting with bravery, behold
    righteousness.
Though pure light illumines the eye, it's like being lost from home.
Though clarity turns the body, it falls into a rank.
We Zen students have nothing to rely on!
The same life, the same death—which of them is best?
Warm tidings bursting the plum buds, spring comes to the icy branches.
A chill blast drops the leaves, fall clarifies the water puddles.

In this koan, Kyozan (whom we met in Case 15), points at a white snow lion and asks us to go beyond its color.

In the Lotus Sutra, it says, "Pure, uniform, unmixed plainness is the character of pure conduct." Pure, uniform, unmixed plainness is like the taste of water or the color white. In physics, white is the basis of all colors, the source of all colors. If you shine white light through a prism, it breaks up into all of the colors of the rainbow. It even transcends the visible spectrum that you can see.

But what's beyond white? What is the source of white? If you call the source of white a color, it relates to the eye. But what is the colorless color that does not relate to the eye? This is what Kyozan is asking us. When I ask, "What is the colorless color?" this might conjure up some image in your mind. But that image is literally just your imagination. Every image that we have is static. As soon as we imagine something, it becomes fixed. Truly going beyond the color white is not an image.

If we reflect upon our life, we see that we have many images about our life—the way it should be, who we are, what we want—and our life is often controlled by these images. Unless we deeply question these images, they become a part of the fiber of our life, and we base all of our actions on these images rather than on things as they are.

So, how can we really go beyond those images? How do we go beyond our narrow views? Even if we see something clearly, how do we go beyond *that?* We may think that we should be loving and compassionate and then we create an image "loving and compassionate." And then that image becomes rigid. It becomes something that binds us and hinders spontaneous action and compassion. How can we really be free according to each situation?

In our zazen, we need to cultivate nonjudgmental awareness, noticing what kinds of deep-seated behavior we have, when and how we do things automatically, what attitudes we have that lead to anxiety and unhappiness. Zazen is the perfect opportunity to practice nonjudgmental awareness, to notice when your mind is spinning off in one direction or another and to bring it back. Just notice it; don't criticize, don't judge. Eventually, you'll see certain patterns of behavior, certain routine ways that you do things, that don't particularly lead to peace and comfort. And when you see that pattern, just observe *that.* You don't have to change it; the process of observing will itself cause a certain shift. And eventually, you might see the root of that pattern, the source of your image. But don't rest there; go beyond even that.

Doing zazen is like riding a bicycle. A bicycle is basically unstable; it doesn't stand on its own. When you learn how to ride it, when your body really knows how to ride it, your body is constantly adjusting and can keep the bicycle upright. When it tips one way, you naturally adjust. When it tips the other way, you naturally adjust. When it bumps over a rut in the road, you naturally adjust. Your body is constantly adjusting because you've trained it that way, disciplined it. It's the same thing during zazen when thoughts arise: You need to adjust. If you don't adjust, your mind "falls over" and gets caught in a fantasy world. But if, as different thoughts arise, you just keep adjusting and moving your mind back to your breath, you'll find stability. You can reach a point where you can sense a thought with your whole body even before it becomes a thought. It's like a sprout: You can even feel the ground begin to budge before the sprout pushes through. Then move your focus back to your breathing. The thought doesn't even have to form. When you discipline your mind, you sense the arising of thoughts and can allow your body and your mind to naturally return to their original resting place.

That is the place beyond the color white. Keep getting in touch with that place.

When I was studying with Sochu Roshi, I was living in London where the sun rarely shines. Sochu Roshi was giving a talk in broken English, and he said, "The sun is shining! The sun is shining!" It was a typical gloomy London day. I was sitting next to him, and I said, "Where is it?"—and he punched me right in the gut. Right there! That's where it's shining! It's always shining; we just don't see it because we cloud it over.

But don't even get stuck in that realm beyond color. That's why Ummon comments, "Right then, I'd push it down for him." Push it down, let it go and go beyond that color. If you get stuck there, you have to push that down, too. Setcho says, "He only knows how to push it down, not how to raise it up." Another teacher said, "There's a time when you push down. There's a time when you raise up." Eventually, raising up and pushing down are simultaneous and then raising up and pushing down don't appear at all. What do you do then? You buy some sandals and go on a pilgrimage for thirty years. This is our life, not something that we're doing just to pass the time. That's the meaning of Kyozan's thirty-year pilgrimage.

The verse says, "We Zen students have nothing to rely on." Kyozan, Ummon, and Setcho are encouraging us not to get stuck in any place. As soon as you get attached to one place, you can't move. It's like nailing one foot to the ground. What's it good for? Walking in a limited circle, that's all. Yet the circle of life is boundless. So don't fiddle around with insignificant things. Don't dwell in your small circle. You can't rely on it.

CASE 27

Hogen Points to the Blind

PREFACE TO THE ASSEMBLY

When doctors are numerous, diagnosis is confused; when rules are set up, trickery is born. Although to cure sickness where no sickness exists is extreme compassion, when cases exist, such cases are presented; why then not present an example?

MAIN CASE

Attention! Hogen pointed with his hand to the blind. There were two monks present at the time. They both went and rolled up the blind. Hogen remarked, "One gains, one loses."

APPRECIATORY VERSE

Pines are straight, briars are bent.
Cranes are tall, ducks are short.
King Gi's people forgot both peace and war.
That peace—a submerged dragon in the abyss;
that freedom—a soaring bird freed of tethers.
Nothing can be done about the Ancestor's coming from the West.
Right here gain and loss are about half and half.
According to the breeze a mugwort leaf twirls in the air;
cutting across the stream a boat touches the bank.
If there's a sharp Zen student here, observe Seiryo's expedient means.

This koan also appears in the *Gateless Gate* as Case 26, and it addresses issues of gain and loss. In a relative sense, of course, everything we do has gain and loss. At every juncture in your life, you're making a choice. When you go down one road, you're not going down the other one. Every choice contains both advantages and disadvantages.

When Hogen was studying with Master Jizo, Jizo said, "Speaking from the point of view of Buddhism, everything presents itself." Everything, as it is, presents itself. At this, Hogen had his great realization. Even though everything always presents itself, we constantly try to gain something. My comments always have both gain and loss in them. You would be advised to wash my words from your ears. You may realize something, and you may attach to something else. Coming to sit zazen has gain and loss as well. You could be out on a picnic, but you chose to sit zazen.

Only if you see clearly into advantage and disadvantage, gain and loss, can you be free of them. If you're not attached to gain and loss, you can see it clearly. When you sit, just sit. When you stand, just stand. The reason we're not free from gain and loss is that we cling to gain and we fear loss. It's not as obvious, but we fear gain, too. Whatever we gain isn't quite enough to overcome whatever feelings of inadequacy we have. Our stubbornness and pride prevent us from accepting ourselves as we are.

This vicious cycle just leads to a yearning for love, approval, and affirmation. Our practice is to appreciate ourselves. Accepting ourselves as we are, we can see the patterns we have. If we don't accept ourselves, we'll never get free of them.

The *Daodejing* contains the line, "One gains by losing and loses by gaining." The more you gain, the more you have to protect. The more you let go, the freer you are. All of the preferences, the ideas, the comparisons we carry in our minds are like heavy boulders. Set them down. Be persistent and courageous and make right effort to stop, look, and listen.

The appreciatory verse for this case says: "Pines are straight, briars are bent. Cranes are tall and ducks are short." That's pretty straightforward. Some of you are tall, some of you are short. I don't think a duck complains that it has short legs, or a crane brags that is has long legs. A violet isn't jealous of a rose.

If you want to avoid misery, rely on your own lot. In the Genjo koan, Master Dogen says, "When the need is large, it is used largely. When the need is small, it is used in a small way. Thus no creature ever comes short of its completeness. Wherever it stands, it does not fail to cover the ground."

When you eat, you do not fail to cover the ground. When you roll up the blind, nothing is excluded. Where is the gain or loss?

CASE 28

Gokoku's Three Shames

The person without clothing is indeed a naked heretic. The person who doesn't chew a grain of rice is for sure the burned-face demon king. Even if you were born in a holy place, you can't avoid falling from the top of the pole. Is there anything to cover up this shame?

MAIN CASE

Attention! A monk asked Gokoku, "When a crane stands upon a withered pine, then what?" Gokoku said, "On the ground below, it's a shame." The monk then said, "When dripping water freezes, what then?" Gokoku replied, "After sunrise, it's a shame." The monk then said, "At the time of Esho's persecution of Buddhism, where were the good gods to protect the Dharma?" Gokoku said, "For the two guardians of the triple gate, it's a shame."

APPRECIATORY VERSE

Vigorous in the prime of life, one's temples are not yet grey;
a man who doesn't exert himself is not awarded nobility.
Instead recall the family members of unbroken honor;
the brook for washing ears is not for watering the ox.

Gokoku lived in the twelfth century, and was in the Rinzai lineage. In this koan the monk is talking about different states in his practice, and Gokoku is telling him, "If you stay there, it's a shame." We can appreciate the poetic expressions used in this case, most of which come from Chinese legends, but what's true is that right now for each one of us, if we get stuck in any place, it's a shame.

Master Tozan previously said, "The spirit tree is sublime, but the crane doesn't stay there." This relates to the first question, where the monk said, "When a crane stands upon a withered pine, then what?" The monk thinks he's realized something. The withered pine represents the state of emptiness. But Tozan reminds us the crane doesn't stay there, and in his comments on this case, Master Bansho says, "This monk took this little bit of scenery and stuck it on his forehead, showing it to everyone he met." He is saying, "Look at me! I've realized something!"...and that is a shame.

Gokoku replies, basically saying, "I'm standing down here on the ground, and you're up on this lofty place, and from this position, your position looks like a real shame." Then the monk says, "When dripping water freezes, what then?" He's presenting another stage: being able to stop all mental and physical activity. Gokoku replied, "After sunrise, it's a shame." When the sun comes out, what happens to your freezing water? If you are working on this koan with a koan teacher, the master might ask you, "What is the sun?"

Regarding Gokoku's comment, one master wrote, "When the ice melts, it exposes the dead body within." Don't dwell in cutting off all activity, otherwise it's a shame.

Next the monk says, "At the time of Esho's persecution of Buddhism, where were the good gods to protect the Dharma?" In the 840's, there was an emperor named Esho who forced a quarter of a million Buddhist monks and nuns to leave the monasteries and assume the lay life, and 4,600 monasteries were destroyed. Within a year of this proclamation, Esho died and Buddhism was restored. Did the good gods fail to protect the Dharma? When the monks and nuns left the monastery, did they leave the Dharma behind? The skillful means of the gods do not fall within the realm of sacred and profane. Since the Buddha Way is without limit, how can it flourish and decline?

Gokoku replied, "For the two guardians of the triple gate, it's a shame." Every Buddhist monastery in China had three gates at the entrance, and it's a shame if you think the Dharma is restricted to one side of those gates. Wherever you are, it's there.

Chinese Buddhism in general did not recover from the persecution, but since Zen Buddhism was practiced in remote places and the monks were self-sufficient, it recovered more fully. Sometimes a pruned tree becomes more vibrant. If you plant a seed, and give it the right amount of nutrients, water, and sunshine, it will grow strong, but if you don't tend it, it won't. Still, the Dharma doesn't depend on rise or decline, on sprouting or withering. As long as you're stuck to clarity and cloudiness, freedom and restriction, you're creating all kinds of conditions. How can you be free of those conditions? If you feel there's a barrier in front of you, how do you pass that barrier? If you think that barrier is not "you," then where is "you"? You're the source of everything in your life. Pleasure and pain originate with you. You have to be patient in looking at it, not judging or criticizing yourself. Be non-judgmental, and then in a clear state of mind, you'll see it.

The Way is vast and wide. Don't restrict it. As soon as you think you've accomplished something, you're stuck. As soon as you think you're not worthy of accomplishing something, you're stuck. And that's a shame! This practice is not just about seeing clearly into the nature of our true self. That's a very important part of it, but if you stay there, as this monk did, it's a shame. To actualize and manifest that realization in your life, moment after moment, is our practice.

CASE 29

Fuketsu's Iron Ox

PREFACE TO THE ASSEMBLY

Playing chess slowly and dully rots the axe handle. Rolling the eyes and loosing one's head, the ladle is snatched away. When dwelling in a demon's cave, and holding fast to a deadly snake's head, is there any chance of transformation?

MAIN CASE

Attention! When Fuketsu was staying in the governmental quarters in Ei Province, he ascended the high seat and said, "The characteristics of the Ancestors' mind-seal is like the functioning of the iron ox. Taking the seal off leaves an imprint. Leaving the seal on covers the imprint. But neither taking it off or leaving it on, is it right to seal this, or right to not seal it?" At that, Venerable Rohi stepped forward and said, "I have an iron ox's function. I beg you, Master, don't stamp your seal." Fuketsu replied, "Used as I am to scouring the ocean and catching whales, I regret that instead there's a frog floundering in the mud." Rohi was bewildered. Fuketsu shouted, "Venerable one, why don't you proceed?" Rohi hesitated. Striking out with his whisk, Fuketsu said, "Don't you remember the subject of our talk? Try and let's see." Rohi started to open his mouth and Fuketsu struck out with his whisk again. Then the governor, who was present, said, "Buddhadharma and ruler's Dharma are one," and Fuketsu said, "What is it you see?" The governor replied, "If you don't cut off when you should cut off, you invite disorder." At that, Fuketsu stepped down from his seat.

The iron ox's function: leaving an imprint, covering the imprint.
Leaving, he goes beyond even the top of Vairochana's head.
Sitting, he comes back on the tongue-tip of the Nirmanakaya Buddha.
Fuketsu checked the balance: Rohi met defeat.
The stick above, the shout below;
    lightning flashes and flint sparks.
Clear and bright, a pearl rolls upon the tray.
Knit your brow, and you'll stumble.

Fuketsu lived in the tenth century, and he was a great-grandson in the Dharma of Master Rinzai, and he also studied for a while with Seppo. The first part of the case is the characteristics of the Ancestors' mind-seal, which is the transmission of the Dharma from mind to mind, from teacher to student. Fuketsu says, "If you lift it, you leave an imprint. If you leave it, you cover the imprint. So what do you do?" This is reminiscent of Kyogen's comment in the *Gateless Gate* Case 5: "If you do not answer, you fail to meet the questioner's need. If you do answer, you lose your life." How do you respond without falling onto one side or the other?

The monk Rohi responds, "I have an iron ox's function." In other words, "I understand it clearly, so you don't need to stamp your seal. You don't need to approve me. I'm all set." Fuketsu tests the monk's state of mind by replying, "Used as I am to scouring the ocean and catching whales, all I see is a little frog floundering in the mud." Now Rohi is bewildered and doesn't know how to respond, so Fuketsu keeps at him: "If you really understand the Ancestors' mind-seal, how are you going to respond to that? Come on! Don't be shy. Say something!" Rohi hesitated, and Fuketsu struck out with his whisk. He hesitated again, so Fuketsu said, "Come on! Don't you remember what we were talking about? Try and let's see." Even before Rohi could open his mouth, Fuketsu hit him again.

Rohi is slow and dull-witted like the woodsman, mentioned in the preface, who was playing chess and took so much time between moves that the handle of his axe rotted. Fuketsu saw right through Rohi. Can he also see through you? When you are ready for the seal will it leave a brand for everyone to see and admire or will it be hidden from everyone, even you? The real challenge is to receive the seal but be free of any imprint.

The last part of this koan is also important to appreciate. The governor says, "Buddhadharma and ruler's Dharma are one." The governor was watching Fuketsu take care of Rohi, and he realized, "Hey! That's what I do, too!" And Fuketsu stepped down from his seat. He didn't say anything more.

Are the king's law and the Buddha's law the same or different? If they are the same, how are they the same? If they are different, how are they different? The king governs the country, but how about the laws with which you govern your own life? Dharma can mean reality, or all phenomena, and so we can also ask this: Is the reality of the Buddha the same as the reality of your life? The governor did not understand this point.

The king, the Buddha, each of us, and all beings intrinsically share the same essential nature—but if we don't live our life in accord with the Buddha's wisdom, we live in delusion. There is a Zen poem: "If the king's name is known, then the country is in disorder. When the king's name is not known, then there is harmony."

Consider this modern example: There was one manager in a certain company, and every project she worked on was on time and successful and all the workers felt alive to their tasks. At one point, when the upper management was looking to downsize the company, they started examining people. They looked at this woman and asked, "Well, what does she really do?" Other people had specific tasks—programmer, designer, and so on—but the upper management couldn't identify anything concrete the manager was doing. Yet what she was doing was supporting the whole team by doing whatever she saw needed to be done. If people had to work late, she would go out and buy coffee and Chinese food for them; if they seemed frustrated she would encourage them; she would check if they were on track; and she would inquire if they had any problems in the rest of their life. If there were problems between people, she'd take care of it, and work them out. But she did it so effectively that she was invisible to upper management—her name was not known—and so the upper managers decided to let her go. And what happened? All those projects started to fail. When the king's name is known, everybody fears the king.

We usually get trapped in our ideas about how things should be and we prevent ourselves from reacting spontaneously and naturally to each situation as it arises. In this case, Rohi wasn't reacting spontaneously. He wasn't adapting to the circumstances. When Fuketsu moved the chess piece in another way, he couldn't adapt to it. How do these fixed ideas arise? That's what each one of us has to look at. We have all kinds of ideas, images, and projections about how things should be. If things don't go according to our preconceptions, then we don't know what to do.

The verse says, "Leaving, he goes beyond even the top of Vairochana's head." Vairochana is the Cosmic Buddha. By walking over Vairochana's head, Fuketsu shows that the transcendence of the reality-body of the Buddha is not stuck in the ice cave where zazen is frozen in one position and dwells in emptiness. When Venerable Rohi says, "I have realized the wisdom of the Ancestors," Fuketsu says, "Well, go beyond that! Walk over Vairochana's head. Don't get trapped in the ice cave."

Master Rinzai, talking about himself, said, "This mountain monk's perspective sits on and cuts off the heads of the manifest Buddhas." And of course there is the familiar expression, "If you meet the Buddha on the road, kill him!" But what does that really mean? There is a story about Soen Nakagawa encountering a Westerner who had heard that expression about killing the Buddha. He visited a temple where Soen Roshi was offering incense to the Buddha and bowing. The visitor asked, "Why are you venerating this image? Why don't you spit on it?" Soen replied, "If you want to spit on it, you can. I prefer to bow." What does it mean to cut off the head of the Buddha, to walk on the head of the Buddha? If you say, "I am the Buddha" the Buddha is cutting off *your* head!

Each of us needs to look carefully. In Case 38 Rinzai says, "Within this lump of red flesh lies a true person of no rank." It's a person holding onto nothing, with no position. If you have no position, then you can adjust spontaneously to every circumstance that comes up.

The verse also says, "Sitting, he comes back on the tongue-tip of the Nirmanakaya Buddha." Nirmanakaya Buddha is the manifest Buddha that appears in many forms. After descending into the depths of your being where there is no mind, no Buddha, and no thing, ascend to manifest your life such that the king's law truly is the Buddha's reality.

CASE 30

Daizui's Kalpa Fire

It extinguishes all relativities and cuts off duality. To break off the ball of doubt, what phrase can be adopted? Choan is not more than a tiny step away. Taizan's weight is only three pounds. Tell me: According to what principle does one speak thus?

MAIN CASE

Attention! A monk asked Daizui, "In the raging of kalpa fire, chiliocosms are together destroyed. I wonder if *this* is destroyed or not destroyed?" Daizui said, "Destroyed." The monk asked, "If so, does everything go with it?" Daizui said, "Everything goes with it."

The same monk later asked Ryusai, "In the raging of kalpa fire, chiliocosms are together destroyed. I wonder if *this* is destroyed or not destroyed?" Ryusai replied, "Not destroyed." The monk asked, "Why is it not destroyed?" Ryusai replied, "Because it is the same as the chiliocosms."

APPRECIATORY VERSE

Destroyed and not destroyed, everything goes with it—chiliocosms.
The phrase didn't function as hook and chain at all;
the feet with brambles are hindered greatly.
Understood and not understood.
The crystal-clear matter—so long-winded!
Those who know when taking it up shouldn't barter;
in my story whether to buy or sell is up to you.

In Buddhist terminology, a *kalpa* is a vast period of time (see Case 23). The kalpa fire is a great conflagration that comes at the end of a kalpa, destroying everything. There then follows a kalpa of emptiness, and then a universe arises again and exists for a kalpa until it is destroyed.

Chiliocosms are described in this manner. Mount Sumeru, which is at the center of the universe and is the dwelling place of the gods, along with its surrounding continents, the eight seas, and the ring of iron mountains, with heaven above and hell below, form a small world. Even though the universe with Mount Sumeru at its center is so vast as to have no inside or outside, it is nonetheless one small world among many. A thousand "small" worlds are said to form one "small" chiliocosm. A thousand small chiliocosms are said to form one medium-sized chiliocosm, and a thousand of these form a large chiliocosm, which consists of a billion small worlds. The kalpa fire destroys everything, the whole universe. Yet the monk asks, "Is *this* destroyed, or not destroyed?" What is *this*? The monk asks this question twice: One teacher says it's destroyed, the other says it's not destroyed. Which is it?

Daizui lived in the tenth century, and was a successor of Isan Daian, who was a successor of the great Master Hyakujo. Isan Daian is not the famous Isan Reiyu who appears in many koans. Ryusai is in the lineage of Master Seppo, a master who was very plodding and was so dull that they called him "the black lacquer bucket." Eventually, Seppo became enlightened and a number of well-known masters are in his lineage, including Ummon who is among the brightest lights of the Golden Age of Zen.

The Buddha's birth legend holds that when the Buddha was born, he stood up and walked immediately. He pointed one hand to the heavens and one hand to the earth, and he exclaimed, "Above earth and below heaven, I alone am the World-Honored One." According to this legend, his words reached the farthest end of the chiliocosm, and all living beings rejoiced, realizing they too were destined to be Buddhas. Is this chiliocosm destroyed or not?

Not too long ago I read this newspaper headline: "After Father's Death, Chopra Ponders Impermanence of Life." Deepak Chopra, as you may know, is quite famous, the author of many books on self-realization. In this article, he's asked, "What new ideas are occurring to you as a result of your father's death?" And he responds, "I'm beginning to question the whole idea that there's such a thing as a person." Is a person destroyed or not destroyed? What is a person?

Chopra goes on to say, "For all eternity, we are there in that primordial quantum soup, and for a few years, which is like nothing, the flicker of a firefly in the middle of the night, we're individuals. We identify with that flicker, instead of the real home we have. If we'd identify with our real home, I think we'd have a lot more love and compassion."

Our real home is the one body that encompasses all things. It is our unity and inseparability. The trees are our lungs, the earth is our body, the water is our circulation. They are not your environment; they are your boundless body. They are you!

Everything is impermanent, and yet we try to make something fixed. As soon as it becomes fixed, what happens? It becomes congealed, blocked, rigid, stiff. The Japanese teacher Takuan said, "You can't wash your face and hands with ice." The ice is rigid, frozen. If you substitute your true self for some kind of confused mind, it doesn't flow like water. As soon as you let go of your ideas that you are this small body, your life will become expansive and your words will reach to the farthest end of the chiliocosm.

When asked about the meaning of permanence and impermanence, the Sixth Ancestor said, "What is impermanent is Buddha Nature. What is permanent is the mind that discriminates all things, good and evil." The student said, "The sutras say Buddha Nature is permanent, yet you say it's impermanent. Good and evil thoughts are impermanent, yet you say they're permanent. This contradiction is causing the students to be confused." The Ancestor said, "If Buddha Nature were permanent, how could differences exist? What good or evil or anything could you think about? I say it is impermanent. That, indeed, is the way of true impermanence as taught by the Buddha."

If you say anything is permanent, it becomes congealed, even Buddha Nature. This is what the teachers in this case are saying. If you say it's permanent, it's destroyed. It goes along with the destruction. If we totally identify with the universe, can it be destroyed? Whether we're destroyed or not destroyed, if you make it fixed, you're fixed to one place. Master Dogen said, "To study Zen is to study the self, and to study the self is to forget the self." If you forget the self, where's the person? What is there to be destroyed?

Is a person destroyed by raging kalpa fire? Who is that person? Daizui says *this* is destroyed, and everything goes with it. He's very careful to not say what the "this" is that's destroyed. As soon as you name it, it becomes something else. So when Ryusai says *this* is not destroyed, he means that *this* is the same as the chiliocosm, the same as the raging fire.

Late in his career the great quantum physicist Schroedinger was investigating the nature of mind and self. He wrote: "The reason one cannot find a self independent of the world can be summed up in a few words: The self is the world." I agree—but what is it when everything is destroyed?

In the appreciatory verse it says, "Destroyed and not destroyed, everything goes with it." When one says everything goes with it, and one says it's the same as the chiliocosm, what's the difference? "The phrases didn't function as hook and chain at all." Each one of their expressions doesn't stick anywhere. "The feet with brambles are hindered greatly." If you get stuck in the brambles, or fall in the weeds, you're hindered.

"Understood, or not understood, the crystal-clear matter, so long-winded." It's crystal clear whether you understand it or not, but they were so long-winded. Don't talk about it; just enjoy the day. "Those who know when taking it up shouldn't barter. In my story, whether to buy or sell is up to you." There's nothing to barter about. It just is as it is. If you want to buy it, go ahead, but when the raging kalpa fire occurs, who are you going to barter with?

Why do we keep creating that split, that separation in our mind? It's the same as the chiliocosm, whether destroyed or not destroyed. Everything that is born, lives for a while and then dies. So, if it is not destroyed, how does it live? If it is destroyed, how does it die?

CASE 31

Ummon's Free-Standing Pillar

The sole function of the ultimate: a crane soars in the firmament. The sole path of the evident: the falcon's already passed Korea. Your eye may be a shooting star, still your mouth resembles a bent-down carrying pole. Tell me: What sort of Zen point is this?

MAIN CASE

Attention! Ummon addressed the assembly, "The old Buddha and the free-standing pillar are mingled together. What level of activity is this?" The assembly said nothing. So Ummon himself answered, "In the South Mountain clouds rise. In the North Mountain, rain falls."

APPRECIATORY VERSE

The one way of divine light: it's never been concealed.
Transcending relative views, it's affirmed without affirmation.
Going beyond commonsense thought, it's adequate without adequacy.
The pollen of cliff flower—hives of bees become honey.
The nutrients of wild grasses—musk deer make their scent.
According with kind, three feet or sixteen feet.
Whatever you touch is brilliantly magnificent.

When the old Buddha mingles with the free-standing pillar, your True Nature is revealed. Ummon asks us, "What level of activity is this?" Ummon could be referring to the levels or stages of development of the bodhisattva. There are ten stages from the lowest to the highest, but to penetrate this koan we do not need to be concerned about such matters.

The free-standing pillar represents the world of form. To see this koan, you have to realize who you are and what your relationship to the world is. In order to do that, look inside and experience what's there. You have to be the Old Buddha himself or herself, and don't add anything extra.

The verse says, "According with kind, three feet or sixteen feet." The rudder is three feet, the mast is sixteen feet. The wind blows and the boat sails. Sometimes we're happy, sometimes we're incensed. That understanding is fine as far as it goes, but how do you get to the source of your True Nature without getting caught in some fixed emotional state?

In the Christian Bible it says that Jesus died to purify our sins. Ummon says, "In the South Mountain clouds rise. In the North Mountain, rain falls." Jesus died on Calvary Mountain and we're saved on the Rocky Mountains. If you understand that, the resurrection is revealed. When Jesus mingles with the free-standing cross, what level of activity is this?

In Buddhism, to purify our twisted karma, we atone for it, we chant, "Now I atone for it all." The way to atone is to die on your cushion and experience the Great Death. Let your self-grasping ignorance wither away and you will experience the Great Rebirth, the Resurrection. If you don't understand this point, you miss the profound meaning of all religions.

Let's turn our attention to the verse, which is particularly useful in this case: "Transcending relative views, it's affirmed without affirmation." If we are trying to follow some external teaching, trying to "resist temptation" or "be obedient" or even "gain enlightenment" that's attempting to affirm affirmation using somebody else's understanding.

"Going beyond commonsense thought, it's adequate without adequacy." As soon as you believe that your understanding is "adequate," it's no longer adequate.

"Whatever you touch is brilliantly magnificent"—because "the one way of divine light has never been concealed." Commenting on this, Bansho said, "When it is thrust in your face, there's no place to hide." Ummon thrusts it in our face with his comment: "In the South Mountain clouds rise. In the North Mountain, rain falls." But who is South Mountain? Who is North Mountain? When I call you, you answer. What level of activity is this?

CASE 32

Kyozan's State of Mind

PREFACE TO THE ASSEMBLY

The ocean is the realm of the dragon, who sinks and emerges with tranquil sport. Heaven is the home of the crane, who flies and calls in perfect freedom. Why does an exhausted fish remain in the shallows? Or a sluggish bird live among the reeds? Is there any measure of gain or loss to be made of this?

MAIN CASE

Attention! Kyozan asked a monk, "Where were you born?" The monk replied, "Yu province." Kyozan said, "Do you think of it?" The monk replied, "I think of it always." Kyozan said, "Subjective thought is mind. Objective thought is the environment. Therein, there are such things as mountains, rivers, the great earth, towers and buildings, people and animals. Reflect upon the mind that thinks. Isn't something there?" The monk said, "As far as that, I don't see anything at all." Kyozan said, "As a belief, that's all right. As a person, that's not all right." The monk said, "Osho, do you have any particular instruction?" Kyozan replied, "To say I have something particular or not misses the point. As for your view, it reaches only one mystery. In taking a seat and wearing robes, observe it for yourself later on."

APPRECIATORY VERSE

Embrace without separation; fly without impediment.
Gate and fence tower high; barrier and chain weigh heavy.
When drinking is abundant, the guests go to sleep.
When bellies are full, the farmer is destitute.
Shooting in the vast sky, the wind flaps the Garuda bird's wings.
Stamping the waves in the blue sea, thunder sends off the sporting dragon.

Kyozan lived in the ninth century, and was a student of Isan. The two of them appeared together in Case 15.

Isan once told Kyozan, "When thoughts are exhausted, you have arrived at the source, where the True Nature is revealed as eternally abiding. In that place there is no difference between affairs and principles and the true Buddha is manifest."

What is the place Isan is talking about? To reveal it, we have to exhaust our thoughts. Subjectively we have thoughts about who we are; thoughts about who we should be; who we want to be. Objectively we think about the nature of others and of things and our relation to them. In our reactions to situations that arise in our life we are often protecting some kind of image or picture of who we think we are. That's why Kyozan says, "As a belief, that's all right. As a person, that's not all right." You have to dwell in that place where the true person is manifest. In this case, the monk says, "I don't see anything at all." And Kyozan responds, "Yet, filling the eye are mountain and rivers." Kyozan is asserting that you're not a complete person until energy is flowing freely through you. It's "not all right" because it's stuck.

Kyozan taught his students, "In my shop, there is a wide range of goods. If someone comes looking for mouse turds, then I give them some. If someone comes looking for real gold, then I give it to him." A monk said to him, "I don't want mouse turds. May I have the master's real gold?" Kyozan said, "You can try to bite the head of a flying arrow until the Year of the Ass but you won't succeed." The monk couldn't respond to this and so Kyozan added, "If you want to exchange something, we can make a deal. If you don't want to exchange anything, then we can't."

If you're looking for mouse turds, that's what you'll find. If you're looking for gold, you'll find that. But if you are looking for your true self, it is not a thing to be found. Exhaust your thoughts and discard whatever you're holding onto, and your true self will naturally be revealed.

The monk in this koan is what we call a "board-carrying fellow"—like somebody walking down a street with a huge piece of wood on his shoulder. The board gets in his way and blocks his view, and he only sees one side. "What a funny town this is! It only has buildings on one side of the street!" he thinks to himself. Here, the one side the monk sees is emptiness, and he's become attached to it. Or as another Zen saying has it: "He's delighting in the road, but ultimately will fail to reach home." The monk thinks he's really something special, even beyond his teacher in understanding. But Kyozan puts the element of doubt in him: "Later on, when you take a seat and wear robes, observe it for yourself."

Letting go of attachment to emptiness, one arrives at the stage of a person far beyond discrimination. The body and mind are without attachment; gain and loss are cleared away. As for this absolute state, if you try to discuss it, you fail. Just as the eye cannot directly see the eye, it doesn't fall in the scope of your mental function to see the true person. In order to reveal the emptiness, you have to *be* the emptiness. In order to reveal the person, you have to *be* the person.

When I was on the faculty at the University of California, we joked that graduates in the biology department could only distinguish a mouse from an elephant by looking at their DNA. If you're full of your own limited ideas, your view will only reach part of it. You should immediately know the difference between a mouse turd and gold!

CASE 33

Sansho's Golden Carp

Encountering strength, one is meek. Encountering tenderness, one is tough. When two strengths collide, there is always damage. Tell me: How should they accommodate each other?

MAIN CASE

Attention! Sansho asked Seppo, "A golden carp passes through the nets—I wonder what he has for food." Seppo said, "I'll wait until you get out of the net, then I'll tell you." Sansho said, "A good teacher of fifteen hundred monks doesn't even know what we're talking about?" Seppo replied, "For this old monk, as head of the temple, affairs do multiply."

APPRECIATORY VERSE

At first, ascending the three waterfalls;
clouds and thunder both give the send-off.
Jumping, leaping splendidly, his great function is seen.
Burning his tail, he clearly passes beyond the Gate of U.
Fine fish are never kept in a pickle jar.
The mellow old man does not startle the crowd.
Used to meeting great opponents, he is fearless from the start.
Flapping as lightly as a flag in the wind, he weighs more than a thousand
    pounds.
His name is known across the Four Seas. Is anyone his equal?
Though the Eight Winds blow, he stands alone, unmoved.

This koan is about skillful means, about skillfully responding to every situation as it arises. As it says in the preface, when somebody comes on strong, retreat is effective. In the face of conciliation, strength is called for. When two people respond with strength they collide and there is always damage.

Perhaps you are in chronic disagreement with your partner or spouse and there is no room to maneuver. This is like two massive pillars leaning on each other. What should you do? If you are able to retreat from your position, the other pillar has no resistance and has to fall—and then there is space for your partner to also shift position.

Sansho, a well-accomplished disciple of Rinzai came to Seppo and boasted: "A golden carp passes through the nets. I wonder what he has for food." In other words, "I've passed through the barrierless barriers set by the Buddhas and Ancestors. What are you going to do with me now?" Seppo points out he's still stuck in his arrogance and pride: "I'll wait until you get out of the net. Then I'll tell you." But Sansho meets him again with strength, "A good teacher of fifteen hundred monks doesn't even know what we're talking about?" Seppo seems to retreat but there are thorns in the mud. He says, "I'm very busy. I have a lot on my mind."

Is Seppo conceding to Sansho? We have to know how to respond appropriately to the conditions as they present themselves. Acting the same way in every situation isn't appropriate. Every situation is different; every student is different. Responding appropriately is called skillful means and it's probably one of the most difficult and dangerous aspects of our practice. If one is deluded about one's understanding, "skillful means" can be used as an excuse for one's own abusive behavior.

It's not easy to know how to swallow and digest our practice. It's not always easy to take. To integrate it as our life is even more difficult. We always want some safe refuge that we can hold onto, so that we can always know beforehand what's appropriate. We want to hold onto this ego-grasping self in order to feel more comfortable but it doesn't work—we continue to suffer and we continue to cause harm. We all know it doesn't work, but still we keep doing it.

Seppo could beat the student around the ears if he wanted to. But instead he just says, "For this old monk, as head of the temple, affairs do multiply."—basically, "I'm too busy to continue this conversation." Is this meek old man really a teacher of fifteen hundred monks?

At the end of the *Gateless Gate*, Master Mumon cautions, "The further you advance on the path, the more confused it becomes. In the end, if you retreat, the less clearly you perceive the path. If you neither advance nor retreat, you're like a breathing dead person. So how do you practice this living Zen?" Master Mumon is cutting off all our avenues of escape, just like Seppo is doing to Sansho.

In the end, like Sansho, you have to ultimately face yourself. Seppo was not releasing Sansho from further accomplishing himself. Seppo's words were not ceding to Sansho. They cut off Sansho's swollen head and gave him no leg to stand on.

Having no safe place to rest, how can you be the golden carp that passes through the netless net?

CASE 34

Fuketsu's Speck of Dust

PREFACE TO THE ASSEMBLY

Open-handed and empty-fisted, he makes a thousand changes and ten thousand transformations. Though he can make something from nothing, how can he escape fiddling with the relative to make a semblance of the real? Tell me: What is the basis of this?

MAIN CASE

Attention! Fuketsu spoke, saying, "When a speck of dust is raised, the nation prospers. When a speck of dust is not raised, the nation is destroyed." Regarding this, Setcho held forth a staff, saying, "Is there any Zen student who has this same death and same life?"

APPRECIATORY VERSE

Is it to be grey-haired standing up from fishing in Ishwi River,
or is it to be the men who chose to starve on Shuyo Mountain?
Within a speck of dust diverse features are distinguished.
Their fame and exploits are hard to forget.

Fuketsu and Setcho are both ancient Chinese masters but Setcho was born about a hundred years after Fuketsu, and so their lives actually didn't intersect. Fuketsu was in the Rinzai lineage and it's said that through him, Rinzai's teachings were preserved and transmitted to later generations. Setcho was the compiler of the *Blue Cliff Record* koan collection. In this koan, Setcho is commenting on Fuketsu's teaching many years later.

The speck of dust in this case could be the activity of your mind, and the nation is the entire phenomenal world. When the activity is raised, the nation prospers. When your mind is busy, all kinds of things grow. And when your mind is still, the nation is destroyed; it falls away completely and there's nothing to be gained or lost.

When the energy flows freely through your body and your mind, you don't think about it. It's only when you have pain in your gallbladder, for example, that you think about your gallbladder. But your gallbladder doesn't require your thinking about it to function. Even being completely ignorant of your body it still functions. But what is this body and mind? What do you identify as mind and what as world? What do you identify as self and what as other? Identification with others is one aspect of the path of the bodhisattva. The bodhisattva path is the path of service to others, of foregoing one's own enlightenment in order to liberate others. But when you completely identify with others, where are they?

One of the ten grave precepts in Zen is not to elevate oneself and put down others, and another precept is not to speak of other's errors and faults. Maezumi Roshi told me about an incident at the Zen temple at which his father, Baian Hakujun, was the priest. One of the parishioners was stealing things from the temple for some unknown reason, and another parishioner came to Baian Hakujun and said, "So-and-so was stealing from the temple!" Baian Hakujun said, "Don't talk about him like that!" When we identify with others, how can we elevate ourselves and put others down? It's only when we create that gap, that separation which comes from fear, that we can do it.

Regarding all of this, Setcho held up a staff and said, "Is there any Zen student who has this same death, and same life?" What does that mean? There is one staff and that staff covers the whole universe. Sometimes it gives life and sometimes it takes life away. If you call it a staff, you are stuck in a fixed position. If you don't call it a staff, you deny the fact.

How can you have the same life and the same death as the one staff?

CASE 35

Rakuho's Acquiescence

PREFACE TO THE ASSEMBLY

Swift action and fluent speech crush heretics and demons. Going beyond formalities and transcending sectarianism is expediently used for a superior, clever person. What happens when you encounter a man who doesn't turn his head even when struck a blow with a stick?

MAIN CASE

Attention! Rakuho went to visit Kassan. Without bowing, he stood and faced him. Kassan remarked, "A chicken lives in a phoenix nest. He's not in the same class. Get out!" Rakuho said, "Your fame has made me come from afar. I beg your indulgence." Kassan replied, "There's no one before me, and no old monk here." At that, Rakuho gave a shout. Kassan said, "Stop! Stop! You shouldn't rattle on like that. The moon and the clouds are the same. Valleys and mountains are different. It's not that you can't cut off tongue tips of everyone under heaven, but how can you make a tongueless person able to talk?" Rakuho had no reply. Kassan struck him. Henceforth, Rakuho acquiesced.

APPRECIATORY VERSE

Head wagging, tail swishing, the red-finned carp
could utterly and independently change its form.
Though he has had technique to cut off tongue tips,
he was subtly led by the nose to realize mind.
Illuminating night outside the blinds, the moon appears as if at noon.
Before the cliff of a withered tree, wildflowers are always in spring.

Tongueless man, tongueless man—an intimate phrase fully reveals the
  right decree.
Walking solitary in one's fiefdom, all is clear. May all under heaven be
  happy and joyful!

Kassan lived in the eighth century and was a successor in the Soto lineage
of Seigen Gyoshi. He was ordained as a very young boy and intensively
studied the Tripitaka, the Buddhist cannon.

One day, when he was lecturing and answering questions from the assembly, a visiting monk, Dogo Enchi, started laughing. Kassan asked him why,
and Dogo said that Kassan needed a teacher, and that, while what he was
saying about the Tripitaka was interesting, it missed the point. Kassan was
humble enough and his heart was open enough that he was able to recognize
the truth that he didn't really have a clear eye.

Dogo suggested Kassan go see the Boatman Monk, Sensu Osho, who
was Dogo's Dharma brother. Kassan did this and eventually became Sensu's
successor. The Boatman Monk, as soon as he gave transmission to Kassan,
disappeared, and was never heard from again. Kassan was his only successor.

Kassan taught: "The Way is without a single teaching, a single Dharma."
A monk asked him, "There has always been meaning attributed to the teachings of the Buddhas and Ancestors. Why does the Master say there isn't any?"
Kassan said, "Don't eat for three years and you won't see anyone hungry." The
monk said, "If no one is hungry, why can't I gain awakening?" Kassan said,
"Because awakening has confused you." That's what this koan is about: the
confusion of awakening. Awakening has confused Rakuho.

Rakuho first studied with Master Rinzai and even served as his attendant.
He's an interesting character because he started out in the vigorous Rinzai lineage, and then he came to study under Kassan, a master in the Silent Illumination Soto School.

When Rakuho left Rinzai, he went to live in a hut on the same mountain
where Kassan's monastery was. Kassan knew of this and wrote Rakuho a letter and instructed one of his attendants to take it to him. When the attendant presented the letter to Rakuho, he took it and, without reading it,
extended his hand to the monk as if asking for something else. "What else did
you bring me?" When the monk didn't say anything, Rakuho hit him and

told him to go back to his master. When the monk told this to Kassan, Kassan said, "If he opens the letter, he'll be here in three days. If he doesn't open the letter, nobody can save him." This exchange was a prelude to what happened later at Kassan's place. Rakuho did arrive in three days, and that's when this case took place.

Rakuho came and stood in front of Kassan but he didn't even bow—as if to say, "Well, here I am. What are you going to do with me?" When Kassan responds, "A chicken is living in a phoenix nest. He's not in the same class. Get out!" he's calling Rakuho to task for his rudeness. But Rakuho knows how to deal with this—somewhat—and says, "Your fame has made me come from afar. I beg your indulgence." So Kassan said, "There's no one before me, and no old monk here." With these words Kassan is telling Rakuho that his eye is still not clear, that he should not stick to anything, even his own enlightenment.

Rakuho responds with a shout, just like he surely did with Master Rinzai. I really admire Kassan's response to that: "Stop! Stop! You shouldn't rattle on like that." There's another koan that says, "One shout! Two shouts! Then what?"

Kassan goes on to say, "It's not that you can't cut everything off, but how can you give life?" As a Zen student, you can go to a place where you find peace and tranquility when you're sitting on your cushion in a dim room where everything supports you, but how are you going to deal with the myriad difficulties that arise in life, the things that you've suppressed in your zazen? Sure, you can kill your pain by cutting it all off with your zazen, but how are you going to use that pain to give life to your life, a life that's free and unfettered?

If we think we have some understanding, we get stuck to that. And if we have an image of how we should be, we get stuck to that. It's a very human distortion to identify with a limited aspect of the self. The reality is that you are neither your negative traits, including the part that punishes yourself for not living up to your expectations, nor are you your positive traits.

We like our positive traits and so we try to show them off. We don't like the negative aspects so we try to hide them—and that creates more harm than exposing them. In exposing them, you are able to see them and take responsibility for them. If you acknowledge the parts that you don't want to acknowledge, it opens you up. Every time we expose something negative that we find within ourselves, we'll contribute not only to unifying ourselves, but also to the universal process of wholeness—with ourselves and all sentient beings, and all insentient beings as well.

Rakuho thought that he had had some great realization, but when Kassan said, "You only see part of it. You can cut off, but how are you going to give life?" he had a genuine realization and accepted Kassan as his teacher. In that moment, Rakuho was able to admit that he didn't know everything, and so he was able to learn.

This is what each of us must do continually.

CASE 36

Baso's Illness

Though you investigate apart from mind and consciousness, there's still *this*. Though your study leaves the road of common and holy, you are still in danger. The iron barb is jerked out from the red-hot forge. Though your tongue is like a sword and your lips are like spears, it is still difficult to open your mouth. Without damaging the spear point, please try to present it and see.

MAIN CASE
Attention! Great Master Baso was ill. The temple priest asked, "Osho, how is your health these days?" Baso replied, "Sun-faced Buddha, Moon-faced Buddha."

APPRECIATORY VERSE
Sun-face, moon-face.
Stars fall, thunder crashes.
With regard to shape, a mirror is selfless.
The ball on the tray rolls by itself.
Don't you see?
Before hammer and anvil, gold of a hundred temperings.
Beneath scissors and ruler, a bolt of silk.

Baso Doitsu lived at the end of the eighth century. It's said that Baso was a large and imposing man, with the piercing look of a tiger and the powerful gait of a bull. And apparently his tongue was so big he could stretch it out and almost cover his whole face. The unique style of Zen teaching using

Dharma dialogues, the kind of back-and-forth discussions like those in koans, supposedly originated with Baso—as did using the staff to beat students to enlightenment. This case also appears in the *Blue Cliff Record* as Case 3.

In this case, Baso's health is failing. The temple priest asked him how his health is, and Baso replies, "Sun-faced Buddha, Moon-faced Buddha."

There's a scripture which is called the Butsu Myoko, which means the "Names of the Buddha Sutra." In this sutra there are 1,193 names of the Buddha, among them are the Sun-faced Buddha and the Moon-faced Buddha. The Sun-faced Buddha is said to live for eighteen hundred years, and the Moon-faced Buddha is said to live only a single day and night. Yet both are Buddha. Sometimes one is well for many years. Sometimes one is sick for many years. Sometimes one gets sick and recovers quickly. Sometimes one never recovers. When feeling well, we're the Well Buddha; feeling ill, we're the Ill Buddha.

In the Vimalakirti Sutra, Vimalakirti talks about his sickness, "My sickness comes from ignorance, and the thirst for existence, and it will last as long as do the sicknesses of all living beings.... Were all beings to be free from sickness, I also would not be sick. Why? For the bodhisattva, the world consists only of living beings, and sickness is inherent in living in the world.... Whence comes my sickness? The sickness of the bodhisattva arises from great compassion." Is that the sickness Baso is referring to?

Don't become attached to the body but at the same time don't abandon it. Don't be attached to the mind but at the same time don't abandon it. Be peaceful but don't seek some absolute state of peace. "Sun-faced Buddha, Moon-faced Buddha."

When he was very ill and near the end of his life, Suzuki Roshi spoke to his students. "We may believe that zazen will make us physically strong, and fundamentally healthy, but a healthy mind is not just a healthy mind in the usual sense, and a weak body is not just a weak body. Even though I die, it's all right with me. That is Buddha. If I suffer when I die, that's all right. That's Suffering Buddha. No confusion in it. We should be very grateful to have a limited body, like mine or like yours." Sun-faced Buddha! Moon-faced Buddha!

So, tell me, how is your health these days?

CASE 37

Isan's Karmic Consciousness

Taking out the farmer's ox, lead him by the nose. Snatching food from a starving man, clasp your hands around his throat. Is there any one who can mete out such poisonous means?

MAIN CASE

Attention! Isan asked Kyozan, "How would you examine someone who happens to ask you, 'All sentient beings have unceasing karmic consciousness, but there is no basis on which to depend.'" Kyozan replied, "If this monk were to come, I would call him by name, saying, 'So-and-so!' If the monk turned his head, I would say, 'What is that?' I'd wait for him to hesitate, and then say to him, 'Not only is karmic consciousness unceasing, there's also no basis on which to depend.'" Isan remarked, "Good."

APPRECIATORY VERSE

Call once and he turns his head: Does he know the self or not?
The full moon imperceptibly turns to a crescent.
When the child with a fortune in gold sinks low,
the road of poverty subtly brings grief.

Kyozan was known for calling out to a student and when that person turned his head, Kyozan would ask, "What is it?" Rinzai was known for raising his staff and poking at everyone in the hall, chasing them out, then just as they were running out of the door, calling to them, "Hey, you guys!" When they turned, he'd say, "What is it?"

My first teacher, Sochu Roshi, spoke very poor English. We'd be walking down the street, and he'd look at me and say, "What is? What is?" Now I ask you the same question: What is it?

Kyozan once asked Isan, "What is the true abode of Buddhas?" Isan says, "Think of the unfathomable mystery. When your thoughts are exhausted, you've arrived at the source." That's what our practice is about.

In this case, Isan says, "All sentient beings have unceasing karmic consciousness." Karma is the law of cause and effect. As long as we have a body and a mind, we are subject to karmic causation and there are karmic consequences of everything that we do. If we put a hand in the fire, it burns and hurts; if we work hard, we can earn money with which to live. What we think, what we believe, and what we say are also subject to karma. That is karmic consciousness.

Isan goes on to say, "There is no basis on which to depend." We imagine that if we do certain things we should get certain kinds of rewards. But that isn't always the case, is it? Why? Because there is no basis on which to depend. Sometimes righteous people come to grief and evil people prosper.

Master Hakuin makes an analogy of a ship: The ship is ready to sail, and all of the oarsmen are fit, well-fed, and strong. They are ready to pull on their long oars. The tide is right. The wind starts coming up and the night falls. The captain gives the order to set sail. All night long, the oarsmen are rowing steadily, and the wind is blowing the sail. But when the sun comes up the next morning they see they are still right there at the dock—somebody forgot to throw off one of the mooring lines! One little line held back this massive ship, with its massive sails and its hundreds of massive oarsmen. They didn't move more than a few feet. What is that small line, that rope that holds us back?

Always, it comes down to one thing: self-grasping ignorance. We dearly want to find some fixed thing we can grasp in ourselves. We keep looking for something to make us secure or to make us special. Yet, there's no basis upon which to depend. When we stand, we stand. When we sit, we sit.

Don't think that if you just sit enough hours, that the original self will be revealed. There is no basis upon which to depend. You have to let go of all of your ideas about original self. The original self isn't something out there that you will find. The original self is always right where you sit, but it's covered over with all kinds of notions, beliefs, opinions, and judgments.

There is also a tendency, when we see our judgments, to beat ourselves up if we don't like them or to praise ourselves if we do like them. Just notice them. Expand the context of who you are, and just be aware of that tendency. Notice it. What are you holding onto, right now? What is there when you let go of that? If I call your name, and say, "What is it?" what do you see? What do you feel?

When you think, "Who am I?" what is it? When you don't think, "Who am I?" then what is it? If you really see it, it will come out without any hesitation. "Call once and he turns his head." Right there, it's manifest. If you blink your eyes, you miss it. Just keep watching. Keep attentive. Don't let down for even a moment. Falling into your old patterns and old habits; just notice! Just watch! Be aware!

"What is it?"

CASE 38

Rinzai's True Man

PREFACE TO THE ASSEMBLY

Taking a thief for a son, perceiving a servant as master. A broken wooden ladle—how can this be the dried skull of an Ancestor! A donkey saddle cannot be the lower jaw of a grandfather. When the land is split up and the thatch roof is partitioned, how do we distinguish the master?

MAIN CASE

Attention! Rinzai addressed the assembly, saying, "There is a true person of no rank. He is always leaving and entering the gates of your face. You beginners who have not witnessed him: Look! Look!" Thereupon, a monk asked, "How about this true man of no rank?" Rinzai got down from the seat and grabbed him. The monk hesitated, and Rinzai pushed him away, saying, "This true man of no rank; what a shit-stick he is!"

APPRECIATORY VERSE

Delusion and enlightenment are mutually opposed.
Subtly conveyed, it's simple:
In spring, the hundred flowers bloom by a zephyr;
in strength, nine oxen are turned about with a jerk.
It's hopeless to dig a hole in the mud—it won't stay open.
Clearly the sweet spring's eye has been closed.
Suddenly dash out and it freely gushes forth.

Master Tendo added, "Danger!"

No rank is "no basis on which to depend" from Case 37. It doesn't matter what station or understanding you achieve, you can't pull rank in Zen just for the sake of control. "Because I am the boss, I said so!" does not work here.

Many Zen students work on the koan, "Who am I?" The natural tendency is to list all of the items on your life's résumé. I am a mother. I am a brother. I am an artist. I am a carpenter. I am a Zen student. I am a *good* Zen student. I am a Zen master. All of these categories are labels that do not penetrate to the essence of who you are.

We find security in our credentials. We are proud of our accomplishments and continually want recognition. When a Zen student penetrates in a particular koan, he or she puts it into his or her basket of accomplishments, like a trinket that can be brought out and displayed as a symbol of status. Any hint of accomplishment or of feeling better than someone else is like putting chevrons on your sleeve and displaying your rank. No rank means to strip away all of your credentials and then see who you are.

In this koan, we encounter Master Rinzai. Maezumi Roshi was empowered by teachers in both the Rinzai and the Soto Schools, so we could say that we belong to the Rinzai School. If we say so, then it becomes a rank. Really we're Soto, but we're not that either. It's just practice: pure, clear practice with no basis on which to depend. A fellow teacher once asked me if I belong to the Rinzai or the Soto School. I answered that "I belong to the half-breed school." I am a mutt. I am both Soto and Rinzai. But even this isn't it.

The true person of no rank is continually entering and leaving the five sensory gates of your face. Rinzai gave a clue about how to reveal that true person: "Followers of the Way, mind is without form and pervades the ten directions. In the eye, it's called seeing. In the ear, it's called hearing. In the nose, it smells odors. In the mouth, it holds conversation. In the hand, it grasps and seizes. In the feet, it runs and carries. Fundamentally, it is one pure radiance. Divided, it becomes harmoniously united spheres of sense. Since the mind is not existent, wherever you go, you're free." One ancient asked, "And so what is it in the eyebrows?"

Using the sense gates freely wherever you go, you are free. But somehow we bind ourselves up with credentials and rank which fundamentally are nonexistent.

In the eye, it's called seeing. The Buddha was enlightened through seeing.

He saw the morning star and had his great enlightenment. That moment occurred, though, after years of hard ascetic practice.

There's another well-known story of a Chinese teacher named Reiun Shigon who was enlightened when he saw the peach blossoms fall. He wrote this poem.

> For thirty years, I've looked for a sword master.
> Many times leaves fell. New ones sprouted.
> One glimpse of peach blossoms.
> Now, no more doubts.

Commenting on this, Koun Ejo, a successor of Dogen said: "The flowers bloom every year. Nevertheless, not everyone attains his enlightenment by viewing them. Only through the virtue of long study and continuous practice, with the assistance of diligent effort in the Way, does one realize the Way or clarify the mind. This does not occur because the color of peach blossoms was particularly profound. Although the color of peach blossoms is beautiful in itself, they open with the help of the spring breeze.... What jewel glitters from its inception? Who is brilliant from the outset? You must polish and refine, so do not demean yourselves, and do not relax in your practice of the Way."

In the ear, it's called hearing. There is a famous story of Kyogen who studied long and hard but had no insight. Disappointed, he left his teacher, Isan, and ended up at the grave site of the National Teacher. I can imagine Kyogen tending this grave site with tremendous care and precision and love. His inner struggle intensified, and continued day and night. He was just so still and so attentive that the slightest thing would cause a great explosion. One day he was sweeping the ground with a rake, and a little pebble touched the bamboo, and that noise opened his mind. He had a great enlightenment. Just the sound of a pebble against the bamboo. He went to his hut, and took off his working clothes and put on his monk's clothes. He burned incense, and prostrated in the direction of Isan and said, "The compassion of Isan is greater than my parents. If he would have told it to me, I would never have had this great joy today."

By polishing away our credentials, our cherished views, our status and position, the true person of no rank will appear. On whose door does the moonlight not shine? Who is *not* the true person of no rank?

CASE 39

Joshu's Bowl-Washing

PREFACE TO THE ASSEMBLY

When food comes, fill the mouth. When sleep comes, close the eyes. When washing your face, you rub your nose. When taking off straw sandals, you touch your feet. At such times, if you miss the point, take a light and search hard in the depths of the night. How will you meet this?

MAIN CASE

Attention! A monk asked Joshu, "Your student has just entered the monastery. Please, Master, instruct me." Joshu said, "Did you finish your rice gruel?" The monk replied, "I have finished eating." Joshu remarked, "Then wash your bowls."

APPRECIATORY VERSE

When the gruel's finished, have him wash the bowl.
Suddenly the mind-ground naturally meets itself.
Right then the monastery's guest is replete.
Tell me: Is any enlightenment in there or not?

We all know Master Joshu. He's in Case 1 of the *Gateless Gate*. He also appears in several other cases in the *Gateless Gate*, as well as in the *Blue Cliff Record*, and elsewhere in the *Book of Equanimity*. A Dharma heir of Nansen, he lived to be 120 years old. Near the end of his life, he wrote this verse:

The cock crows in the early morning.
Sadly, I see as I rise, how worn out I am.
I haven't a skirt or a shirt, just this semblance of a robe.
My loincloth has no seat. My pants, no opening.
On my head are three or five pecks of grey ashes.
Originally, I intended to practice to help save others.
Who would have suspected that instead, I would become an idiot?

We can imagine that here Joshu is describing the five grey hairs on his head and what is probably the same robe he'd worn for eighty years. It's said that he practiced "lips and tongue Zen"—the Zen of illuminating words. In fact, it is said that flashes of light would appear whenever he spoke. Some of his contemporaries would shout and hit their students, but Joshu just offered turning words to reveal and eliminate self-grasping ignorance.

On one level this koan is about taking care of the details of your life. Those of you who cook for your family know that the meal is over only after the kitchen is clean—not after the last bite is eaten. We leave a lot of things half-done. In the preface it says, "When food comes, fill the mouth. When sleep comes, close the eyes." When you eat, there is nothing in the universe but eating. When we clean, we clean. But there's also more going on in this koan.

The monk says, "Instruct me." Joshu asks, "Have you finished your rice gruel?" Another way of hearing this question is as, "Have you accomplished anything at all?" Then the monk answers, "Yes, I have." And Joshu responds, "Well, then wash it away."

There are all kinds of obstacles in the way to our practice. We talk primarily about the three poisons of greed, hatred, and ignorance. They touch just about everything. Greed is manifest in our attachment; hatred in our reactions when things don't appear the way we want them to be; and ignorance in our not seeing clearly. But there are other impediments or poisons as well. One of them is called sloth. Sometimes, we just really don't feel that we have the determination, the impetus, and the energy to do what needs to be done. It's important to realize that what we experience as *low* energy is not a *lack* of energy but rather blocked energy that is not flowing. There is an intimate connection between this sloth and laziness and feelings that we haven't fully experienced. In this practice, we begin to face things that we haven't faced yet, to dissolve barriers. But we want to be somewhere else because we're not fully contented where we are.

What if part of where we are is great pain? How can we heal the pain of deep wounds? We can't heal wounds by "trying to put them behind us" or by "just moving on" or "letting go"—we have to go right into it. We can all use pain to liberate ourselves rather than to bind ourselves into our suffering by trying to avoid it. We have all kinds of blockages and barriers and if we don't face them, they will persist. It doesn't matter whether you sit one year or twenty years. Somehow, we have to deal with everything that obstructs our living a liberated life. It's not a question of our behavior being "good" or "bad"—it has to do with dropping our resistance to getting in touch with ourselves at the most intimate level.

"Then wash your bowls" Joshu tells us. It is to lead an ordinary life, just as it is, ordinary—and *that* is truly extraordinary. But we must not confuse a Zen life with a "Zen-like" life, a life that conforms to our ideas of what we think Zen should be, and a life in which we try to act like a "Zen student" or, worse still, a "Zen master." In this koan, Joshu is telling us just to let our life express itself and naturally come out in all our activities.

Do not let the word *Zen* delude you. Intimately realize that Zen is nothing other than what you do, and what you are, morning, noon, and night. As long as you think it is something else, somewhere else, then you are trapped in a tomb with no way out.

CASE 40

Ummon's White and Black

PREFACE TO THE ASSEMBLY

When the wheel of activity turns, the wisdom eye is still bewildered. When the jewel mirror opens, not the tiniest speck of dust adheres. When the fist opens, nothing drops to the ground. Being in accord with things, one knows the right moment. When two swords cross, how will they interplay?

MAIN CASE

Attention! Ummon said to Kempo, "Your answer, please, sir!" Kempo replied, "Did you meet this old monk yet?" Ummon said, "If so, then I'm too late." Kempo remarked, "Is that so? Is that so?" Ummon admitted, "Instead of Kohaku, you're really Kohoku."

APPRECIATORY VERSE

Bowstring and arrow-notch interlock.
The net's jeweled knots reflect each other.
A hundred bull's-eyes shot with not an arrow lost.
Myriad shapes are perceived with ray after ray unhindered.
Obtaining the *dharani* of words, dwelling in the samadhi of play.
How subtle it is! The seeming and the real intermingled.
How surely it's thus! Everywhere to be oneself.

There's an old story about a great king, King Malinda and a famous monk, the Venerable Nagasena. The king said, "I'm going to pose a question. Can you answer?" The monk said, "Please ask your question." The king said, "I've already asked." The monk responded, "I've already answered." Then the king said, "What did you answer?" Nagasena countered, "What did you ask?" The king said, "I've asked nothing." And the monk replied, "I've answered nothing."

While it may seem at first glance nonsensical or pointless, this dialogue and the dialogue in the koan are actually very subtle. They're conversations that don't hold onto anything, that don't leave any traces. It sounds like foolishness, and doesn't seem to elevate us in any sense—if we don't really see what they're doing. Dialogues such as these often make uninitiated people frustrated with koans and with the way Zen uses language.

Ummon was born in 864 and died at the age of eighty-five. He is considered the last of the great masters of the Golden Age of Zen. He appears in five cases in the *Gateless Gate* (which has forty-eight cases altogether), he appears eighteen times in the *Blue Cliff Record* (which has one hundred cases) and he appears thirteen times in the hundred cases in this collection. Ummon was a master of great accomplishment.

Although we don't know much about Kempo, we can see from this dialogue that he too was well accomplished.

Ummon starts the encounter by saying, "Your answer please, sir."—rather an odd way to begin. If someone said that to you, what would you do? When I was attending Maezumi Roshi he would often look at me and say, "Shishin?" I would say, "Yes, Roshi." "Tell me!" I'd say, "Sure, Roshi. I'll tell you. What do you want me to tell you?" "Tell me!" he'd shout again! At the time, I completely missed it.

So Kempo says, "Have you met this old monk yet?"—which can also be understood as a reference to enlightenment. Ummon replies, "If so, then I'm too late."—"If I say I have, then it's already passed."

The Diamond Sutra says, "The mind of the past is ungraspable. The mind of the present is ungraspable. The mind of the future is ungraspable." With our discriminating mind, it's obvious that the mind of the past is ungraspable, because it's the past, it's no longer here. The mind of the future is ungraspable because it hasn't arrived. But why can't we grasp the mind of the present? We've all heard the phrase, "Be here now" but if the mind of the present is ungraspable, how can you do even that? As soon as you say, "I'm here now," you're no longer here now. That moment is already passed. So where is now? As soon as you say it, you're too late, the bus has pulled out of the station.

Kempo remarks, "Is that so? Is that so?" That's a nice expression. Maezumi Roshi, when students would argue or make some definitive statement, would say, "If you say so..." In one way, it doesn't commit you to anything but, at the same time, it's communicating something very significant. If you are really open, a response like that might make you look at what you just said.

Here, Ummon replies, "Instead of Kohaku, you're really Kohoku." Literally those words mean "white-head" and "black-head" but they're also references to a couple of famous characters in Chinese literature. Kohaku was known as a real scoundrel, a trickster, and a great liar. He could trick anyone out of anything. And Kohoku was trickier still; he could trick Kohaku even as Kohaku was in the midst of perpetrating a fraud. So Ummon is essentially laughing, "I thought I was conning you, but really you are conning me" or maybe, "I thought I left no traces, but you wiped up my mess." Ummon is giving a response without giving anything away, without leaving any traces.

How can you really reach this place where you leave no traces?

Elsewhere, Ummon has said, "A true person of the Way can speak of fire without burning his mouth. He can speak all day without moving his lips or uttering a word. The entire day he just wears his clothes, and eats his food, but never comes in contact with a single grain of rice or a shred of cloth."

Chant without using your voice, play instruments without using your hands. If you can do that, then everything will be naturally harmonious. That's part of the deeper meaning of this koan.

The verse says: "How surely it's thus! Everywhere to be oneself." On one level, how can you not be who you are? But on another level, how can we truly be ourselves, no matter what the situation, no matter what the circumstance? We take on so many roles and then obscure reality according to the roles that we assume. We put on many false identities. In one position, we're one person; in another position, we're somebody else. So who are we really? How can we truly be who we are everywhere, throughout space and time? The challenge is to see through all the masks and personae.

This kind of koan is very subtle, calling on us to reveal a deeper understanding after we've penetrated all the superficial layers of understanding.

Really though, there's not too much one can say. Then, thunderous silence says it all.

CASE 41

Rakuho's Last Moments

PREFACE TO THE ASSEMBLY

Sometimes out of loyalty, one drives oneself to unspeakable hardship. Sometimes when disaster befalls, other men fail to get the point. Humbly stooping down at the time of departure, his last moments are utterly kind. Tears flowing forth from his tender heart are still more difficult to hide. However, is there someone here with cool eyes?

MAIN CASE

Attention! Rakuho, on his deathbed, addressed the assembly, saying, "Now I have one matter to ask you about. If you approve this, you're putting another head on top of your own head. If you disapprove this, you're seeking life by cutting off your head." Thereupon, the head monk said, "The green mountain always raises its leg. In bright daylight, you don't raise a torch." Rakuho scolded, "What occasion is this that you should say such a thing?" The monk Genju stepped forward and said, "Leaving aside these two roads, please Master, don't question." Rakuho replied, "Partly, but say some more." Genju admitted, "I can't say it all." Rakuho said, "I don't care if you say it all or not." Genju said, "Being your attendant, Osho, it's hard for me to reply."

When evening came, Rakuho summoned the monk Genju and said, "Your response today makes very good sense. You should experience what my late master said: 'Before the eyes no Dharma. Mind is before the eyes. This: It's not Dharma before the eyes. It's something that ear and eye cannot reach.' Which phrase is guest? Which phrase is host? If you can make the distinction, I'll hand over the bowl." Genju said, "I don't know." Rakuho said, "You should know." Genju said, "I really don't know." Rakuho said cuttingly,

"Tough, isn't it? Tough, isn't it?" The monk said, "Osho, how about you?" Rakuho answered, "The boat of compassion is not poled over the waves of purity. In the rapids of the steep ravine one toils in vain to release the wooden goose."

APPRECIATORY VERSE

With clouds as bait, and moon as hook, he fishes in pure water.
Burdened with years solitary and hard, and no fish yet.
After the tune "Riso" dies away,
on the river Bakira, a lone man awakens.

We met Rakuho in Case 35 where he was a brash young monk. In this case Rakuho is on his deathbed and thus has mellowed out quite a bit. But even now, as he is about to die, he's still trying to help his students come to realization. My own teacher was the same way: There wasn't a single moment when he wasn't trying to draw something out from his students, there wasn't a time when he wasn't showing it.

In this case, Rakuho asks his assembly, from his deathbed, whether they approve or disapprove. He sets a trap: To approve or affirm anything—your practice, your understanding, your awareness—is adding something extra, like a useless appendage. If you have two heads you become a side-show freak. But disapproving, denying it, is cutting off your own head, negating reality. What would you say?

The head monk gives a poetical reply that basically means that morning until night, we do what we do, and that's the functioning of our true self. He says that Rakuho is using a flashlight to find his way in broad daylight. But Rakuho scolds him: "What occasion is this that you should say such a thing?"

The appropriate response to any situation always depends upon the conditions. There is no fixed response that is universally appropriate. In the conditions at hand, with Rakuho on his deathbed, is the monk's response appropriate? The head monk wasn't obnoxious, but he wasn't quite appropriate. It's like somebody coming to you and saying that her parents just died, and you say, "Life and death are empty!" Is that an appropriate response? No! It might be correct, but it's not an appropriate response. That's what we have to look at. What's an appropriate response according to the conditions?

Rakuho challenges Genju to say something appropriate to the conditions. Responses to koans demand the same appropriateness. When addressing a particular koan in dokusan, you might say something that's generally true but not appropriate or precise to the koan at hand. Working on koans is like looking at all the facets of a diamond, one at a time. Maybe you understand *that* facet but your teacher might want you to see *this* facet.

Eventually Genju comes out with, "Leaving aside these two roads, or these two options, please Master, don't question." But Rakuho isn't quite pleased with that and squeezes him a little bit to see if he could say some more, and Genju said, "I can't say it all." In a way, that's true: If you say it, that's not it. But Rakuho presses on and Genju still can't respond appropriately.

Then, getting even weaker and sicker, Rakuho summoned the monk to his room that evening. He wasn't ready to die without giving every last ounce of energy that he had. He said, "Before the eyes, no Dharma. Mind is before the eyes." Everything is empty, yet this mind manifests in all kinds of shapes and forms. "This: it's not Dharma before your eyes." Since it's not before your eyes, it's something that ear and eye cannot reach, so what is it? If, as the Heart Sutra says, there's no eye, no ear, no nose, no tongue, no body, no mind, what is it that's hearing? What is it that's seeing? What is it that's tasting? What is it that's touching? "Which phrase is guest? Which phrase is host?" These are terms designating the relative and the absolute, self and other. Then Rakuho tells Genju that if he can answer, Rakuho will "hand over the bowl" and thus name Genju his Dharma successor.

Genju responds, "I don't know." There are different kinds of "I don't know." There is not-knowing that forgets all attachment to ego, and there is not-knowing that holds on. Which is this? Sometimes when you say, "I don't know" you are clueless of something knowable. On another occasion you might say, "I don't know" because the subject cannot be known. Rakuho ends up saying, "Tough, isn't it?" It is tough. It's not only tough for the student but it's tough for Rakuho too. Here he is, putting every last ounce of his life into teaching and all his student can say is, "I really don't know."

Rakuho's answer—"The boat of compassion is not poled over the waves of purity. In the rapids of the steep ravine one toils in vain to release the wooden goose."—amounts to telling Genju that he'll have to do it himself. The wooden goose is a piece of wood that is sent down the rapids to determine the turbulence in the water so that rafters can plot a safe course through the rapids.

Rakuho is telling Genju, "You have to do it. Don't hold onto the wooden goose. Let go."

No one is going to do it for you. You're the wooden goose. Follow the flow through the ravine. Do it yourself.

The verse uses a metaphor of catching fish for the process of teaching. Rakuho threw out the line, but he didn't reel in Genju. "No fish yet." Actually, Rakuho had eleven successors—but Genju wasn't one of them.

CASE 42

Nanyo's Washbasin

PREFACE TO THE ASSEMBLY

Washing bowls and filling the washbasin are both Dharma gates and Buddha's affair. Carrying wood and drawing water are nothing but marvelous activity and supernatural power. Why can't one obtain releasing effulgence in shaking the earth?

MAIN CASE

Attention! A monk asked National Teacher Chu of Nanyo, "What is the original body of Vairochana?" The National Teacher replied, "Go and fetch me the washbasin." The monk brought the washbasin to him. The National Teacher said, "Now, go put it back." The monk asked again, "What is the original body of Vairochana?" The National Teacher remarked, "The old Buddha is long gone."

APPRECIATORY VERSE

A bird soaring in air. A fish dwelling in water.
Rivers and lakes both forgotten, he aspires to clouds and heaven.
A thread of doubting mind, and they're facing ten thousand *li* apart.
How many people understand and requite benevolence?

The National Teacher Chu of Nanyo lived from 675 to 775 in China and was a successor of the Sixth Ancestor, Huineng. He taught three different emperors of China during the Tang Dynasty.

The preface highlights the point of this koan: "Washing bowls and filling the washbasin are both Dharma gates and Buddha's affair." Everything you do manifests your original face. It's easy to say that but what does it mean? You might understand that chopping wood and carrying water are Zen activities, but how do you realize your True Nature while driving the car on a busy highway? How do you realize your True Nature while fighting with your parent or partner? How do you realize your True Nature while feeling lonely or unworthy?

"What is the original body of Vairochana?" Vairochana is Cosmic Buddha, present everywhere, and is one of the manifestations of Buddha. His name means "He who is like the sun." Get caught in your ideas and it's long gone. You missed it. Even if you say that you see it, it's long gone. The Buddha is long gone. Blink your eyes, and you miss him. How many times have you said, "I should have done this," or, "I should have said that"? Each of us should reflect on every moment we've missed the Buddha!

Pay attention to each moment. Don't look for the original body of Vairochana somewhere else. If you can appreciate that, what's the problem?

CASE 43

Razan's Arising and Vanishing

PREFACE TO THE ASSEMBLY

A drop of the elixir of life and iron becomes gold. A word of the ultimate principle and the commoner becomes a sage. If you know that gold and iron are not two and that the commoner and the sage are basically the same, then obviously not even a drop is needed. Tell me: What drop is this?

MAIN CASE

Attention! Razan asked Ganto, "How about when arising and vanishing are ceaseless?" Ganto scolded, and said, "Who is this arising and vanishing?"

APPRECIATORY VERSE

Cutting old brambles, smashing the fox cave.
A leopard shrouded in fog has its spots changed.
A dragon riding lightning has its bones transformed.
Tut! Rising and vanishing snarled up. What is it?

All phenomena arise, persist, then decay. Everything arises and vanishes. When you meditate and watch your thoughts, you see them arise and vanish, arise and vanish. Razan asks, "What about when it's ceaseless?"

In another koan, Razan asks this same question to Sekiso, who replies, "Be cold ashes, a dead tree: one thought for ten thousand years, pure and spotlessly clear." A version of this answer is presented in Case 96. This is the state of being free and when you are free, there's no-thing. You would only know the arising and vanishing if you are separate from them. As long as you're sitting there and *watching* the arising and vanishing, then there's a duality. When it is ceaseless, then one thought, instead of arising and vanishing, lasts ten thousand years. How can you achieve that state?

But Razan didn't get it and so he brought the question to Ganto, who responds, "Who is this arising and vanishing?" It's not enough to be one with the absolute. You're not just the absolute. You're everything altogether. When subject and object vanish, who are you? When box and lid perfectly join, there is no discernible seam. When absolute and relative interpenetrate, there is no gap. Finally Razan got it and eventually became a successor of Ganto.

Much later a monk asked Razan, "When in front of you is a ten-thousand-foot cliff, and behind you are tigers, wolves, and lions, then what?" Razan replied, "Be there!" Where else can you be? Razan's sentiment arose from his realization of the ceaseless arising and vanishing.

The "enlightened life" that Ganto and Razan embody is as available to you as your willingness and readiness to venture into it. You must be willing to face your fears without piling more fear on top of them. You must be ready with a steady practice of zazen, able to quiet your mind and not identify with your thoughts even as they are arising and vanishing. Zazen is essential to creating the atmosphere you need to go into the abyss of your fright, loneliness, helplessness, pain, anger.

"Cut the brambles" of your conditioned responses, as the verse to this koan says, "smash the fox cave" and really be free. When the fox is free, it transforms into a wolf, which transforms into a leopard. When the leopard's spots change, it transforms into a tiger. When it takes to the air, it becomes a dragon. When that dragon rides on lightning, even its bones are transformed. How can you smash that fox cave? If you're a fox, be a fox with all of your flesh, bones, and pores of skin, then you could be transformed into a high-flying dragon.

CASE 44

Koyo's Garuda Bird

PREFACE TO THE ASSEMBLY

The lion attacks the elephant; the Garuda strikes the dragon. Soaring or crawling, king and minister are discerned. We monks should maintain host and guest. When a person debases heavenly dignity, how do you cut him off?

MAIN CASE

Attention! A monk said to Ho Osho of Koyo, "A dragon-king leaves the ocean, and heaven and earth are calm. Meet him face to face and then what?" The master replied, "The Garuda attains the universe. At such a time, who would dare stick his head out?" The monk countered, "When the head sticks out, then what?" Koyo answered, "It's like a falcon seizing a dove. If you don't understand, check in front of the balcony and know the truth." The monk then said, "Well then, I clasp my hands on my chest and retreat three steps." And Koyo remarked, "Blind turtle pinned under Sumeru. Don't get hit on the forehead and scarred again!"

APPRECIATORY VERSE

The imperial order descends; the general's order disperses.
Within the fortress, the emperor; outside the walls, the general.
Thunder doesn't wait for the astonished bugs to crawl out.
You'll never know the wind has stopped the flowing clouds.
The loom's lower warp is continuous and golden needle and jeweled
    thread are naturally there.
Plain and vast before sealing, originally there's no ideograph, or
    worm hole.

This case is a classic example of a Dharma combat, a spirited back-and-forth Zen dialogue in which each participant tries to present a live Zen phrase that not only quiets the opponent, but elevates his spiritual understanding and that of everyone else. There are no recorded dates for the birth and death of Koyo Ho, but it's known that he succeeded Taiyo Kyogen in the Soto lineage, and that Kyogen lived in the late tenth century and the beginning of the eleventh. Koyo was one of fifteen successors of Kyogen, and all fifteen of them died before Kyogen—and did so without leaving a successor. So, at the age of eighty, despairing that his lineage might die with him, Kyogen took a very unusual step, and he entrusted his lineage to a prominent Rinzai teacher of the day, Fuzan Hoen. When Kyogen died, the essential teachings of the Soto lineage remained with Fuzan. After many years, Fuzan encountered Tosu Gisei, a Soto-ordained monk, whom he deemed a worthy Dharma vessel for Kyogen's teachings, and Fuzan transmitted to him the lineage he had held for Kyogen. Thus the main Soto lineage took a little jog over to the Rinzai, and then came back again to maintain the integrity of the Soto lineage.

On the face of it, this koan seems pretty straightforward: a confrontation between a young upstart monk and an unrelenting teacher. The first lines of the case mention the dragon-king, who would be the complete ruler of all the oceans; in the ocean, the dragon-king is all-powerful and invulnerable.

We can draw an analogy to sitting on your cushion in the meditation hall: You're ruler of that realm, you're safe on your zafu. But what happens if the dragon leaves the ocean, what happens when you get up off your cushion? The dragon only has one foe: the Garuda bird. When the Garuda bird is hunting, it spreads its massive wings, and fans the waves, and separates the waters of the ocean. It sees the dragons crawling around on the ocean bottom like insects, and then dives down and preys on them. Thus the master in this case says, "The Garuda attains the universe. At such a time, who would dare stick his head out?"

When you rise from your zafu, what is the one thing (or are there many?) that spoils your tranquility and invincibility? Is it the girlfriend Garuda, the boss Garuda, the baby Garuda, the ex-spouse Garuda, the crazy-driver-in-front-of-you Garuda, or just some generic Garuda who happens to penetrate your protective shield? We all have our comfort zones where we feel safe and secure. It takes courage and faith to extend the boundaries of that zone to step into the unknown. That is what our practice is about. We must continually face all situations with open hearts and minds; we must continually face Garudas around every corner. When we fall into old habits and patterns, the Garudas swoop down upon our heads.

So, when the Garuda's on the prowl, how do you deal with it? Do you just stick out your head and confront it? The Garuda is all-powerful and will eventually beat you down. Do you just hide? Tell me: What do you do?

The monk here throws all caution to the wind. Discretion is the better part of valor, but the monk says, "When the head sticks out, then what?" For Koyo, this was too easy. He answered, "It's like a falcon seizing a dove. If you don't understand, check in front of the balcony and know the truth." In ancient China, when a subject offended the emperor, he'd cut off the subject's head and hang it in front of the balcony. So the master here is saying, "If you don't understand this thing, take a look at the bodiless heads hanging in front of the balcony, and know this isn't a game." Every time you sit zazen, it is a matter of life and death!

Yasutani Roshi used to describe *shikantaza*, the practice of just sitting, by saying that it's like walking in a crowded marketplace, balancing a jug of water on your head, trying not to spill a drop. You need to be aware of everything. If your mind just focuses on one thing, you miss something else; if you just focus on the kid on the pogo stick in front of you, you don't notice the donkey with its huge baskets of dried peppers walking on the other side and it will bump you and cause you to spill your water. You have to be aware of everything: all of the merchants, the shoppers, the children, the animals. If you are too loose, and you're not paying attention, you'll spill the water. If you're too tight and somebody just slightly bumps you, you'll spill it too. You need the right tension to help you concentrate. To this graphic description of shikantaza, Yasutani Roshi would add, "And there's a soldier walking behind you with a drawn sword. If you spill a single drop, he'll cut off your head." That's how much energy you should be putting into your zazen. The more energy you put in, the more energy it gives back to you.

The monk in this case goes on to say, "Well then, I clasp my hands on my chest and retreat three steps." That's supposed to be an indication of withdrawal and submission—the appropriate thing to do here, if it's sincere. But the master doesn't think it is, and replies, "Blind turtle pinned under Mount Sumeru. Don't get hit on the forehead and scarred again!"—"The

Garuda already cut off your head! Grow back another one, and I'll scar that one too!"

These koans are not just stories that took place in ancient China. To really do koan study effectively, you need to take each one and apply it to your life. So, what about your arrogance? What about your condescension? What about your insecurity? How do you deal with those? Can you leave the safety of the water without getting swooped up by the Garudas?

The monk here is pinned under Mount Sumeru. I ask you: What does he need to do to get free?

The Sutra of Complete Awakening

PREFACE TO THE ASSEMBLY

A manifest koan depends solely on right now. The absolute manner distinguishes only itself. If you try to set up gradations or intentionally strive, then all of this is painting eyebrows on chaos, or attaching a handle to a bowl. So how is tranquility achieved?

MAIN CASE

Attention! The Sutra of Complete Awakening says, "Be at all times without deluded thoughts arising. Moreover, with regard to all deluded states of mind, do not try to extinguish them. Dwelling in the realm of delusion, do not add discriminating knowledge. When knowledge is absent, do not distinguish reality."

APPRECIATORY VERSE

Sublime, magnificent, courageous, magnanimous;
piercing your head in bustling places;
walking along in tranquil places;
Underfoot, string cut away—I'm perfectly free.
Stop cutting. The mud's gone from the nose.
Don't be disturbed.
A prescription on a thousand-year-old paper.

This case, based on an ancient sutra, explains how to function, how to focus your mind—and how to sit zazen. It makes it absolutely clear.

The first line says, "Be at all times without deluded thoughts arising."

Deluded thoughts are the same thing as dichotomous thoughts, dualistic thoughts. You're separating yourself not only from everything else, but also from yourself. For instance, you may think you're inadequate, "I can't do this." When that thought arises, you believe it is true. Eventually your thoughts become basic beliefs that control your life. It all starts when you identify yourself with your thoughts. But any time a deluded thought arises, don't grab it. Just observe it and let it pass.

This verse from the Sutra of Complete Awakening can raise many questions for us: What is the nature of thought? What is the source of thought? What is the nature of knowledge? What is the nature of reality? It brings up all kinds of things, if we really think about it. Dogen says, "To study Zen is to study the self." To study the self is to look at the nature of these thoughts, and see them arising and dropping away.

We all want to have a peaceful mind, a mind completely at rest—that was what Master Eka said to Bodhidharma, "My mind is not at rest. Please pacify it for me."—but the sad truth is that there's no such thing as a peaceful mind! As long as you cling to "mind," then you're stuck. No-mind is what's peaceful. When we think that this "I," this mind that we identify as ourselves, has to be satisfied, we will never have peace. We all have our highs and lows; sometimes the mind is moving and sometimes it is at rest. How can we find peace no matter what the circumstance?

The first line of this koan tells us to avoid deluded states of mind. But that's not always possible, and so the second line tells what to do if they do arise. "With regard to deluded states of mind, do not try to extinguish them." Let them follow their own course. Don't grab onto them. What happens when you grab onto them? That's what the next line is about: "Dwelling in the realm of delusion, do not add discriminating knowledge." Grabbing onto them, evaluating them as to whether they're good or bad, real or unreal, true or false—you're adding needless interpretation. First thoughts arise. Then you have thoughts about thoughts. Altogether, this process gives an illusion that there's an independent self holding it all together. Yet if you don't cling to thoughts and quiet your mind, at moments there are no thoughts arising. Without thoughts, who are you?

Consider the word *shikantaza*—the practice of "just sitting." *Shikan* means "just" as in "just this." Maezumi Roshi says there is another implication to the word *shikantaza*: to "stop and observe." Just stop all of this chatter going on in your head and observe. Hold the whole universe as your zazen. Just being—not thinking about it, not analyzing—that's what shikantaza is, that's how you really become aware.

We fall into the realm of delusion when we are caught up in our heads, when we use our minds to foster our own self-image. This is like adding frost on top of snow.

The last line of the koan says, "When knowledge is absent, do not distinguish reality." Don't get stuck anywhere. When knowledge is absent, you can't get stuck anywhere because it is most intimate. In Case 20 Jizo says, "Not knowing is most intimate." Don't argue about what's true and what's not true. After all, what's the basis for that? Thinking is not precise enough to distinguish reality.

Sochu Roshi said that steady zazen is like an oven. It will burn up anything. Just keep putting your thoughts into the oven of your zazen. There are soft, pliable thoughts, like balsa wood, and hard, durable thoughts, like oak or maple. You'll consume it all. Just do it over and over and over again.

Literally, *zazen* means "sitting meditation" but the Sixth Ancestor added his interpretation: "*Za* means externally relating one's self to others, not a thought arises. *Zen* is seeing into one's own nature and being unmovable, unshakable." Now "unshakable" doesn't mean that you disengage yourself from everything. Quite the contrary: You are completely engaged. You may even have strong feelings—but don't blame others for them. Don't put yourself up and put others down.

The appreciatory verse for this case says: "Don't be disturbed—a prescription on a thousand-year-old paper." Take each moment just as it is. Just this. Nothing else. Just this. Do not be disturbed. Just sit. Don't judge. Don't criticize. Don't evaluate. A thousand-year-old paper's prescription.

Now it's a 2,500-year-old-prescription. Let's fill it, and administer it right now.

CASE 46

Tokusan's Completion of Study

PREFACE TO THE ASSEMBLY

The pure ground without an inch of grass for ten thousand *li* still deludes people. The clear sky without even a speck of cloud deceives you. Though wedges are driven in and pulled out, this does not impede holding up and supporting space. A hammer blow on the back of the head. Let's look at a skillful expedient.

MAIN CASE

Attention! Great Master Emmyo Tokusan addressed the assembly saying, "Exhaust the end and there's instant attainment. The mouths of all Buddhas of the three times might as well hang upon the wall. Now, there's a person who roars with laughter. Ha! Ha! When you know this one, the essence of your exhaustive study is completed."

APPRECIATORY VERSE

Gathering. Seizing the throat collar.
Winds burnish. Clouds sweep.
Chilling water, heaven turns to autumn.
Don't say a fish scale lacks taste.
Catching all the ocean's fish with a crescent moon.

This Emmyo Tokusan is not the Tokusan that we're familiar with from Cases 14, 22, and 55 and from the *Blue Cliff Record* and the *Gateless Gate*. Emmyo Tokusan lived in China from 910 to 990, and was a student of Master

Ummon. Interestingly, he is also the great-grandson in the Dharma of the better-known Tokusan.

The preface points to the nature of emptiness, the main theme in this case. Even if you see emptiness clearly, you can still be deceived.

There's another koan where Master Shakyo Ezo asks Master Seido Chizo, who was his senior, "Do you know how to comprehend universal emptiness?" Master Seido answers, "Of course I do." "How?" And Seido grasped a handful of air. Master Seido demonstrated the first two lines of this preface. "The pure ground without an inch of grass for ten thousand *li* still deludes people. The clear sky without even a speck of cloud deceives you."

After Seido showed how he grasped emptiness, Master Shakyo said, "Aha! You don't know how to grasp it!" And so Seido challenged Shakyo to show him how to grasp universal emptiness, and Shakyo grabbed Seido's nose and yanked it. Seido cried out in pain. That's the last two lines of the preface. "Though wedges are driven in and pulled out, this does not impede holding up and supporting space." In other words, don't get lost in this emptiness. You can drive wedges in and out. After he yelled out in pain, Seido said, "Now I've got it!" And Shakyo replied, "Yes! Now you know what it is!"

What is it? These two are playing with it: grasping empty space, grasping the nose. In either case if you think there's something there to grasp, you're deceiving yourself. In this case, Tokusan says, "Exhaust the end and there's instant attainment." Is there an end to exhaust? How would you do it? If you can exhaust it, then "the mouths of all Buddhas of the three times might as well hang upon the wall." Take all of the sayings, everything the Buddhas have ever said, and put them on the wall like a picture. There's no way that they can even express *it*.

Dogen's teacher, Tendo Nyojo said, "The entire body is a mouth hanging in the air." When Tokusan says that the mouths of all of the Buddhas of the three times might as well hang on the wall, he's saying even the Buddhas can't express this exhausted end. When Tendo Nyojo says the entire body is a mouth hanging in the air, he's saying, "You're expressing it all the time." It can't be expressed, and yet you're expressing it all the time. As soon as you think you've grabbed it, it's moved. And yet, you're constantly expressing it. Why? Tokusan says, "There's a person who roars with laughter." And then he laughs. "Ha! Ha! When you know this one, the essence of your exhaustive study is completed."

Even if you can't express it, there's still one who laughs, who cries, and who vows to save all sentient beings. In Case 38 Rinzai said, "There's a true person of no rank who continuously enters and leaves the openings of your face. For those who have not yet met this one, look! Look!" The true person of no rank is the one who roars with laughter. We need to know this one. When you're sitting facing the wall, what is the wall teaching you? When you're facing the wall, if you think it's you facing the wall, then what is it? When you can let go of that separation between you and the wall, then what's revealed? If you don't realize it, then it's just an idea up in your head. You have to see how it functions when you're facing the wall.

When the entire body and mind are facing the wall, the wall is facing the wall. The entire body and mind is a mouth hanging in the air. When you speak, use your whole body and mind. If your body and mind are the entire body and mind hanging in space, it is the body and mind of the universal emptiness. And if not, it's just some kind of an idea, some kind of concept, a false basis that depends on your own image of who you are.

Sometimes we laugh. Sometimes the one who's roaring with laughter cries. Sometimes we sit. Sometimes we stand. Yet we want to make something more out of it. To see the one who roars with laughter, exhaust the end! Just look into yourself and see. Water bubbles from the fountain. Heaven turns to autumn. The leaves fall. Just see who you are. And in seeing who you are, let that manifest as your life.

CASE 47

Joshu's Cypress Tree

PREFACE TO THE ASSEMBLY

The cypress tree in the garden. The flapping flag on the pole. As a blossom bespeaks the boundless spring, a drop bespeaks the ocean's water. The five-hundred-year-old Buddha clearly leaves the usual stream. Not falling into speech or thought, how do you express it?

MAIN CASE

Attention! A monk asked Joshu, "What is the meaning of Bodhidharma's coming from the West?" Joshu answered, "The cypress tree in the garden."

APPRECIATORY VERSE

Eyebrow-banks snow tipped.
River-eyes embracing autumn.
Ocean-mouth booming out waves.
Sail-tongue drifting downstream.
Riot-quelling hand, peace-making strategy.
Dear old Joshu! Dear old Joshu!
Stirring up the monastery, he's not yet taken rest.
Uselessly rendering aid, making a cart and entering the well-worn ruts.
Basically untalented; he blocks up ravines and fills ditches.

This koan is short, and it appears in many places, such as Case 37 in the *Gateless Gate*. Master Dogen devoted a whole chapter of the *Shobogenzo* to this koan. We should pay careful attention to it.

This question of Bodhidharma's coming from the West has many implications. It could be: "What is the meaning of Zen?" or it could be, "What is my true self before my parents were born?" The cypress tree in the garden! There's a classic Zen verse, which I've modified a little bit, which points to this koan.

> The golden aspens in the fall.
> The whispering of the pines.
> They are all the voice and body
> of our dear Shakyamuni.

When Shakyamuni Buddha saw the morning star, he was enlightened and exclaimed, "I, all beings everywhere, the Sun, the Moon, the stars, and the great Earth are simultaneously enlightened." What better way to honor the enlightenment of our dear Shakyamuni than to see him eye to eye in the Sun, the Moon, the stars, and the great Earth?

Master Joshu was called "little Shakyamuni." This koan occurs when Joshu's eyebrows were as white as the mountain peaks in the Rockies. It's stated in the preface to the assembly that one blossom testifies to a boundless spring. One drop of water testifies to the vast ocean. This expression of Joshu's, the cypress tree in the garden, contains everything—if you really see it. One cypress tree attests to the meaning of Bodhidharma coming from the west, to the ultimate meaning of Zen, to your true self before your parents were born.

The Record of Joshu contains a longer version of this koan: A monk asked Great Master Joshu, "Why did the First Patriarch come from the west?" Joshu said, "The cypress tree in the front garden." The monk said, "Oh priest, you shouldn't talk to me of external things." Joshu replied, "I didn't." The monk asked again, "Why did the First Ancestor come from the west?" Joshu said, "The cypress tree in the front garden."

Master Dogen commented on this dialogue: "Although this koan originated with Joshu, it was created by the entire body of all the Buddhas. Who is the master of this koan? We should know that the principle of the cypress tree in the front garden, and why did the First Ancestor come from the west, does not belong to the objective world. Furthermore, the cypress tree is not the objective self. Because we have in this dialogue, 'Oh priest, you shouldn't talk to me of external things,' there is the reply, 'I didn't.' How can the priest become attached to the priest? If he's not attached, he becomes 'I' and how can 'I' become attached to 'I,' and if 'I' is attached, he becomes a human."

Thus if you're attached anywhere to an external, objective tree, then it becomes the concrete world, the objective world. If there's an object, there is also a subject. The subject is our ego-grasping mind full of its concepts. We become attached to those concepts and ideas and then we become deluded. We begin to believe our thoughts, our ideas, and our images.

Joshu had a large number of students. One of them, whose name was Kaku Tetsu, was on a pilgrimage, and he went to Hogen's monastery. Hogen said, "Where have you come from?" Kaku Tetsu said, "I came from Joshu's." Hogen said, "I hear that Joshu has a saying, 'the cypress tree in the garden.' Is it so?" Kaku Tetsu said, "No." Hogen said, "Everyone who's been around says that a monk asked him the meaning of Zen, and Joshu said, 'the cypress tree in the garden.' How come you say no?" Kaku Tetsu said, "The late master really didn't say this. Please, don't slander him!" If you want to honor your live experience, don't cling to the words of a deceased master.

A monk asked Joshu, "Does the cypress tree have Buddha Nature or not?" Joshu said, "Yes, it has." The monk said, "When does the cypress tree attain buddhahood?" Joshu said, "Wait until the great universe collapses." The monk said, "When does the great universe collapse?" Joshu said, "Wait until the cypress tree attains buddhahood." We spend our energy trying to keep the universe from collapsing. What is the universe that we're propping up? It's not the true universe. It's not the true cypress tree. It's the universe that we invent in our thoughts. When that universe collapses, freedom is manifest, and the cypress tree attains buddhahood. There are all kinds of universes, and there are all kinds that have to collapse.

A koan reveals hidden structures beneath the surface, the ones that are propping up our notions of what's true and what's false. Keep penetrating further into your fundamental belief system that's propping up this false universe that you have created in your mind. You'll discover that ultimately it's built on quicksand. It's eventually going to sink—so why not now? What are you holding onto?

Why did Bodhidharma come from the west? What is the cypress tree in the garden? The deeper we look into these questions, the more unfathomable they become. Therefore our answers are always incomplete. It's confusion after confusion, piling up, and our speech is like a meaningless echo.

If you see that there's no objectivity or subjectivity, then you'll see that the cypress tree in the garden is rooted in complete freedom.

CASE 48

Vimalakirti's Nonduality

PREFACE TO THE ASSEMBLY

Marvelous activity may be limitless, but there is a place where the hand cannot reach. Speech may be unimpeded, but there's a time when the mouth can't be open. As Ryuge was a handless man who used his fist, so Kassan, a tongueless man, used words to cause understanding. To liberate the body when halfway down the road: Who is such a person?

MAIN CASE

Attention! Vimalakirti asked Manjushri, "What about a bodhisattva entering the nondual Dharma gate?" Manjushri replied, "As I understand it, with regard to all dharmas, there are no words or speech, no revelation or knowledge, and it is separate from all conversation. This is entering the nondual Dharma gate." Thereupon, Manjushri questioned Vimalakirti, saying, "All of us bodhisattvas have each had our say. Venerable Sir, now you should expound about a bodhisattva entering the nondual Dharma gate." Vimalakirti maintained silence.

APPRECIATORY VERSE

Manjushri's sick call to old Vaisali.
The nondual gate opens. Look at the adept.
Rough outside, genuine inside—who appreciates him?
Forgetting before and losing after, don't lament.
Trying hard to offer a stone, the offender was punished at So's palace.
In recompense, the luminous jewel: the wounded snake at Zui's castle.
Stop inquiring! It's beyond flaws.
Totally lacking worldliness—that's worth a little.

This case comes from the Vimalakirti Sutra, a Mahayana sutra written a couple of thousand years ago. Vimalakirti was a famous and highly enlightened layperson, who lived at the time of the Buddha. The Vimalakirti Sutra emphasizes nonduality—between monastic and lay, woman and man, enlightened being and ordinary being—and thus became one of the foundational sutras of Mahayana Buddhism. Of course, the old institutions of Buddhism still maintain those distinctions, but the teachings of the Mahayana don't.

In the beginning of the sutra, Vimalakirti is sick in bed. The Buddha hears about this and says to his followers, "Vimalakirti is sick. Someone should go inquire after him." Scanning all of the bodhisattvas in his assembly, he asks, "Who is willing to go?"—but the Buddha doesn't get any volunteers. He asks one after another, but they all beg off because they had previously encountered Vimalakirti in a Dharma dialogue, and he had bested them. His realization was so deep that they were afraid to even encounter him. Finally, the Buddha settles on Manjushri, the bodhisattva of wisdom. An extraordinary bodhisattva of great stature, Manjushri can't back out. But Manjushri says, "Alright, I'll go. But I want all the other bodhisattvas to go with me."—and so they all went to visit Vimalakirti in his little ten-foot-by-ten-foot sick room. Into that room arrive thirty-two bodhisattvas and 32,000 arhats, enlightened beings.

Vimalakirti asks each of the thirty-two bodhisattvas present to speak about the Dharma gate of nonduality. The first thirty-one each took dualistic views of doing and not doing, of right and wrong, and merged them into a monism or a view of oneness, which they considered to be the Dharma gate of nonduality. When it was Manjushri's turn, the extraordinary bodhisattva of great spiritual stature says, "As I understand it, with regard to all dharmas, there are no words or speech, no revelation or knowledge, and it is separate from all conversation."—you won't find it in words. Manjushri is correctly pointing out that as soon as you say something, you create something else, a picture, an image. Master Engo commented on this: "Since the other thirty-one had used words to dispense with words, Manjushri used no words to dispense with words. At once, he swept everything away, not wanting anything, and considering this to be the Dharma gate of nonduality. He certainly didn't realize that this was the sacred tortoise dragging its tail, that in wiping away the tracks, it was making traces." A sea tortoise comes out of the sea and lays her eggs in the sand. When she heads back into the sea, she tries to cover up her flipper-steps by wiping them away with her tail—but then she's leaving the traces of her tail in the sand. Manjushri is trying to wipe everything away, but he's still leaving traces.

In response to this, Vimalakirti remains silent. Does that silence reach it? Sometimes silence is very loud, reaching everywhere. But sometimes silence isn't appropriate; it can be an evasion of truth. You can say that silence is just the other side of speech, one half of a dichotomy, so how can silence be the entry into the nondual Dharma gate? What is nondual? Is nondual the opposite of dual? If it is, then it too is just another duality. How do we transcend all dualities?

Engo, further commenting on this, said, "Don't misunderstand. If it is the Dharma gate of nonduality, only by attaining together and witnessing together can there be a common mutual realization and knowledge."

Vimalakirti concurs: Elsewhere in the sutra he says that in order for his sickness to be healed, all sickness has to be healed. We have to attain enlightenment together, and bear witness together. Is it possible then to function in this life in a nondual way? Vimalakirti says that it is. Buddha says it is. Manjushri says it is. Countless Buddhas and Ancestors have said it is. Even I say it is.

In his silence, Vimalakirti is vividly displaying nonduality. Each one of us, right where we sit, is continuously shining with the light of nonduality. Do you see it?

CASE 49

Tozan Offers to the Essence

Sketching it doesn't succeed. Coloring it doesn't either. Fukei turned a somersault. Ryuge revealed only half his body. In the end, what are the features of *that* person?

MAIN CASE
Attention! When Tozan was conducting a memorial service to Ungan's essence, he related the story of how he once asked Ungan to reveal his essence and Ungan had replied, "Just *this*." A monk who was present at the memorial asked, "What did Ungan intend by saying 'Just *this*'?" Tozan replied, "At that time, I almost completely misunderstood my late teacher's intent." The monk then asked, "Did Ungan know of 'Just *this*'?" Tozan replied, "If he didn't know, how could he speak thus? If he did know, why did he speak thus?"

APPRECIATORY VERSE
How could he speak thus?
Fifth watch, and a cock crows: dawn in the forest of houses.
Why did he even speak thus?
Thousand-year-old crane and cloud-piercing pine together grow old.
The jewel mirror lucidly tests Absolute and Relative:
the bejeweled loom, with shuttle flying.
See the unstopped finish.
The school's style prospers greatly; rules mosey along.
Father and son transforming throughout,
their charisma expanding.

As a young monk, Tozan studied for twenty years with Nansen and then Nansen suggested that he go study with Ungan. In China at that time, which is known as the Golden Age of Zen, it was not uncommon for students to study with different teachers. Apparently Nansen sensed that it would be best for Tozan to go study with Ungan instead of continuing just with him. Maybe they were in some kind of a stuck relationship, and Nansen felt that he had to help Tozan break free from it.

At Ungan's monastery, Tozan had a realization and eventually succeeded Ungan's Dharma—but Tozan still wasn't totally clear even at that point. When Tozan was taking leave of Ungan, he asked him what he should say if asked, "Can you still recall your master's true face?" Ungan remained silent for a while, and then replied, "Just this one is." In other words, just *this*. After another pause, Ungan said, "In carrying out this charge, exercise your utmost circumspection and care." The present koan recalls this dialogue.

In this koan, Tozan comments, "At that time, I almost completely misunderstood my late teacher's intent." Only when Tozan was on a pilgrimage after taking leave of Ungan, as he was looking at his reflection in a mountain stream he did realize "Just this one is." At that time he composed this verse:

> Do not seek him anywhere else or he will run away from you.
> Now that I go on all alone, I meet him everywhere.
> He is even now what I am; I am even now not what he is.
> Only by understanding this way can there be a true union with the
>   self.

In the Record of Tozan, there's another dialogue which is very similar to the one in this case: Tozan was conducting another memorial service for Ungan, and the monk said, "What instruction did you receive at your late teacher's place?" Tozan said, "Although I was there, I didn't receive his instruction." What is there to receive? What is there to give? The monk continued, "Then why conduct a service for him?" Tozan replied, "Even so, how dare I turn my back on him?" It's a sad thing when students turn their backs to their teacher, especially if they've become teachers themselves. Then the monk said, "You rose to prominence at Nansen's. Why do you instead conduct a service for Ungan?"

My late teacher, Maezumi Roshi, had three teachers. Baian Hakujun, his father, was his first teacher and gave him Dharma transmission in the Soto lineage. Then, Hakuun Yasutani Roshi, a Soto teacher with Rinzai training, also transmitted the Dharma to him. And finally Musu Koryo Roshi, a lay teacher in the Rinzai lineage, also approved Maezumi as a Zen master. At the Zen Center of Los Angeles, we did regular services for all three.

Tozan may have also done a service for Nansen, but nonetheless the monk asked, "Why are you conducting a service for Ungan?" Tozan said, "I do not esteem my late teacher's virtues, or his Buddhist teachings. I only value the fact that he did not explain everything to me." If his teacher had told him everything, he never could have realized it for himself. He would only have thought that he understood. Next the monk said, "You succeeded to the late teacher. Then, do you agree with him or not?" And Tozan said, "I half agree, half don't agree." The monk asked, "Why don't you completely agree?" Tozan said, "If I completely agree, then I would be unfaithful to my late teacher." There's a Zen saying that if the student is only as good as the teacher, then the teaching will decline. Thus Tozan said, "If I completely agree, then I'd be unfaithful." When Tozan was taking leave of Ungan, as his successor Ungan said, "In carrying out this commitment, exercise your utmost circumspection and care." If we just parrot what our teachers tell us, what are we expressing? So Tozan half agrees. Is that arrogance? Be careful not to be arrogant; that's one of the worst things we can do with our Zen training.

In the present koan, the monk asks, "Did Ungan know of 'Just *this*'?" "If he didn't know, how could he speak thus? If he did know, why did he speak thus?" If he didn't know the essence, how could he say anything about it? If he did know the essence, for what reason would he say anything about it? What would you say?

The verse to this case says, "The jewel mirror lucidly tests absolute and relative." Tozan presented a short verse called the "Jewel Mirror Samadhi." Look at Tozan's answer in light of this verse:

> The teaching of thusness has been intimately communicated by
> Buddhas and Ancestors.
> Now you have it, so keep it well.
> It's like facing a jewel mirror. Form and image behold each other.
> You are not it; it actually is you.

It's like a baby in the world, in five aspects complete.
It does not go or come, nor rise, nor stand.
Baba wawa! Is there anything said, or not?

Baba wawa is the sound of baby babbling. Is there anything said or not? Babawawa. The wooden man sings. The stone woman gets up and dances. Everywhere we meet it. How could it admit of consideration and thought? How could it admit of "Just this is it"?

CASE 50

Seppo's "What's This?"

The last word ultimately reaches the impenetrable barrier. Above, Ganto, being confident, did not approve his closest teacher, and below, did not concede anything to his Dharma brother Seppo. Is he trying to create an echelon, or is there some other vital function?

MAIN CASE

Attention! When Seppo was dwelling in a hut, two monks came and both made prostrations. Seppo, having seen them come, threw open his hut door, burst outside, and shouted, "What's this?" One monk repeated, "What's this?" Seppo hung his head and went back inside the hut. The monk later arrived at Ganto's monastery, and Ganto asked, "Where have you come from?" The monk replied, "Reinan Province." Ganto asked, "Did you visit Seppo?" The monk answered, "Yes, I did." Ganto asked, "Did he have anything to say?" The monk related the previous incident, and Ganto asked, "Was there anything else?" The monk replied, "He said nothing, but hung his head and went back inside the hut." Ganto remarked, "Ah, I should have told him the last word that one time. If I had told him, no one under heaven could do anything with him." At the end of the summer practice session, the monk again repeated the previous story and this time asked for some guidance. Ganto said, "Why didn't you come sooner?" The monk replied, "It's not an easy thing to ask." Ganto remarked, "We were born of the same branch, but we will not die of the same branch. If you would know the last word, it is just this."

Cutting, carving, polishing, grinding; transforming and veiling.

Kafi pond's stick transformed to a dragon.

Toka's shuttle hung on the wall.

Many are born of the same branch but few die of the same branch.

The last word is just this.

A wind boat, having loaded the moon, bobs on autumn waters.

So, what's *this*? Seppo comes out of his hut and shouts, "What's this?" In our lives, we all have this kind of knee-jerk reaction to things. How often do you ask yourself, "What's this?"

Your mother says something to you, your boyfriend or girlfriend responds in some way, your boss makes some request: How often do you stop and ask "what's this?" It doesn't even have to be a question, it could be an exclamation. *What's this!*

Ganto and Seppo were Dharma brothers, they trained together. In this case, Ganto is referring to an incident that is recorded in this book as Case 55. Tokusan, who is the teacher of both Ganto and Seppo, was carrying his bowl to the dining hall for the afternoon meal, and Seppo was the cook. He said, "Old Master, the bell has not rung, and the drum has not yet struck. Where are you going with your bowls?" Tokusan at once turned around and went back to his room. Seppo related this incident to Ganto, in a bragging way, saying, "I really got one over on the old boy this time!" Ganto said, "Great master though he is, Tokusan has not yet grasped the last word of Zen."

Hearing of this, Tokusan sent his attendant to bring Ganto in and said, "Do you not approve of me?" Ganto whispered in his ear his intention, and Tokusan was satisfied and silent. The next day, Tokusan appeared on the rostrum, and sure enough his talk was different from the usual one, and Ganto came in from the assembly, laughing heartily, clapped his hands, and said, "What a joy it is! The old master has now grasped the last word of Zen!" Ganto and Tokusan were trying to bring Seppo out.

In the *Gateless Gate* Case 13, Master Mumon wrote a poem about this case:

> If you understand the first word of Zen, you will know the
>   last word.
> The last word or the first word—*IT* is not a word!

One time when Ganto and Seppo were on pilgrimage together, Ganto helped bring Seppo to realization. Thus Ganto remarked, "We were born of the same branch, but we will not die of the same branch. If you would know the last word, it is just this." Born of the same branch could mean that they practiced together at Tokusan's, but they each led their life differently, taught differently, had different ways of expressing their realization. That is a lame explanation. What is the living branch?

In this case, it's important to notice that the monk spent a whole summer training period with Ganto, ninety days, before asking for guidance about the incident he had related. What's that about? He was holding onto his own ideas, opinions, and judgments and was afraid to really expose himself.

Maezumi Roshi often asked me to look at these koans from two perspectives: the intrinsic and the experiential. Intrinsically, everything is perfect as it is. The sky is blue: it's perfect. The grass is green: it's perfect. The grass is brown: it's perfect. You are the Buddha: perfect just as you are, yet you don't always feel perfect. You don't believe that you are Buddha. In Case 67 the Buddha says, "All beings everywhere have the wisdom of the Tathagatha,"—but if you haven't experienced yourself as the Buddha, it doesn't matter what the Buddha says. If it's not your experience, then it's not really helpful. The Buddha might as well have been talking to a pack of donkeys. Your understanding is not complete unless you have the experiential understanding to go along with the intrinsic understanding. They have to come together. A testing question for this koan is, "What's the difference between the first word and the last word of Zen?" Intrinsically, of course, the first word is perfect and complete, and the last word is perfect and complete. So, what's the difference? Mumon says, "If you know the first word, you know the last word." Intrinsically, that's true, but is it true for you experientially? Is your first word of Zen the same as your last word of Zen? Is your first sesshin the same as your last sesshin? Surely your first day of zazen isn't the same as your last day of zazen. Only when there's no difference between the intrinsic reality and the experiential reality can you say that you understand the last word of Zen.

When I was beginning my practice, I was struck by a phrase in "Faith in Mind," the famous poem usually attributed to the Third Ancestor of Chinese Zen: "To come directly into harmony with this reality, just simply say, when doubt arises, 'Not two.' In this 'Not-two' nothing is separate, nothing is excluded." I took part of that phrase, and I wrote "NOT TWO" on a little piece of paper and put it above my desk. When I would get annoyed at some of my coworkers I would recite in my head, "Not two!" When I saw someone doing something that I disliked, I would say, "Not two." But now I say, "What's this!" Whatever's arising: What's this! When something's perceived: What's this! Projections, opinions, beliefs, images: What's this!

My first word of Zen was "Not two." Ganto's last word is "Just this." Right now, my last word is "What's this!" Next week I'll have a new last word! Experientially the first word is not necessarily the same as the last word. What are your words?

CASE 51

Hogen's "By Boat or Land"

PREFACE TO THE ASSEMBLY

Worldly dharmas enlighten many people. Buddhadharma deludes many people. Suddenly become one: Can there be any delusion or enlightenment?

MAIN CASE

Attention! Hogen asked Kaku Joza, "Did you come by boat or by land?" Kaku Joza replied, "By boat." Hogen said, "Where is the boat?" Kaku answered, "The boat is in the river." After Kaku left, Hogen asked the monk beside him, "Tell me: Did that monk who was just here have the Zen eye or not?"

APPRECIATORY VERSE

Water does not wash water;
gold does not trade for gold.
Ignoring its color, obtain a fine horse.
Without its strings, enjoy a lute.
Tying a knot, divining with sticks—
Then there is this matter:
Utterly lost is true, innocent, ancient mind.

In this koan we again encounter Master Hogen, the founder of the Hogen School, one of the five schools of Zen in China, during the Golden Age of Zen. He often went on pilgrimage, here and there, traveling by boat and by land. Once, a blizzard forced him to end up at Master Jizo's monastery. Case 20 of this collection records his encounter with Jizo: Jizo said, "Where are you going?" Hogen said, "On an outward pilgrimage." Jizo said, "Why do you go on this pilgrimage?" Hogen said, "I don't know." Jizo said, "Not knowing is most intimate." At those words, Hogen experienced some awakening.

Knowing makes us feel comfortable. In the ancient Zen monasteries, they had an expression for those monks who came there just to be comfortable: cat and dog monks. Like a pet, they came to sit and be taken care of. This real practice of Zen is about continuously stepping into the unknown and allowing yourself to be enlightened by the worldly dharmas.

The preface to this case says, "Worldly dharmas enlighten many people." The comings and goings of our everyday life are enlightening. How does it enlighten many people? And the next line says, "Buddhadharma deludes many people." Buddhadharma deludes many people as soon as we think, "Oh, I understand that! If I'm just empty, then I'm free." As soon as you say, "I'm empty," then you've just filled yourself up with *I'm empty*. Relating to the Buddhadharma, how can one truly *not know*?

A monk once asked Hogen, "What is the particular thing an advanced student should attend to?" Hogen said, "If the student has anything that is particular, he can't be called advanced." Whatever it is that you think qualifies you as "advanced" is what is preventing you from being advanced! Not knowing is most intimate.

There's a story about a Zen monk who lived in a cottage, and above his door he wrote the word *mind*. Above his window, he wrote the word *mind*. On his wall, he wrote the word *mind*. Hogen commented on this, saying, "Above his door, he should have written *door*, and above his window he should have written *window*, and on his wall he should have written *wall*."

Kaku Joza, who appears in the present case, answered Hogen genuinely: A wall is a wall; a window, a window; a door, a door. Kaku was a fairly well-established monk when he visited Hogen. Hogen asks him, "Did you come by boat, or by land?" Kaku Joza replies, "By boat." Hogen says, "Where is the boat?" Kaku answers, "The boat is in the river." At that point, if Kaku wanted to engage Hogen in Dharma combat, he might have answered, "Here!" or "Just this!" But this isn't what he does. And then, after Kaku leaves, Hogen asks his attendant: "Did that monk have the Zen eye or not?"

In contrast consider Case 15 in the *Gateless Gate*: Tosan came to an interview with Ummon, and Ummon said, "Where have you been recently?" Tosan said, "At Sato, Master." Ummon said, "Where did you stay during the last Ango period?" "At Hozu, of Konan," replied Tosan. "When did you leave there?" "On the twenty-fifth of August." Ummon exclaimed, "I give you sixty blows with my stick!" What's the difference? Why did Hogen say, "Did he have the Zen eye or not?" Ummon says, "I'm going to give you sixty blows!"

The next day, Tosan came up again to the master and said, "Yesterday, you gave me sixty blows of your stick. I do not know where my fault was." Ummon cried out, "You rice bag! Have you been prowling around like that from Kosei to Konan?" At that, Tosan became enlightened. Why does Ummon respond so differently to a seemingly natural response? Why was Hogen so gentle with Kaku Joza and Ummon so hard with Tosan? What's the difference? It's not just the words that we say; it's where we are coming from, our fundamental attitude, when we say them. Do we answer with a mind of not-knowing or a mind of grasping? Life itself is the Dharma, but if you think it's Dharma, it's not. Don't get caught up in the Buddhadharma. Just be who you are, be natural.

In *Thoughts Without a Thinker*, Mark Epstein recounts a funny story about an encounter between Seung Sahn, a famous Korean Zen master, and Kalu Rinpoche, a prominent teacher of Tibetan Buddhism. The representatives of the two traditions were each going to demonstrate their understanding of the Dharma, and investigate the other's. At one point, Seung Sahn, famous for hurling questions at his students to bring forth the mind of not-knowing, reached into his robe and drew out an orange. He held it in front of Kalu Rinpoche and demanded: "What is this! What is it!" Kalu Rinpoche paused, and then through his interpreter asked their host, "What's the matter with this fellow? Don't they have oranges in Korea?"

Kaku Joza is so natural in his responses, it is hard to distinguish his level of attainment. That is why Hogen questioned his attendant. If he has the Zen eye, why is he so ordinary? If he does not have the Zen eye, how could he be so ordinary? Don't let the bright sun of enlightenment blind you so you don't know if you come by boat or by land. It is simple. The ground is firm and the water flows.

CASE 52

Sozan's Dharmakaya

PREFACE TO THE ASSEMBLY

All knowledgeable persons are able to learn by parable and analogy—but when comparisons cannot be made and when it's impossible to find something similar or identical, how can it be expressed?

MAIN CASE

Attention! Sozan asked Toku Joza, "Buddha's true dharmakaya is like the vast sky. Its conforming to things and manifesting shapes is like the moon in the water. How can this principle of conforming be expressed?" Toku said, "It's like the donkey seeing the well." Sozan remarked, "Well said, but that's only eighty percent of it." Toku rejoined, "How about you, Osho?" Sozan replied, "The well sees the donkey."

APPRECIATORY VERSE

Donkey sees the well; well sees the donkey.
Wisdom contains without exception,
purity permeates more than enough.
Behind the elbow, who discerns the sign?
Within the house, no books are kept.
Loom threads don't hang, a matter of the shuttle.
Patterns emerge every which way.
The intent differentiates of itself.

Sozan was the successor of Tozan, and cofounder of the Soto School, which takes its name from the first syllable of each master's name. In this koan Sozan says that the Buddha's true dharmakaya—the "reality body" of the Buddha—is like the vast sky. In other words, your true self is vast and boundless, conforming to things and manifesting shapes like the moon in the water.

If you totally realize yourself like the vast, empty sky, you see that you manifest according to circumstances—but the truth is, whether you realize it or not, that's what's happening. In *The Record of Transmitting the Light*, Master Keizan calls this, "Manifesting according to circumstances without falling into thought."

The part of this koan about the donkey and the well calls to mind an interview with Maezumi Roshi. The interviewer asked him, "Do you think scientists will ever fully understand the functioning of the brain?" This is the usual way of seeing things—the donkey looks at the well. Maezumi Roshi said, "No, I think the brain is using the scientists in order to understand itself."—the well looks at the donkey!

We can also view Toku's comment about the donkey looking at the well as an expression of a state of meditative accomplishment: The original mind is like a mirror reflecting whatever comes in front of it, without putting up filters, without putting up projections or ideas. But Toku's still holding onto something: Even the donkey is extra. "The well sees the donkey" pulls that away.

Master Tozan expressed the various stages of Zen practice using a teaching that has come to be called Tozan's Five Ranks. There are two sets of Five Ranks—one based on the relation of the absolute and the relative; and the second, which is lesser-known, is called *Kokan Goi*, the Ascending Five Ranks. First there is a *shift* where the student vows to realize his/her true self against whatever odds. Then there is *submission* where the student surrenders his/her puny self to the boundless, true self. It means to let go of attachments to our views, images, and projections. Jesus said, "Give, and ye shall receive." To give is to give up one's self. Give up your small attachments, and you'll receive the boundless life like the vast sky.

The third of the ascending Five Ranks is *awakening* which means to "forget the self." It also means "the donkey sees the well." Tozan wrote a verse for each rank and one line for this stage says, "Hunting a unicorn, a man rode backward on a jade elephant." The unicorn represents True Self but could also represent the external world or all phenomena. Riding backward on a jade elephant is being free and unencumbered. Then you are not tossed around by the phenomena of life, but freely use them according to circumstances. When the donkey sees the well, a donkey appears. When the jade elephant sees the well, a jade elephant appears. Where is the loss or gain in that? Leaving aside whether it lifts up or tears down, what is your living expression of "the donkey sees the well"?

"The well sees the donkey" touches on the fourth rank, *collective awakening*, which Tozan versifies:

> Buddhas and living beings do not hinder one another.
> The mountain is high and the water is deep.
> In the midst of contraries, clear understanding wins the way.
> A myriad fresh flowers blooming where the partridge calls.

The donkey does not hinder the well and the well does not hinder the donkey. The donkey is the donkey and the well is the well. Yet, the myriad flowers bloom where the partridge calls. That is only eighty percent of it. How would you express "the well sees the donkey"?

The fifth of the ascending Five Ranks is *absolute awakening*. Tozan versifies, "The far distant empty eon—no one has known it yet." When you finally get down to it, what do you really know? When you realize, "the donkey sees the well" there is nothing to know. When you realize, "the well sees the donkey" there is no one who knows. When there is no subject and no object, your body is "like the vast sky conforming to things and manifesting shapes like the moon in the water"—but that is only eighty percent of it.

CASE 53

Obaku's Dregs

Having opportunity and not seeing a Buddha: Great enlightenment has no teacher. Human emotions are eliminated by the sword that regulates heaven and earth. Holy understanding is forgotten in the activity that catches tigers and buffaloes. Tell me: Whose stratagem is this?

MAIN CASE

Attention! Obaku addressed the assembly, saying, "All of you without exception are eaters of wine-dregs. Going on pilgrimage here and there, when will there ever be a day for you? Don't you know there are no Zen teachers in all of Tang China?" At that time a monk who was there stepped forward and said, "What about those everywhere who have disciples and lead assemblies?" And Obaku remarked, "I don't say there's no Zen, just that there are no teachers."

APPRECIATORY VERSE

Roads being split, threads being dyed—how bothersome!
Catching at leaves and lining up flowers ruins the Ancestors.
Subtly grasping the handle that educates Southerners,
the cloud-and-water inscribing tool is on the potter's wheel.
Tangles and shards removed and crushed, downy hairs razored off.
Balance scale, bright mirror, jeweled ruler, golden sword:
Old Obaku even divines autumn fur,
cutting off the spring breeze, not allowing arrogance.

Obaku was an heir of Hyakujo and teacher of Master Rinzai. He lived in the ninth century in China. When he was studying with Hyakujo, Hyakujo told him, "If your understanding equals that of your teacher, you will cut his merit in half. Only when your wisdom exceeds that of your teacher are you worthy to pass on the transmission." Obaku is said to have been a very imposing man, with a hard knot on his forehead from bowing down repeatedly to the hard floor. People called that knot a pearl, the symbol of wisdom.

Obaku had a very direct way of teaching. Once a student asked, "What is the Way, and how must it be followed?" Obaku said, "What sort of thing do you suppose the Way is, that you wish to follow it?" He is snatching away all ideas. Then the student said, "What instructions have the masters everywhere given for meditation, practice, and the study of the Dharma?" Obaku said, "Words are used to attract the dull of wit, and are not to be relied upon." The student didn't give up and said, "If those teachings are meant for the dull-witted, I have yet to hear what Dharma's been taught for those of high capacity." And Obaku replied, "If you're really of high capacity, where could you find a teacher to follow?" Do not look to what is called the "Dharma-by-preachers," for what sort of Dharma could that be?

Obaku concluded this exchange with some clear instruction: "Look at the void in front of your eyes; how can you produce it or eliminate it? Observe things as they are and don't pay attention to other people. There are some people who act like mad dogs, barking at everything that moves. Not even distinguishing between the wind that moves among the grass and the wind in the trees."

In the present case Obaku says, "I don't say there's no Zen, just that there are no Zen teachers." Master Hakuin, who lived almost a thousand years later and revitalized Rinzai Zen in Japan, commented on Obaku's assertion: "This statement of Obaku's is poison on the water. Whoever drinks it, dies. I misunderstood this for twenty years, so don't take it lightly. This saying is hard to penetrate. It's in the same mold as he who has a habit-ridden consciousness."

Our practice is about letting go of that habit-ridden consciousness. Hakuin says that if you penetrate Obaku's statement, you'll know it means to let go of habits. Like Obaku said, "Observe things as they are," not as you project them to be or you'd like them to be, or you imagine them to be, but as they are.

Before you say there are no Zen teachers, you need to clearly understand what a Zen teacher is. A teacher is like a mirror, encouraging you to trust yourself at the deepest levels possible. To work at the profound level where you're not holding back requires unconditional commitment. A good teacher can see where you are holding on. If a teacher challenges you, see what comes up, and let *that* process *you*, rather than the other way around.

The preface says, "Holy understanding is forgotten in the activity that catches tigers and buffaloes." It is forgotten in the activity that changes diapers and mows the lawn. If you are running around looking for holiness, when are you going to find peace and tranquility? Where do you think you'll find this place? If you try to find it in someone else's words, you are a wine-dreg-eating fool—greedily slurping up the crud that's left in the bottom of the bottle after you've decanted the good stuff. Seeking after teachers is like being a dreg-slurper.

And yet, a teacher is essential. In the *Shobogenzo*, Master Dogen encourages us to find a qualified teacher if we really want to know the Dharma. But how can we do this if Obaku is right that there are no Zen teachers? What does this really mean? And what is the role of the teacher? When you trust and surrender to a spiritual teacher, it is not the same as guru worship. In guru worship, you hope that the teacher will somehow do all of the hard work for you. But a real teacher, a worthy teacher will push you back on your own resources so you can eventually be free of the teacher's influence.

The verse says, "Catching at leaves and lining up flowers ruins the Ancestors." When we idolize the Ancestors—or even our own teacher—and hold onto their teachings, that too is like slurping after dregs, ruining the bouquet of flowers. By "lining up flowers" we are setting up schools and setting up lineages and setting up the position of teacher and thus creating institutions that will become stale and stagnant. Holding the staff of authority we are "subtly grasping the handle that educates Southerners." What about when there is no authority to depend on? Look at the void in front of you. How could you produce or eliminate it? Observe things as they are.

A Buddhist teacher once said, "Wisdom is for yourself to watch and develop. Take from the teacher what is good. Be aware of your own practice. If I am resting while you all must sit up, does that make you angry? If I call the color blue, red, or say male is female, don't follow me blindly. One of my teachers ate very fast. He made noises as he ate, yet he told us to eat slowly and mindfully. I used to watch him and get very upset, I suffered, but he didn't." Looking outside the self, you will not find happiness, nor will you find peace if you spend your time looking for the perfect teacher.

On the other hand, I have met some students who have sat on their own for years and believe they have deep understanding when all they have really done is mistaken the smoke for the fire. Do not think that Obaku is denying the value of a teacher; he just does not want you to cling. True mind is the true teacher. Learn from the teacher what it is to be adequate, appropriate, and don't cling to ideas of what teachers should be or what students should be. Realize the Dharma. Realize the true mind as your true teacher. That is the vow of the Buddha.

CASE 54

Ungan's Great Compassionate One

The eight compass points bright and clear. The ten directions unobstructed. Everywhere, bright light shakes the earth. All the time there is marvelous functioning and the supernatural. Tell me: How can this occur?

MAIN CASE

Attention! Ungan asked Dogo, "What does the great compassionate bodhisattva do when she uses her manifold hands and eyes?" Dogo said, "It's like a man who reaches behind him at night to search for his pillow." Ungan said, "I understand." Dogo said, "What do you understand?" Ungan said, "All over the body are hands and eyes." Dogo said, "You've really said it—you got eighty percent of it." Ungan asked, "Elder brother, how about you?" Dogo replied, "Throughout the body are hands and eyes."

APPRECIATORY VERSE

One hole penetrates space. Eight directions are clear and bright.
Without forms, without self, spring follows the rules.
Unstopped, unhindered, the moon traverses the sky.
Clean, pure, jeweled eyes and virtuous arms:
Where is the approval in "throughout the body"
    instead of "all over the body"?
Hands and eyes before you manifest complete functioning.
The great function is everywhere. How could there be any hindrance?

The great compassionate bodhisattva is Avalokiteshvara and she manifests in each one of us. The Japanese name for the bodhisattva of compassion is Kannon or Kanzeon, and the Chinese is Guanyin. It is said that Avalokiteshvara is the mother of all Buddhas. *Avalokiteshvara* means "the one who *sees* the cries of the world." She hears all painful laments for help and has the wonderful ability to help all beings in danger and misfortune. According to legend, as Avalokiteshvara looked down at the suffering of the world, her head literally burst from pain; her spiritual father, Amitabha Buddha, put the pieces back together as nine new heads—and her wish to help all beings caused the bodhisattva to grow a thousand arms, with an eye in the palm of each hand. With her manifold eyes, Kannon can perceive the suffering of all beings and with her thousand arms she can act to free them without limit.

Ungan and Dogo are Dharma brothers who appear together in a number of koans, such as Case 21. Ungan was the teacher of Tozan, and thus can be regarded as the Dharma grandfather of the Soto School. Although in this case Ungan and Dogo just talk about hands and eyes, the Buddha said that all of the six senses and all of their functioning can be interchanged. Avalokiteshvara's name itself attests to this: she is the one who *sees* the cries of the world. So Ungan and Dogo's "hands and eyes" are more than just hands and eyes.

When Tozan was studying with Ungan he wrote the following verse:

How wonderful, how very wonderful—
the preaching of the insentient is inconceivable
listening with the ear, it is difficult to understand
hearing with the eye, then you can know it.

In this koan, Dogo says the functioning of compassion is like someone who reaches behind him at night to search for his pillow. It's a nice image: Totally asleep at night, somehow your head slips off the pillow and you grope around, trying to find it, without thinking, without discrimination— like the mother who unhesitatingly cuddles her crying child. You don't care if the pillow has a satin pillowcase or a coarse linen one; you embrace any and every pillow without discrimination. In the same way, Avalokiteshvara embraces every being without discrimination, with total freedom of activity.

Not limited by ideas of enlightenment or delusion, self or other, just embrace that pillow.

Ungan says, "I understand," demonstrating that his hands and eyes are working. Dogo asks, "What do you understand?" Ungan replies, "All over the body are hands and eyes." Is he referring to the one body that encompasses all things? Hands and eyes transcend the body. We use them to save all sentient beings. These hands and eyes are not bound by observation, behavior, or words; they're not limited by ideas or images. For the bodhisattva, they function freely.

An ancient master said, "If there were no sentient beings and no mundane suffering, not even a finger would remain, much less a thousand or ten thousand arms. Not even an eyelid would be there, much less a thousand or ten thousand eyes. All over the body and throughout the body—there seems to be shallow and deep but really, there's no loss or gain."

Dogo goes on to say, "You've really said it—but you got only eighty percent of it." It's never complete, never finished. If you used a billion words, maybe you could express a little more of it, but in Zen we say that it's better to express eighty percent of it with a few words.

Dogo says, "Throughout the body are hands and eyes." Does this express the whole thing, or just eighty percent? Is it the same as Ungan's? Superficially it appears that Ungan is talking about the surface of the body and Dogo is talking about inside and outside. That is not necessarily so. The body itself is hands and eyes—but what body is it? Our body is not limited to this space and this time, thus the preface alludes to "the ten directions unobstructed" and the verse refers to a hole that penetrates all of space. Where is this body? Where are its hands and eyes?

The verse says, "The great function is everywhere. How could there be any hindrance?" Each one of us has to see our own hindrances, and yet the great compassionate bodhisattva uses her manifold hands and eyes freely giving life and taking it away. A small life only hangs onto its own self-aggrandizing ignorance. How can you function freely? How can you effectively use your manifold hands and eyes?

CASE 55

Seppo the Rice Cook

PREFACE TO THE ASSEMBLY

Ice is colder than water. Green derives from blue. When one's viewpoint excels that of the teacher, one is ready for transmission. If the children who are raised are not equal to their parents, the family will decline in a single generation. Tell me: Who is the one who snatches up the father's function?

MAIN CASE

Attention! Seppo served as cook while at Tokusan's monastery. One day the meal was late. Tokusan arrived at the Dharma hall holding his bowls. Seppo remarked, "Old fellow, the gong has not yet rung. The drum has not yet sounded. So where are you going with the bowls?" At that, Tokusan returned to his quarters. Seppo told Ganto about this, and Ganto remarked, "As you might expect, Tokusan does not yet understand the last word." Hearing of this, Tokusan called an attendant to summon Ganto, and asked, "Don't you approve of this old monk?" Ganto whispered his intended meaning, whereupon Tokusan desisted. The next day, when he went to the Dharma hall to speak, Tokusan was not the same as usual. Rubbing his hands and laughing, Ganto cried, "Luckily, the old fellow has understood the last word. From now on, no one under heaven will be able to prevail over him."

APPRECIATORY VERSE

The last word: understood or not?
Tokusan, father and sons, are exceedingly abstruse.
Within the group there's a guest from Konan.
Don't sing the partridge's song before men.

This case also appears in the *Gateless Gate* as Case 13. The incident in this story takes place when Seppo is forty-one years old, Ganto is thirty-five, and Tokusan is eighty. Ganto, though he was six years younger than Seppo, was a brighter light, but he burned out more quickly, living fewer years. Whereas Seppo burned for a long time and had a number of great heirs, such as Ummon and Gensha.

Tokusan, their teacher, was brash when he was younger but here he has aged and mellowed. In his youth as a teacher, Tokusan was renowned for being quick with a heavy stick—yet here he just returns to his room without saying a word, after having been confronted by Seppo. Why is that? This is the first testing point of this koan.

Seppo is rude to Tokusan and then seems to brag to Ganto, "I sure showed up the old boy this morning! He didn't have a word to say to me after I shut him up!" and Ganto replies, "Great as he is, he still doesn't understand the last word of Zen." That's another point. Tell me: What is the last word of Zen? Do you ever reach the last word? It is like the concept of infinity. If you say infinity is the biggest thing there is, if I add one to it, it's even bigger than that. If you say the last word, I can say something else—and *that* becomes the last word. Of course, the last word may not be a word at all!

Tokusan summons Ganto, and says, "You're creating disharmony in the Sangha, putting down the teacher in front of another student. What are you doing? Don't you approve of me?" Ganto whispers his intention into Tokusan's ear, and Tokusan desists. What did he whisper and why was Tokusan satisfied? All of these questions are essential points to see.

Ganto was quite well accomplished, and Tokusan was without question very well accomplished—so what kind of thing can they talk about? There's a Zen expression for this: "Meeting without bringing it up." As soon as you pay attention, you know what exists. That's not very American. We have to analyze things to death, particularly in relationships. "Why did you do that? What about this, and what about that?" There is value to doing that, but at some point you have to let it go. If you really pay attention, then you see what it is. So in this case, I want you to really pay attention. What did Ganto whisper in Tokusan's ear?

The next day Tokusan goes to give his talk, and it is different than usual. The next point: What was different about this talk?

So, Ganto says, "Ah, now he understands the last word. Nobody can mess with him." Master Mumon comments, "As for the 'last word of Zen,' neither Ganto nor Tokusan has ever heard of it, even in a dream. If you examine it carefully, they're like puppets on a shelf."

So the last word, is it understood or not? If you understand it, what do you understand? If you see clearly into it, there's nothing to understand, and no one to understand it. But if you don't understand it, you're only half a person. When he was younger, Tokusan put it like this: "If you say this is a stick, I'll give you thirty blows. If you say it's not a stick, I'll give you thirty blows. So, what do you call it?" So, do you understand the last word or not? If you say you understand it, I give you thirty blows. If you say you don't, I give you thirty blows. So what is it?

The verse to this case says, "Tokusan, father and sons, are exceedingly abstruse." Tokusan is of course the father, and his sons are Seppo and Ganto—and they're all abstruse, concealed. What does this mean? Mumon just says, "The last word of Zen? Bah!" Outwardly, in this koan it's clear what's going on. It's a nice story and you can understand it. But inwardly, what is going on? The verse continues: "Within the group there's a guest from Konan." Konan, apparently, is renowned for the partridges that live there, and these partridges have a beautiful song. So partridges live in the land of Konan—but what about people? How are we going to deal with them? The last line of the verse tells us: "Don't sing the partridge's song before men." The partridge's song; what does that mean? It too is abstruse. If you want to talk to people, use their language. If you want to talk to a horse, use its language. But if you come before us and sing like a partridge, will we get it? Don't sing the partridge's song before people. Still we try! Expressing the whole thing, first word to last word, is exceedingly difficult.

CASE 56

Mishi's White Rabbit

Although one is forever sinking down, one doesn't seek the sage's liberation. In the Hall of Constant Torment, Devadatta experienced the joy of the third stage of Zen. From the Heaven above, Udraka Ramaputra fell down into the body of an otter. Tell me: Where is the gain or loss?

MAIN CASE
Attention! When Mishi Haku was accompanying Tozan, he saw a white rabbit run across in front of them. Mishi Haku said, "How quick!" and Tozan said, "How's that?" Mishi Haku replied, "It's like a commoner being appointed magistrate." And Tozan chided, "As great and experienced a person as you using such words!" Mishi Haku said, "How about you?" Tozan said, "The Ancestors' crown has sunk low for a time."

APPRECIATORY VERSE
Contending strength with frost and snow,
footsteps alike in cloud and heaven:
Kake left the country; Shojo crossed the bridge.
Shoso's strategy made the Han dynasty prosper.
Sokyo's body and mind wanted to avoid Gyo.
Favor and disgrace do unsettle.
Have firm faith in yourself.
The genuine spirit—mingling footprints, mixing with fishermen
   and woodcutters.

There are always two aspects of our practice and realization, the intrinsic and the experiential. Intrinsically, you see through the eyes of the Buddha. You hear with the ears of the Buddha. You sit in the seat of the Buddha. When you are sad, heaven and earth are sad, and when you shake with laughter, the earth spins on its axis. I tell you this as fact—yet, if you don't experience it, you are like a ghost trying to satisfy your hunger with a picture of a rice-cake.

Usually, in the Zen tradition, we awaken through our steady practice, through focusing and quieting our mind, allowing our concentration to develop ever more deeply into samadhi, single-pointed attention—and then through some cause or another we suddenly have an awakening experience. That's called "entering sagehood from ordinariness" or as Mishi Haku, Dharma brother of Tozan and successor of Ungan Dojo, says here: "It's like a commoner being appointed magistrate." He was called Uncle Mi by Tozan's students.

Realization is a place to get stuck. But having such an experience, letting go of it, refining it, and maybe having additional realizations and letting go of them is called "entering ordinariness from sagehood." It means not holding onto anything. Then the crown of realization temporarily abides in the ordinary—but nonetheless the power is there when needed: As Tozan says in this case, "The Ancestors' crown has sunk low for a time."

Have you ever seen a rabbit run? When someone's chasing it, it zigzags as a diversionary tactic to confuse its pursuer. If you try to grab it here, suddenly it's over there. The rabbit changes directions very quickly—just like your mind. When you try to control and discipline it, it changes directions. You try to confine it, and it pops out somewhere else. How quick! It cannot be grasped; it cannot be controlled.

Yet ultimately there's no thing there to control. When you realize that, then you'll be, as the preface says, like Devadatta in the Hall of Constant Torment experiencing the joy of the third *dhyana* heaven. Devadatta was the cousin of Shakyamuni Buddha, and was one of the early followers of the Buddha—but at a certain point he became jealous of Shakyamuni and attempted to murder him. This act plunged him into Avici Hell, where he suffered ceaselessly. The Buddha, in his compassion, went into hell to rescue him, to bring him the True Dharma—and even in the Hall of Constant Torment, even without seeking guidance, Devadatta had a realization. That is "liberation in the Hall of Constant torment." Elsewhere, Master Gensha has said, "Even in the dark mountain cave of demons there's complete liberation." It's like a commoner being appointed magistrate.

The preface says, "From heaven above Ramaputra fell down into the body of an otter." In the heavenly realm, everything is beautiful, everything is easy. But amid a life of total ease, we become complacent—and fall into the realm of animals, where we become completely consumed with pursuing our physical comfort with no thought of the consequences. If you attain some realization you may feel like you've risen into heaven, but if you hold onto it, then you fall into other realms—the Ancestors sink low for a time.

One teacher commented, "It's easy to ascend to the solitary peak. But it's difficult to climb back down." Climbing up the mountain, the view gets increasingly broad, increasingly beautiful, and we may want to stay there. But our practice is to descend back into the noise and hubbub of our daily life.

Master Tozan wrote a verse, as his teaching of the ultimate stage of practice:

> Who can be tuned to that beyond what is and what is not?
> Though all persons want to leave the ever-flowing stream, each
>   returns to sit among the coals and ashes.

What is beyond what is and what is not? If you name it, it falls into the relative. If you don't name it, it's useless. All people want to leave the ever-flowing stream of life and death, the world of samsara, of suffering, and enter instead into a world of peace, into nirvana. But, Tozan tell us, "Each returns to sit among the coals and ashes."—not among the satin pillows and the fragrance of flowers! To sit among the coals and ashes is the compassionate activity of the bodhisattva. For the bodhisattva, there is no separation. Everything is one body. Coals and ashes, satin pillows, potpourris, the snow and ice, falling leaves are all expression of this one body.

The verse says, "Favor and disgrace do unsettle: Have firm faith in yourself." Favor and disgrace are disturbing. When you get disgraced, you're disturbed. But you're also disturbed when you gain favor and puff up your pride or become afraid for your continued reputation. But beyond favor and disgrace, with firm faith in yourself, there are no expectations. If you profoundly trust yourself, appreciate yourself, have strong faith in yourself, even being royalty, you can freely mix with fishermen and woodcutters without any pretenses of "being something." How quick! How quickly, it changes directions. Wherever you try to hold on, right there, it's a problem.

CASE 57

Genyo's One Thing

PREFACE TO THE ASSEMBLY

Fiddling with shadows, toiling with forms. It's not understood that forms are the basis for shadows. Raising the voice to quiet an echo. It's not known that the voice is the root of the echo. You don't ride on an ox to look for an ox. This is using a wedge to remove a wedge. How can you avoid this error?

MAIN CASE

Attention! Venerable Genyo asked Joshu, "Where there is not one thing, what then?" Joshu replied, "Throw it away." Genyo said, "With not one thing, what is there to throw away?" Joshu remarked, "Then carry it off."

APPRECIATORY VERSE

Be inattentive to careful moves and you lose to the opponent.
Learn for yourself it's a shame to be surrounded due to carelessness.
The game ended, an axe-handle at the waist has rotted.
Washing clean a bumpkin, sporting with hermits.

When my children were young, about two years old, one of their uncles liked to play a trick on them by putting a piece of tape on one of their fingers and telling them to try to take it off. And of course, when they tried to take it off, it just stuck to their other hand. In a way, that's what this koan is about: How do you remove all of the stickiness of words and ideas, so that you don't stick to anything?

We don't know much about this Venerable Genyo, except for the interesting fact that apparently wherever he lived, there was a snake and a tiger that would eat from his hand. Also he was the only successor of Joshu's who was later recognized as a prominent Zen teacher. In this case, Genyo says, "When there's not even one thing, then what?"

Joshu replied, "Throw it away."—commenting that Genyo was raising his voice to quiet an echo. An ancient teacher remarked, "Bringing not one thing, both shoulders can't lift it up." As long as you think you're bringing not a single thing, that idea itself is vastly heavy. Why not get rid of it? That's Joshu's point: Throw it away! Don't even carry "not a single thing."

Genyo then responds on the obvious level: If there is nothing there, what is there to throw away? This is where Joshu shows his "lips and tongue Zen"—the Zen of quick and cutting words for which Joshu is so well-known. "Then carry it off." Joshu doesn't argue with Genyo, doesn't beat him down, but just gives Genyo space. When we find ourselves in contentious situations, what do we usually want to do? We want to be right, of course, and so we argue to make our point, to elevate our perspective. "If he only saw my point." But can you express it without sticking?

A koan in Zen practice isn't just about "seeing the point," but realizing how to integrate its insight into your life. How can we use this discriminating mind to release this discriminating mind? How can we use a wedge to remove a wedge?

Master Bankei said, "You people try to stop your thoughts of clinging and craving from arising, and then by stopping them you divide one mind into two. The original clinging thoughts that you were able to stop may have come to an end, but the subsequent thoughts concerned with your stopping them won't ever cease. Well, you might wonder, what can I do to stop them? Just let them come. Don't develop them any further. Don't attach to them. Without concerning yourself about whether to stop your rising thoughts or not to stop them, just don't bother with them. And then there's nothing else they can do but vanish. You can't have an argument with a fence. When there's no one there to fight with, things can't help but simply come to an end of themselves."

Bankei is expressing how to make right effort by not adding anything extra, including "effort" itself. Just keep coming back to your breath and let everything go. Don't engage in it. That's what Joshu is doing here, he's not engaging Genyo's "not even one thing" but he's still responding in a way that could be helpful.

The appreciatory verse says, "Washing clean a bumpkin, sporting with hermits." Clean and purify your ordinary bones to play with the immortals, the great Ancestors. Clean all of the stuff that's sticking to you, the sticky-tape of all of your ideas and notions and your fears. Free yourself from the trap of ideas and notions.

And then throw away that idea of "no ideas." And if you can't throw it away, then carry it out.

CASE 58

The Diamond Sutra's Reviling

PREFACE TO THE ASSEMBLY

Depending on a sutra to understand a principle is making false accusations against the Buddhas of the Three Times. Departing from even one character of a sutra is the same as a devil's talk. Does a person who isn't regulated by cause and who doesn't enter into effect still receive karmic consequences?

MAIN CASE

Attention! The Diamond Sutra says if someone is reviled by others it is because that person had acquired negative karma in a previous existence. Because of this past falling into evil ways he is reviled by people in this life, and in being reviled, the karma of the past will be exhausted.

APPRECIATORY VERSE

Success and failure bound together;
cause and effect glued together.
Outside the mirror Enyadata crazily runs;
Hasoda swings the staff and the kiln is smashed.
The spirit comes forth to congratulate him.
Why say you've been beholden till now?

According to the Diamond Sutra, if people hate you, it's because of past negative karma you've accumulated. But then, through thoroughly feeling hated, that karma will be exhausted. But this section of the Diamond Sutra is not just about being hated—it's about all kinds of suffering. In fact, your practice can be said to be a means of dealing with karma and its consequences. Whenever we act with craving or loathing, we are acting according to the causes and conditions of our karma, and as a consequence more karma is created. But we rarely know all of the causes of our past karma, the past causes that lead to our actions. So how should we deal with our karma, how should we deal with being reviled?

There's a Zen story about a monk who was deeply disturbed and disillusioned with Zen when he heard his master scream in pain and fear as he was being murdered by thieves. He thought that Zen was a fraud if it did not teach you to stay calm in the face of death. He expressed his concern to another teacher, later, who opened the young monk's eyes. He said, "Fool! Zen is not about killing all feelings and becoming anesthetized, or numb, to pain and fear. Zen is about being free to scream loudly and fully when it's time to scream." When it's time to scream, we scream; when it is time to laugh, we laugh; when it is time to cry, we cry; when it's cold, we're cold; when you're reviled, be reviled.

As long as we live in this world, there are all kinds of suffering: There is the pain and anxiety caused by life itself; and there is the suffering of sickness, old age, and death. Suffering can be divided into four types: loving someone or something and having to be apart from it; hating someone or something and having to be close to it; wanting what we can't get; and not wanting what we have. Even being healthy, wealthy, young, and strong, there are difficulties.

And so this life is called the Land of Patience—without patience we cannot survive. The Buddha said that being patient is far better even than assiduously maintaining the precepts or practicing asceticism—of course, if you are truly patient, you will find you are naturally maintaining the precepts and avoiding extremes. In one of the Sutras, there's a story about a traveling merchant whose name was Funda. One day he was traveling near where the Buddha was giving a talk, and he heard him speak, and he was so impressed, he immediately became a student and devotee. He was a very devoted and wonderful man, who eventually attained arhatship. An *arhat* is an enlightened being who has accomplished one's own practice. Arhats eventually become bodhisattvas. The Buddha told him, "Now, I wish you to leave and be with the people to expound the Dharma." He told Funda to go to the west of India. The Buddha said, "Those people who live there are very rough and mean people. If they insult you, what are you going to do?" If they revile you, what are you going to do? And Funda said, "I will consider them very good people because they don't hit or kick me." Then the Buddha said, "If they hit or kick you, how are you going to react?" Funda said, "I will still think they are good people because they don't beat me with sticks or throw stones at me." The Buddha said, "If they beat you with a stick or throw stones, what would you do?" Funda said, "I would still think they're good people, because they don't injure me with a dagger or a knife." Then the Buddha said, "What if they do that? How would you react?" He said, "I would still think they're good people because they don't kill me." Finally the Buddha said, "If they try to kill you, what will you do?" And Funda said, "I'll still appreciate them. Among the Buddha's disciples are many who are willing to die, willing to end their lives because life is so painful. If they are going to take my life, I will be glad to let them." The Buddha said, "If you have that much patience, your mission will be successful." And indeed it was.

But we often don't manifest that kind of patience; often even from the tiniest insult, we get upset. To be patient means to be compassionate, to lift your hearts, as we chant in our prayers, to liberate all beings, animate and inanimate altogether.

The verse to this case refers to, "Success and failure bound together; cause and effect glued together." Dogen said, "One success is the result of the ten thousand failures."—success and failure bound together. "Cause and effect glued together."—the cause and the effect are difficult to distinguish.

Sometimes it is said that an enlightened being is no longer subject to cause and effect. Is it true? When you become enlightened, show me. Master Dogen wrote, "Those that believe that enlightened beings are beyond the effect of causality willfully deny the law of causality, and will undoubtedly fall into the three evil worlds. Those, on the other hand, with confidence in the laws of causality realize no person to be beyond its effect. Constantly, they gain relief from all present suffering." We should not doubt this.

You have to have deep faith and belief in causality, in karma, to relieve suffering. You have to be one with cause and effect. The principle of causation means that those who practice oneness, those that truly identify themselves with causes and effects will be released. It's as straightforward as that.

CASE 59

Seirin's Deadly Snake

PREFACE TO THE ASSEMBLY

Leaving, yet staying; dwelling, yet departing. Not leaving, not dwelling: he is without a country. Where can he be met? Anywhere. Everywhere. Tell me: What thing is it that can be so marvelous?

MAIN CASE

Attention! A monk asked Master Seirin, "How about when a student proceeds on the trail?" Seirin replied, "The dead snake hits the great road. I advise you not to bump into it." The monk said, "When it's bumped into, then what?" Seirin answered, "You lose your life!" The monk continued, "When it's not bumped into, then what?" And Seirin said, "There's no place to dodge to." The monk said, "At that very moment, then what?" Seirin replied, "It has been lost." The monk then said, "I wonder where it's gone." And Seirin responded, "The grass is so deep there's no place to seek." The monk replied, "Shield yourself, Osho! Then you'll be all right!" Finally Seirin clapped his hands and exclaimed, "Your poison is equal to mine!"

APPRECIATORY VERSE

The ferryman in darkness turns the rudder.
The lone boat at night turns its bow.
The snow of both banks' reed flowers intermingle.
Smoky waters veil the autumn of one river.
Wind power helping the sail; going without poling.
Flute notes calling the moon; sailing down to Paradise.

Master Seirin lived in the ninth century and was a successor of Tozan. When Seirin left Tozan, he lived in a hut on a solitary peak. After ten years, he suddenly realized something he learned at Tozan's, and he said, "I should try to benefit the many deluded beings. Why limit it to a few!" He left the mountain, and was invited to become the abbot of Green Forest Monastery. The name by which we know him means "Green Forest." Seirin taught his students, "Without careful investigation, the gates of the Ancestors are most difficult to enter. You must practice apart from mind, intention, or consciousness. The essential teaching of the Ancestors is proceeding right now. The Dharma is apparent. What other matter is there?"

In other words, it doesn't have to do with intellectual understanding. Drop away anything you're attached to, anything you're holding onto, any idea that you cherish. If it's not right here, right now, where is it? The Dharma is apparent, right now. See it. Hear it. Maintain it. What other matter is there? What else is there besides this Dharma?

The monk asks Seirin, "How about when a student proceeds on the trail?" What's his mistake in that question? Another translation has it as: "How about when a student takes a shortcut on the trail?" By saying that, it's already the long way round. It's not a shortcut. He's creating separation.

Seirin says, "The dead snake hits the road. I advise you not to bump into it." Already, you're creating some kind of a problem. You're turning away from that black jewel at your feet and looking toward that sky that's filled with anxiety. You're creating something where nothing exists. The monk says, so what if I bump into it? What then? "You lose your life." What are they talking about? In this case, this dead snake is your True Nature. Bump into it and you become alive. What then?

Next the monk says, "When it's not bumped into, then what?"—What makes you think it depends on you? What kind of *you* is it that can bump or not bump? Seirin says that there's "no place to dodge to." You can't jump out of its way; you bump into it everywhere. Right now, right here, you're bumping into it—although, on the other hand, since there is no separation, you're actually *not* bumping into it. Nonetheless, there is no way to avoid it.

Then the monk says, "At that very moment, then what?" Seirin says, "You've already lost it." You bumped into it, but now you've lost it by fiddling with it. Though it's a dead snake, if you handle it, it's suddenly alive. The monk says, "I wonder where it's gone." Seirin said, "The grass is so deep, there's no place to seek." Above Heaven and below Earth, above Earth and below Heaven, it's boundless. It is so vast that there's no outside and no inside.

The monk says, "In that case, you'd better protect yourself, Osho. Then you'll be alright." This monk wasn't afraid of bumping into anything! Seirin says, "Your poison is equal to mine!" His remark is like the Zen phrase, "I thought I'd stolen everything from you, but you've stolen everything from me." Seirin is acknowledging that this monk is pretty sharp.

The preface says: "Leaving, yet staying. Dwelling, yet departing." That's reminiscent of a Zen verse:

> Life is like a floating cloud which appears.
> Death is like a floating cloud which disappears.
> Floating cloud, itself, originally does not exist.
> Life and death, coming and going, are also like that.

Yet, it is met everywhere. In his "Instructions to the Cook," Master Dogen said, "Be very clear about this. A fool sees himself as another, but a wise person sees others as himself. You are not it. It actually is you." Which is the image, and which is the form? Wherever you turn, you bump into it. Yet you are not it. When it is not bumped into, it actually is you.

The verse says: "Smoky waters veil the autumn of one river." Smoky waters are not quite clear. Both sides of the river are indistinguishable. The image and form merge. It's like this conversation between Seirin and the monk. As soon as you think you grabbed onto it, it's gone somewhere else. Or it bites you. So how clear are they, these smoky waters? As clear as the hazy moon in the autumn sky.

The preface asks us, "Where can he be met with? Anywhere. Everywhere." And what thing is it that can be so marvelous?

CASE 60

Ryutetsuma's Old Cow

With splendid noses, each one is endowed with a powerful appearance. With firm, real footsteps, who needs to learn grandma Zen? Penetrate the activity of the ungraspable nose and you will see the method of the true adept. Tell me: Who is such a person?

MAIN CASE

Attention! Ryutetsuma arrive at Isan's place, and Isan said, "Old cow, you've come!" Ryutetsuma said, "There's a big feast on Mount Tai tomorrow, Osho. Are you going?" Isan lay himself down. At that, Ryutetsuma left.

APPRECIATORY VERSE

With a hundred battles' merit, growing old in great peace;
being serene, who's to pick at the details of strategy?
Jeweled whip and golden horse passing the day at leisure;
bright moon and refreshing breeze enriching a lifetime.

Ryutetsuma is one of the few women mentioned by name in the koan collections, and this same case also appears in the *Blue Cliff Record*, as Case 24. She's a Buddhist nun and a student of Isan's. We don't know the exact dates of her birth and death, but Isan lived from 771 to 853. Ryutetsuma's Zen style was called "precipitously awesome and dangerous." Her ability to test the mettle of Zen adepts brought her the name Iron-grinder Ryu. Many monks had mortifying experiences with her in Dharma combat; she ground them to dust. Grinding oats is one thing, but grinding iron is something else entirely!

When Ryutetsuma came to visit Isan, she was not necessarily doing it innocently. She may have come for a visit, or she may mischievously have wanted to arouse Isan and have some fun. She and Isan were very close, both personally and geographically. She had built a hut right next to his monastery and used to come visit him often. When Isan says, "Old cow, you've come!" he wasn't saying it in the same way we might call someone an "old cow." In fact, the character in Chinese refers to a kind of water buffalo. That buffalo is your true self prior to thinking good and evil. It's a very intimate greeting, but there's also a touch of humor in it.

Isan often referred to himself as a buffalo. Before he died, he said, "I, an old monk, will be reborn as a buffalo in front of the temple a hundred years from now. Five words will be written on the buffalo's side: *Monk Isan Such-and-Such*. If you call this Monk Isan, it's a buffalo. If you call it a buffalo, it's Monk Isan Such-and-Such. Tell me: What do you call it?"

In the ten ox-herding pictures, the ox, which represents our True Nature, is also a kind of water buffalo. So, "Old cow, you've come!" is not only "you've come," but also the buffalo has come.

Ryutetsuma invited Isan to a feast on Mount Tai the next day—the only problem is that Mount Tai is hundreds of miles away from Isan's monastery, far too long to make a journey in a day. It's like me saying to you, "Let's go have a feast on the moon."—although actually, the moon is even closer to us than Mount Tai was to them. Astronauts can get to the moon in just three days.

Commenting on this case, Master Kyozan said, "If you beat the drum in China, they dance to the sound in Korea." In response to Iron-grinder Ryu's challenge, Isan just lies down. He already has "a hundred battles' merit" and is "growing old in great peace." As far as the feast on Mount Tai is concerned, Isan has been there and has done that, and furthermore, by lying down he is doing it right now. So as to her expression of the feast on Mount Tai, since Isan did not want to fool around, Ryutetsuma had no option but to leave.

There are a number of koans that don't make sense in terms of space and time if you limit your viewpoint. For instance, "Take a five-story pagoda out of a teapot," or, "What is your original face before your parents were born?" If you totally identify with each moment, with each place, then you are space and time—and won't be fooled by the words. According to an old saying, "The meaning is conveyed, but the words obstruct."

Isan just lies down. But how easy is it to do that? When your life and people, even those close to you, goad you, or criticize you, how easy is it to just let it go? We so desperately want to be right, that we have to defend ourselves, or assert ourselves, and make others wrong. Withdrawal is avoidance, but lying down is a most active expression of Isan's state of mind.

Having been through a hundred Dharma combats, Isan only wants to grow old in peace. He doesn't even want to play with Ryutetsuma. It's only young monks who talk about Buddha! Old generals don't tell war stories.

Ryutetsuma also lets go. She's like a bright jewel on the stand. When a foreigner appears, a foreigner is reflected; when a native appears, a native is reflected. Whatever appears, that's what's reflected.

Tomorrow there's a feast on Mount Tai. How will you go?

CASE 61

Kempo's One Stroke

PREFACE TO THE ASSEMBLY

A roundabout explanation is easy to understand but imparts only the one hand; straightforward talk is hard to understand but opens every direction. I advise you not to speak too clearly. Speak too clearly, and it will be all the more difficult for you to come forth. If you don't believe so, let's have a look at this and see.

MAIN CASE

Attention! A monk asked Kempo, "The exalted saints of the ten directions have one road to the nirvana gate: I wonder where the one road is." Kempo made a stroke with his staff, saying, "Here it is!" The monk later told Master Ummon about this. Ummon remarked, "The fan jumps up to the thirty-third heaven, and whacks Indra's nose. When the carp of the Eastern Sea is clubbed once, the rain is like water from a tipped-over tray. Understand? Understand?"

APPRECIATORY VERSE

Taken in hand, even a dead horse is cured.
Vivifying incense intends to heal your deathly illness.
Exude sweat all over your body only once and surely you'll believe.
At my house, eyebrows are not begrudged.

"Exalted saints" usually refers to *bhagavats*—certain Hindus who worshipped the Lord Vishnu. In this koan, "exalted saints of the ten directions" refers to devotees of Shakyamuni Buddha. These followers of the Dharma have one road to the nirvana gate. The challenge for each of us is to reveal this one road. Thus Kempo says, "Here it is!" The preface warns us that if he says it too clearly, you will begin to think you understand it—and if your understanding is only conceptual, you will make it into some kind of a dogma. It becomes the One Road of My Lineage, or of My Practice, or of My School—and then we get sectarianism.

We don't know very much about this monk Kempo other than that he was eventually a successor of Master Tozan, who lived 807–869. Master Ummon was born in 864 and apparently studied with Kempo before he succeeded to Seppo's Dharma. When Ummon met Kempo, Kempo said, "In the dharmakaya, there are many barriers. You must penetrate them one by one, before you can return to your home and sit solidly. Then you must know that there is yet more pivotal realization."

We invent all kinds of barriers in our minds, and before we can "sit solidly," we have to penetrate each barrier and allow each barrier to penetrate us. In order to do that, we have to become transparent and completely unattached to our notions of self. Ummon asked, "Why does one who is in the hut not know of the affairs outside the hut?" A hut has four walls and a ceiling: it's a box that we put around ourselves. Our zazen too can become a kind of box if when we sit zazen we try to become holy or to escape the mundane.

If we practice like that, we stink of Zen but we don't smell it because we're so used to our own stench. It's a blind spot. How can one shine the light on such a blind spot? Not by trying to escape, but by observing your own mind without attachments or judgments. That is the one road to nirvana. You won't find it on a map. It doesn't know north or south or east or west. It's not far. It's not near. It's not traveled by monks or laypeople, men or women. And if you don't see it, you don't see it even as you walk on it. Even the Buddhas and Ancestors can't grasp it.

An ancient once said, "There are no walls in the ten directions. In the very beginning, there is fundamentally no obstruction." There are no doors in the four quarters, but the entryway is in front of our eyes. Yet we sit inside the hut, and we don't know what's outside because we condition our experience in all kinds of ways. From the very beginning, there are no obstructions, so, where do these obstructions come from? How are we looking?

Kempo says, "Here it is!" He snatches away everything, and Ummon gives it back. If all expressions were the same, we would all be bogged down.

Sometimes we have to hear things with different ears or see things with different eyes in order to perceive them. The preface says, "A roundabout explanation is easy to understand," but it's only part of the story. That's how we usually function, through roundabout explanations which are our stories about this and that. "Straightforward talk is hard to understand, but opens every direction." It's going right to the source. Kempo was very direct. But how much do we really understand him?

From the other direction, Ummon says, "The fan jumps up to the thirty-third heaven, and whacks Indra's nose." We can imagine Ummon was probably holding a fan at the time he said this, and Indra is the deity in the highest heaven. Can you reveal the road he's referring to as the one road to the nirvana gate? The thirty-third heaven is right here. Indra is right here. Ummon's fan is right here. Watch out or you will get whacked on the nose.

"When the carp of the Eastern Sea is clubbed once, the rain is like water from a tipped-over tray." A carp is a sacred animal that, according to legend, can jump up and transform into a dragon. It's clubbed once, and it rains like cats and dogs. The carp is right here. When you are whacked between the eyes, the water starts flowing. Kempo is gathering it in and Ummon is spreading it out.

Teachers shouldn't give students little trinkets to grasp onto. It confuses them. Get to the point. But one ancient teacher says that Kempo is too direct. The very nature of the carp is that it whacks Indra on the nose—why add anything?

The verse to this case says, "Exude sweat all over your body only once and surely you'll believe." This is like the saying, "Suddenly realizing that fundamental nature is empty is like a fever breaking into sweat." You know when you have a fever, you feel achy all over, you feel hot and cold—and then it breaks and you start to sweat profusely. It's like a great release. If you've totally transcended all of these barriers, it's like a fever breaking into a sweat; it's a tremendous joy, even though the body is covered with sweat.

How many roads do you need? How many lives do you need? Maezumi Roshi used to say, "Don't put another head on top of your head." What are you adding to the practice that's extra? Right here is one road. Right here is the one life.

Where else could it be?

CASE 62

Beiko's No Enlightenment

PREFACE TO THE ASSEMBLY

The primary meaning of Bodhidharma's principle muddled Emperor Wu's head. The nondual Dharma gate of Vimalakirti made Manjushri's speech go wrong. Is there anything here of enlightenment to enter and use?

MAIN CASE

Attention! Master Beiko sent a monk to ask Kyozan, "Do people these days have to attain enlightenment?" Kyozan replied, "It's not that there's no enlightenment, but how can one not fall down into the second level?" The monk related this to Beiko, who wholeheartedly approved it.

APPRECIATORY VERSE

The second level divides enlightenment and rends delusion.
Better to promptly let go and discard traps and snares.
Merit, if not yet extinguished, becomes an extra appendage.
It is as difficult to know wisdom as to bite one's navel.
The waning moon's icy disk; autumn dew weeps.
Benumbed birds, jeweled trees, dawn's breeze chills.
Bringing it out, great Kyozan discerns true and false.
Completely without flaw, the splendid jewel is priceless.

Kyozan lived in the ninth century and was a successor of Isan with whom he founded the Igyo School, as I mentioned in Case 15. Not much is known about Beiko. He's listed as a successor of Seppo, although Master Wanshi, the compiler of this *Book of Equanimity*, thinks that this koan indicates that Beiko was really a Dharma brother of Kyozan.

The theme of this koan, like so many in this collection, is not to dwell in any fixed place. This is perhaps one of the most important themes in Zen. Beiko sends the monk to ask Kyozan, "Do people these days have to attain enlightenment?" Kyozan says, "It's not that there's no enlightenment, but how can one not fall down into the second level?" Don't hold onto anything, just let go.

The Diamond Sutra says, "Dwell in no place," but is enlightenment "no place" to dwell? What is "no place"? Tell me! As long as you objectify it, it's the second level. If you say you're enlightened, you've already fallen into the second level since words can't reach it. If you say you're not enlightened, you've fallen into the second level because you deny the Buddha's teachings. Is there a first level? If you say there is, you fall into the second one. And if you avoid the question entirely, you also fall.

Master Keizan, the great popularizer of Dogen's Japanese Soto School warned us in the fourteenth century: "Don't try to seek enlightenment, and, don't say enlightenment doesn't exist." You have some ideas about enlightenment, some kind of a notion, maybe it's not even fully formed—but whatever it is, it's not this life, not this suffering, not this reality. It's something else.

So, where is that place where there's no first level and no second level? Master Keizan wrote this poem:

> Seeking it oneself with empty hands,
> you return with empty hands;
> in that place where fundamentally nothing is acquired,
> you really acquire it.

In that place where nothing is acquired there are no levels. Somehow we return with our hands full of spiritual sprouts which are our attachments to holiness.

Chogyam Trungpa wrote a book, called *Cutting Through Spiritual Materialism*, about all the ways we objectify our practice, making it into something special. As described in Case 36 of the *Blue Cliff Record*, Master Chosha went for a walk. When asked where he went, Chosha replied, "First I went following the scented grasses; then I came back following the falling flowers." How does that compare with the spiritual sprouts invading spring?

The verse says: "The second level divides enlightenment and rends delusion. It is better to promptly let go and discard traps and snares." When the rabbit is caught, you forget the trap. When you realize enlightenment, you let go of all the devices that you've used. As long as you believe there's enlightenment, then there's delusion. Is that what Kyozan is saying in this case?

CASE 63

Joshu Asks About Death

Sansho and Seppo are spring orchid and autumn chrysanthemum. Joshu and Toshi are Benka's Jewel and En's Gold. In the marked scales, both trays balance evenly. In the bottomless boat, they cross over the river together. How about when both people meet?

MAIN CASE

Attention! Master Joshu asked Master Toshi, "When a man who dies the Great Death revives, what then?" Toshi replied, "Going by night isn't permitted. You'd better arrive during the day."

APPRECIATORY VERSE

Even before the mustard-seed, castle and the kalpa stone,
the beginning is to be subtly investigated.
The vital eye illumines the emptiness within the ring.
Not allowed to travel by night, arriving at dawn,
the message does not depend on the goose and fish.

Master Toshi or Tosu Daido (819–914), a Dharma successor of Suibi, settled on Mount Tosu and remained obscure for more than thirty years. Toshi literally means "Teacher To." The reputation of Toshi could not be concealed and had reached Joshu while he was on pilgrimage to deepen his understanding. On his way to Toshi's place, Joshu met him on the road and, thinking he recognized him, asked, "Aren't you the host of Mount Tosu?" Toshi acted like a beggar and said, "I need a coin please, for tea and salt." Joshu just proceeded on to Toshi's hut, and sat down inside. Later, Toshi returned carrying a jug of oil. Joshu said, "Long have I heard of Tosu, but since coming here all I have seen is an old-timer selling oil." Toshi said, "You've only seen an old-timer selling oil, but you haven't recognized the true Tosu." Joshu said, "What is Tosu?" Toshi lifted up the jug of oil and yelled, "Oil! Oil!" Following that exchange the current case takes place.

Joshu says, "When a person who dies the Great Death revives, what then?" The Great Death is dropping away body and mind, totally penetrating through all of the barriers set up by the ancients and by your own self-grasping ignorance. It means letting go of all your defenses, all your projections, and finally letting it all drop away. What about when he revives? That doesn't mean grabbing on again to all these projections and beliefs. It's seeing clearly this life as it is. Great Death releases us to Great Life.

There is a Zen saying: "Let go of your hold on the cliff, die completely, and then come back to life—after that you cannot be deceived." After letting go and coming back again, you live a very ordinary life in a most extraordinary way.

In the present case, Toshi says, "Going by night isn't permitted. You'd better arrive during the day." This is a very subtle phrase. This koan is what we call a *gonsen* koan—a koan that addresses the proper way to use words. As I've said, Joshu was renowned for what is called "lips and tongue Zen"—he always had just the right expression at the right time. Yet in this case Toshi outdoes him. All Joshu could say after that was, "I thought I was a robber, but you stole everything away from me!" Joshu was a great teacher because always he continued to refine his understanding.

Maezumi Roshi used to say that if you clearly see your koan or your life situation, you'll be able to find the right words to express it. We're so used to conceptualizing our words that they have become dead words, not live ones. How can you express yourself in live words? Going by night isn't permitted. You'd better arrive during the day. What's the difference between the night and the day? At night, you can't discern shapes very clearly; during the day there's more illumination. You can see more clearly—but we still can fool ourselves even when we can see. These koans always take us to lucid awareness, to truth without a trace of attachment.

In contrast, in Case 76, Master Shuzan encourages his monk to arrive at night. In that case, "after the moon sets" refers to moving freely in the dark.

Always you have to go beyond the words and penetrate to the spirit of the koan.

The verse says, "Not allowed to travel by night, and arriving at dawn, the message does not depend on the goose and fish." There's a story about a princess who was kidnapped and sent a message to her family by strapping it onto the leg of a goose. When the goose stopped to drink at a lake, a fish jumped up and grabbed the message, and swallowed it. Later, a fisherman caught the fish, and opened it up and saw the message and delivered it to the family. A rather roundabout form of communication! So this phrase means, "Don't beat around the bush; be direct." Toshi had told his monks, "If you ask me, then I'll answer you directly. But there is no mystery that can be compared to you, yourself." But you'd better see it clearly if you're going to talk about Great Death. You had better not arrive at night, not quite sure what it is, clinging onto the ghostly shapes. Come in full daylight when it becomes Great Life.

CASE 64

Shisho's Transmission

PREFACE TO THE ASSEMBLY

Ummon saw Bokushu immediately and offered incense to aged Seppo. Tosu received the Dharma from Enkan and became the Dharma successor of Taiyo. On the coral branches, jeweled flowers bloom. Within the fragrant woods, the golden fruit ripens. Tell me: How does it develop?

MAIN CASE

Attention! The head monk Shisho asked Master Hogen, "Osho, as head of the temple, whose Dharma did you receive?" Hogen said, "Master Jizo's." Shisho said, "Aren't you greatly transgressing against our late teacher Chokei?" Hogen replied, "I don't understand a turning word of Chokei's." Shisho retorted, "Then why don't you ask?" Hogen said, "Among the myriad forms is a solitary, manifest body. What does it mean?" At that, Shisho lifted up his *hossu*, his fly-whisk, and Hogen said, "You learned that as a student at Chokei's place. What is your expression?" Shisho had nothing to say. Hogen said, "As it says, among the myriad forms is a solitary, manifest body. Does it wipe out the myriad forms, or does it not wipe out the myriad forms?" Shisho answered, "It does not wipe them out." Hogen said, "A duality!" The followers of Shisho, the monks on both sides of the Dharma hall, all said, "It does wipe them out!" Hogen said, "Among the myriad forms is a solitary, manifest body. Hah!!"

APPRECIATORY VERSE

Staying away from thought, see Buddha;
rending the dust, bring forth the sutras.
Dharma style manifest as is: Who lays out one's front garden?

Chasing a boat, the moon is led to the clear river's purity.
Accompanying grasses, spring rises from the burned ruin's greens.
Wiping away and not wiping away, listen with care.
Though the three paths are overgrown, he still could come home.
Pines and chrysanthemums of old still have their fragrance and smell.

Hogen started as a student of Chokei's, and eventually he went to study with Master Jizo, who was first introduced in Case 12. Shisho also was a student of Chokei's and was irritated at Hogen because he thought he transgressed against their teacher Chokei since Hogen venerated Jizo. After Chokei died, Shisho became head of the temple. Along with his resentment, Shisho took his fly-whisk, which was the symbol of his authority to teach, and all of his senior monks to go to Hogen's place and confront him. That's when this case takes place.

When Hogen was at Jizo's monastery, he continually spoke about the Way with Jizo trying to demonstrate his understanding. Jizo would always say, "The Buddhadharma isn't like that!" Finally, Hogen said, "I've run out of words and ideas. You have exhausted my mind." Jizo said, "If you want to talk about Buddhadharma, everything you see embodies it." At those words, Hogen experienced great enlightenment and he eventually became a Dharma successor of Jizo.

Together, Shisho and Hogen studied for many years with Master Chokei, and now Shisho feels that Hogen has abandoned Chokei. So he says essentially, "I want to hear it from you: Whose Dharma did you receive?" but Hogen was pretty clever and says he didn't understand a thing Chokei said—although of course, he did understand Chokei intimately. But Shisho misses this and invites Hogen to ask him so that he can clarify Chokei's teachings. Hogen says, "Among the myriad forms is a solitary, manifest body. What does it mean?" Shisho holds up his whisk, his hossu—something he probably saw Chokei doing. Hogen chastises him: "You learned that as a student at Chokei's place. What is your true expression?" Hogen was pushing for Shisho's own understanding. How would you express it?

As I mentioned in the commentary on Case 20, Hogen ended up at Jizo's place because he was stranded in a snowstorm during a pilgrimage. Sometimes it is a matter of circumstances, who we study with, and who we bond with. When I was a university student in the San Francisco Bay Area I often went to listen to Shunryu Suzuki's Dharma talks. Then I moved to England and met Sochu Roshi, continuing my Zen studies with him. Then I returned to Southern California and met Maezumi Roshi. I received something from all these teachers, but I succeeded Maezumi Roshi's Dharma. In China, it was quite common for students to make a pilgrimage from place to place, teacher to teacher. In this country, there are teachers who don't want their students to go see other teachers—some even expel them if they do. The preface says, "How does it develop?" Without having been with Chokei, Hogen wouldn't have been ripe for Jizo. After the dialogue presented in this case, Shisho stayed with Hogen—and he also "transgressed" against Chokei by eventually succeeding Jizo's Dharma through Hogen.

But the essential point of this koan is this: "Among the myriad forms is a solitary, manifest body." The entire world, the trees, the sky, the people, and the buildings: Are the myriad forms effaced or not? Does this single, solitary body wipe out the myriad forms or not?

Master Hogen told his assembly, "Students of Zen need only act according to conditions to realize the Way." What are those conditions but the myriad forms themselves? When it's cold, they're cold. When it's hot, they're hot. "If you must understand the meaning of Buddha Nature, then just pay attention to what's going on. There's no shortage of old and new expedients. But if you spend your time trying to understand form in the middle of non-form, just going on this way, you're missing your opportunity. So, do we therefore say that you should realize non-form in the midst of form? If your understanding is like this, then you're nowhere near it. You're just going along with the illness of the two-headed madness. What use is that? All of you, just do what is appropriate to the moment. Take care." Master Hogen is pulling away all expedients. Don't rely on either form or non-form.

Just take care, pay attention, be attentive. Don't worry about whether it's the myriad forms or the one manifest body, or whether the myriad forms arise from the one manifest body, or the one manifest body arises from the myriad forms. If we go along like that, it's like a two-headed madness. Take care.

The verse says, "Wiping away and not wiping away." Does one wipe out the other? "Listen with care." Master Bansho comments, "Talk of wiping out

and not wiping out is like inviting a wolf home. It will crap on the floor."
Hogen clarifies it for us: "Hah!!!" This transcends wiping out and not wiping
out. Was Hogen being appropriate or inappropriate when he stayed with
Jizo? *Hah!!!*

CASE 65

Shuzan's New Bride

PREFACE TO THE ASSEMBLY

Damn, damn! Neighing, neighing! Ripping, ripping! Carefree, carefree! Zephyrs, zephyrs! Dodging, dodging! Despising, despising! Fooling, fooling! There's nothing to chew well. It's hard to get closer. Tell me: What talk is this?

MAIN CASE

Attention! A monk asked Shuzan, "What is Buddha?" Shuzan replied, "A new bride rides a donkey. Her mother-in-law leads."

APPRECIATORY VERSE

A new bride rides a donkey.
Her mother-in-law leads.
The manner of appearance is quite natural.
How laughable! The neighbor lady imitates the grimace:
facing the people, turning more ugly, she's not attractive.

Master Shuzan lived in the tenth century in China. He is a direct descendent of Master Rinzai, and all modern Rinzai lineages pass through him. His teacher was Fuketsu, and Shuzan was Fuketsu's only successor. He is the one link in the chain that maintained the Rinzai lineage.

"What is Buddha?" is a classic question in Zen. Buddha is the enlightened one, the founder of this great tradition, but there are also other Buddhas constantly manifesting, unifying, and maintaining. The wind in the trees is the voice of Buddha. The fragrant blossoms are the smell of Buddha. Mountains and streams are the body of Buddha. So is the polluted air. Buddha also represents the absolute, ineffable state. Shuzan says, "A new bride rides a donkey. Her mother-in-law leads."

In China, filial devotion is very important and when a man takes a bride, she should honor her husband's mother. So what is she doing riding on the donkey, while the mother-in-law is carrying the reins of the donkey, walking in front? It's backwards; it shouldn't be like that! It makes the people laugh to see such a spectacle.

The preface doubles each word for emphasis. Consider, "Fooling, fooling!" So, if you're not afraid of being a fool, you'll be able to share with everybody. When I was a graduate student in physics at the University of California, we had a seminar each week with a guest speaker. One of the professors, Luis Alvarez, who later won the Nobel Prize, was never afraid to ask questions that a graduate student would be embarrassed to ask. Of course there was always a twist to his question, but on the surface it seemed simple. In the end it elevated everyone's understanding of physics.

Somebody once asked Maezumi Roshi, "What's the purpose of Zen?" He said, "To be stupid." Are you comfortable being stupid? To be stupid, you have to throw away all your ideas about being smart, and your ideas about other people thinking that you're smart! Being stupid is being simple and sincere with your whole body and mind. The 360 bones of your body and the 84,000 pores of your skin need to consent to your understanding—and if they do you will never be deceived by others and never need to rely upon someone else's understanding.

But Shuzan is disrupting the order. He is encouraging us to find freedom within our limitations—and we have a lot of limitations! Shuzan answers the way he does in order to shake the monk from his attachment to the sacred, the holy, and the hierarchical. Whatever the monk is attached to, that's what the master breaks. In our practice and in our life, there is order, but we need to find freedom within that order so we are not constrained by it.

When Shuzan received the Dharma-seal from Fuketsu, it was a very chaotic time in China. The Tang Dynasty was toppling and it wasn't safe to be a Buddhist priest in that environment. Many priests were persecuted and even killed. It was recorded that Shuzan "covered his tracks and concealed his light." In other words, he went into hiding. He came forth only when the conditions were appropriate.

A monk once asked Shuzan, "What is a bodhisattva before he becomes a Buddha?" Shuzan said, "All beings." Then the monk said, "How about after he becomes a Buddha?" Shuzan said, "All beings, all beings." Before manifesting as Buddha, all beings; after manifesting as Buddha, all beings. That includes the drunken bride riding and the sober mother-in-law leading.

In the verse it says, "The neighbor lady imitates the grimace." There's a Chinese story about a beautiful woman named Zishi. She was considered to be most elegant and attractive. Whenever she had a stomach cramp, she would grimace in pain—and everybody thought that she looked even more beautiful. So some of the less attractive girls in the village tried to imitate her, but they only made themselves less attractive still. The verse is cautioning us against trying to imitate someone else. If you hear the Dharma expounded and then you just regurgitate what you've heard, it's ugly. But if you swallow it down and absorb it into your bones, it's beautiful.

CASE 66

Kyuho's Head and Tail

Those with supernatural power and marvelous activity can't step in. Those who have forgotten externals and eliminated thoughts still can't lift up a foot. Let us say that sometimes there are the running dead, and sometimes there are the sitting dead. How can they be made complete?

MAIN CASE

Attention! A monk asked Kyuho, "What is the head?" Kyuho said, "Opening the eyes and not being aware of the dawn." The monk asked, "What is the tail?" Kyuho said, "Not sitting on an eternal seat." The monk asked, "What about having the head and no tail?" Kyuho said, "After all, it's not precious." The monk asked, "What about having the tail and no head?" Kyuho said, "Though satisfied, you are powerless." The monk asked, "How about when head and tail are directly well matched?" Kyuho replied, "A descendent gains power without knowing it."

APPRECIATORY VERSE

A compass for the circle, a ruler for the square.
With use it functions well, with neglect it hides.
Stupid and bumbling: a bird dwelling in reeds.
Backing and filling: sheep caught in a fence.
Eating others' food, sleeping in one's own bed:
Clouds rise and rain falls, dew collects and turns to frost.
The well-aligned jeweled string passes through the needle's eye.
The embroidered thread unceasingly vomits from the shuttle's guts.
The stone woman stops weaving, and night's colors turn toward noon.

A wooden man travels the road, and the moon's silhouette
    moves to half full.

This koan looks at the stages of practice, but also points to how to really be alive. A koan like this requires attention to detail. We need to know precisely every part of a koan like this to understand it. In this case, the head is the absolute, and the tail is the relative. Also, the head is "the state of enlightenment," and the tail could be called "the state of practice."

To the first question—"What is the head?"—Kyuho replies, "Opening the eye and not being aware of the dawn." He's talking about that very state of enlightenment or awakening itself. There is a famous Zen expression: "Before I had realization, mountains were mountains and rivers were rivers, and when I had realization mountains were not mountains and rivers were not rivers. After enlightenment, mountains are mountains and rivers are rivers." Here Kyuho is talking about having realization. If you're in this state of oneness, this absolute state, there's no observer, nothing to observe. So what is there to see when you open the eyes? Opening the eyes refers to an awakening experience. There's no self, no other, no mountains and no rivers; it's all one. You are not aware of the dawn even though the sun is shining on your face.

"If that's the head, what's the tail?" Kyuho replies, "Not sitting on an eternal seat." The tail is not an unchanging state; the tail is practice. But your practice is not to sit there on your cushion for eternity like a clay Buddha. The preface says, "Sometimes there are the running dead, and sometimes there are the sitting dead." If you sit there like a dead person, there is no tail. The tail is the arising of all phenomena. There's no enlightenment without practice, and because of enlightenment there is practice. Master Dogen invented a word for this to indicate that the two are not separate: "practice-enlightenment."

A monk was on a pilgrimage deep in the mountains and he ran across Master Daibai. He said, "How do I get out of the mountains?" Daibai said, "Go on following the flow of water." Zen is not just sitting on an eternal seat, it's following the flow of the water. Just keep going.

Trust yourself and appreciate yourself. Bring together head and tail, inside and outside, as altogether one thing; what kind of practice is this zazen?

This is the zazen of not holding on. If you hold on, if the hand is closed, there's nothing more that it can accept.

Then the monk in this case asks, "What about having the head and no tail?" Kyuho replies, "After all, it's not precious." Kyuho is referring to the "stink of zen" that comes after people have an opening and as a result become arrogant, attaching to their Zen ways and Zen understanding. They think they're better than other people and that nobody can touch them. But because of their clinging to their opening, there is still delusion and attachment to a false sense of self. When Master Hakuin—the great eighteenth-century master who revitalized Rinzai Zen in Japan—had an awakening, he said, "Nobody in the history of Buddhism ever saw as clearly as I do!" and yet a hermit monk snatched his arrogance away and called him a bed-wetting imp! After all, it's not precious. Even at 318 dollars an ounce, gold dust still irritates the eye.

Having the tail and no head means having a strong practice and no realization. Kyuho replied, "Though satisfied, you're powerless." You are powerless to do anything for the sake of others. You don't see clearly, can't act freely. Though you might think you are doing the practice well enough, you are really powerless. People in this state often practice what we call "idiot compassion," just blindly trying to be helpful but ending up ultimately causing harm.

There is a false form of Zen we call *Buji* Zen. Someone who practices Buji Zen might say, "Since everything is perfect as it is, I don't have to practice or have an enlightenment experience because I'm already enlightened." Kyuho doesn't say enlightenment doesn't exist or doesn't need to be realized; he just says it's not precious.

What about when the head and the tail are well matched? Kyuho says, "The descendent gains power without knowing it." But as long as a trace of enlightenment or practice remains, you're stuck there. This state is very difficult to attain and I don't know how many people have actually accomplished it.

Sekiso, Kyuho's teacher, was asked these same questions by his community. When asked, "What's the head?" he replied, "You should know that it exists." There is such a thing as enlightenment. Don't deny it.

When asked, "What's the tail?" he says, "Exhausting the present." That's what our practice is: exhausting the present. Penetrate through every thought, every feeling, every sensation, every conception, every perception. Just be aware of it; don't identify yourself as it. Totally exhaust every corner. If you're holding onto anything, any image of who you think you should be, you're not exhausting it. You have to be willing to totally expose yourself, whatever it is that you're hiding.

When asked what happens if there's the head and no tail?, Sekiso said, "What's the use of spitting out gold?" Everything Midas touched turned to gold—but what a horror when he touched his daughter and she became a gold statue. What's the point of shining brilliantly? To blind other people?

When asked how it is if there's the tail and not the head, Sekiso said that there's still dependence. You haven't quite let go. There's still an idea of a safe haven. When asked how it is when the head and tail are well matched, Sekiso said, "Even if he does understand this, I don't yet approve of him!" If he understands this, there's still something left to understand. Throw it out!

What this koan and these teachers are telling us is that first we raise our intention, raise our determination, then we practice and have some realization, we must then let go of that, and continue to practice. That's what Zen is; there's no beginning and no end. Just practice-realization. Letting go. Further practice. Master Dogen expressed it in the *Genjokoan*, "No trace of enlightenment remains and this traceless enlightenment continues without end."

If you see it clearly you will know that this division into head and tail is artificial, bogus. It's just an expedient means to help you understand what you're going through with practice-realization, and to further clarify it. Later Kyuho said that the head and tail are just means to encourage you to make the most of your life. Once you integrate the head and the tail, there is no further need of them. Basically, there's no head and no tail. They're not two sides. It's your life. Just let it be so. Just reveal who you truly are, and manifest that as your life. Maezumi Roshi used to say, "You're doing it anyway. You might as well appreciate it."

CASE 67

The Avatamsaka Sutra's Wisdom

PREFACE TO THE ASSEMBLY

A speck of dust contains the ten thousand shapes. A single thought is endowed with the three thousand realms. How much moreso a great man crowned by heaven and standing upon earth? A sharp one, who, when you speak of the head, knows of the tail. Don't disregard your very own spirit and bury your family treasure.

MAIN CASE

Attention! In the Avatamsaka Sutra, Shakyamuni Buddha says: "As I now see all sentient beings everywhere, they're endowed with the Tathagata's wisdom and virtue. But because of deluded thoughts and attachments, they do not realize it."

APPRECIATORY VERSE

Covered like heaven, supportive like earth;
making a ball, forming a mass;
suffusing the Dharma realm: it's boundless.
Crushing the tiniest motes, it lacks an interior,
penetrating utterly the subtlest point.
Who can distinguish the pro and con?
Buddhist Ancestors come to repay their debt of karmic words.
Ask old teacher O of Nansen and see.
Every person eats but a single vegetable leaf.

According to the Avatamsaka Sutra, Shakyamuni Buddha uttered the words in the main case of this koan when he became enlightened two thousand five hundred years ago. Everybody without exception has the wisdom and virtue of the Buddha, though "has" is a misleading word, implying that perhaps wisdom is like an object that we can possess. All beings—including you!—are endowed with the Tathagata's wisdom as part of their birthright. But if you don't realize it, then it doesn't really have any significance for you.

The Avatamsaka Sutra is highly revered in the Huayan School of Buddhism. The central image of Huayan Buddhism is Indra's Net: at each one of the junctions of the net, there is a jewel that totally reflects every other jewel. We are all reflecting everything else.

This sutra also teaches that the mind is the universe itself, and that this mind is the Buddha-mind. Here, Shakyamuni says that all beings everywhere have this mind—each one of us without exception. You might imagine this means "everybody else but me" but the sutra is very clear: It means everybody!

Once when I was frustrated with my practice, I asked Maezumi Roshi, "Roshi, can everybody realize their True Nature?" He said, "Sure. Sure. Sure." If one doesn't realize this inherent wisdom it is like a person of magnificent stature who sees himself as feeble, sick, and destitute. As if in a dream, he does not see his true body, blessed with myriad marvelous qualities, but takes the sick and suffering one to be his own. In Case 10 of the *Gateless Gate*, Master Sozan says to monk Seizei, "Having tasted three cups of the best wine in China, do you still say that your lips are not yet moistened?"

Our deluded thoughts and our attachments blind us to our True Nature. A deluded thought is any thought that creates a gap between ourselves and others or other things—or between ourselves and ourselves. In the movie *A Christmas Story* a young boy believes that if only he had a Red Ryder BB Gun with the Double Barrel Action, then his life would be perfect. Each one of us has our own elusive Red Ryder BB Gun. Everyone warned the boy, "Be careful! You'll put out your eye!" As long as we grasp after it, it will definitely put out our eye. We have all kinds of ideas that we're attached to: "I can't do it." "I won't do it." "I'm not as good as everyone else." "I'm better than everyone else." "I am stupid." "I want to be enlightened." "I am enlightened." "Zazen is easy for everyone except me."

Master Dogen expressed it very clearly: "To study the Buddha Way is to study the self. To study the self is to forget the self." As long as you believe that there's a separate self, you won't clearly see. It's very difficult to let go of it because it takes courage to let go of that notion of self. If you let go of the self, then how are you going to function? How are you going to know right from wrong?

We spend all of our energies trying to protect or aggrandize the self, or to pity it. Dogen continues, "To forget the self is to be enlightened by the ten-thousand dharmas." If you can just let go of your attachments to your ideas about who you are, then all phenomena, the ten-thousand dharmas, will reveal your enlightenment, your wisdom, as the virtue of the Buddha Tathagata.

There is an old story of a monk who carries a sack of horse shit around with him. Each time he goes to a monastery, he puts his sack down, looks around, and says, "Boy, this place stinks! I'm not staying here." Then he picks up his sack, and carries it with him to the next place and—surprise!—that place stinks too. There's only one constant in all of the troubles we have in life: ourselves.

We've developed certain ways of behaving, certain patterns, certain habits over our lifetimes. That's how we define ourselves, how we identify ourselves. That's our secure haven; even though we may not be fully satisfied or fully comfortable, at least it's familiar. So this practice requires that we let go of our most cherished views. To forget the self is to be enlightened by the ten-thousand dharmas—including the Dharma of having a difficult time.

Master Ummon told his disciples, "Every day is a good day!" Maezumi Roshi added, "Even having difficulties, every day is a good day." How can that be? "If I have difficulties, it's a bad day! It's not a good day." To forget the self is to be enlightened by the ten-thousand dharmas. Even having difficulties. To be enlightened by the ten-thousand dharmas is to free one's body and mind and those of others, to drop away attachment to our own body and mind as my body and mind! If you realize that your body and mind are not your body and mind, *that* is the universal body and mind. How would you function? Then every day is a good day.

Master Dogen goes on: "No trace of this enlightenment remains, and this traceless enlightenment is realized forever." As long as you have a notion of enlightenment or delusion, it's another idea. So how to really be free?

The verse to the present case says, "Crushing the tiniest motes, it lacks an interior. Penetrating utterly the subtlest point. Who can distinguish the pro and con?" Exhaust the self, exhaust the moment. Examine the minutest detail. Cease to distinguish pro and con. It penetrates everywhere, so where is the mysterious subtlety, other than the turmoil of the moment?

This life is boundless. If you crush it, it has no interior. If you expand it, it has no limit. The preface says, "a single thought is endowed with the ten-thousand realms." One thought creates an infinite number of thoughts. One speck of dust contains the ten-thousand shapes. Don't disregard your own spirit and bury your family treasure. You are the Buddha, let it shine through.

CASE 68

Kassan's Slashing Sword

Inside the castle, it's the emperor's decree. Outside the gate, it's the general's command. Sometimes power is obtained at the gates. Other times reverence is admired within the chamber. Tell me: Who is such a person?

MAIN CASE
Attention! A monk asked Kassan, "How about when sweeping out the dust you see the Buddha?" Kassan said, "Straightaway, slash with a sword. If you don't, the fisherman will live in a nest." The monk then went and asked Sekiso, "How about when sweeping out the dust you see the Buddha?" Sekiso said, "He has no country. Where can he be met?" The monk returned to Kassan and related this to him. Kassan ascended the high seat and said, "In setting up expedients, I am better than he, but as to a profound talk of the principle, he is a hundred paces ahead of me."

APPRECIATORY VERSE
A sword's spirit drives out the bull.
The heavens are washing the soldiers.
To achieve the quelling of a riot: Who is he?
Once, there were battle clouds, the four seas were clear.
With flowing robes, the emperor's governing is naturally effortless.

We met Master Kassan in Case 35. He succeeded Sensu Osho, the Boatman Monk. Sekiso studied with Isan, but left him and went to Dogo, the master who later sent Kassan to the Boatman Monk. The time after Sekiso received transmission from Dogo, there was a period of great unrest in China. It wasn't safe to be a Buddhist monk, so Sekiso spent three years working as a potter's apprentice in order to hide from the marauding armies.

Kassan and Sekiso were asked the same question: "How about when sweeping out the dust you see the Buddha?" When I get rid of all the confusion in my own mind and wisdom manifests in my mind, then what? Kassan says essentially, "Cut that out, otherwise a fisherman will live in a nest." You're getting things all confused. Keep things in order, like it says in the preface: The emperor rules in the castle and the general commands in the field. What's the Buddha doing in your mind? Is that his seat?

You can either cut it out, or you can just let it be. When I first started sitting, I read, "hold your mind against incoming thoughts like a great iron wall." That is cutting it off, and that's one way to practice. In the long run it is better to let it pass through. You can sit like a vast ocean letting everything in. The ocean accepts everything. All streams flow to the ocean and become the single taste of the ocean. If your energy channels are all open, delusive thoughts will pass through. To let them go, we have to illuminate our hidden beliefs. Our hidden beliefs help us maintain our position of arrogance, anger, hatred, laziness, indifference, self-pity. We attach to all of these things in order to protect that self-grasping ego and maintain it. Just let go of all your opinions, and the Buddha appears—but Kassan says, "Don't hold onto it."

Master Sekiso says, "Where would you meet the Buddha?" She has no name, no country, no gender, no occupation, no rank, no sword, no mother, no father, and no lover. She doesn't even have a face. If you say all the dust has been swept, what about that new dust ball you're creating that you call Buddha? You can't depend on it.

Kassan hears Sekiso's words and says, "In setting up expedients, I am better than he, but as to a profound talk of the principle, he is a hundred paces ahead of me." Kassan's expedient means is to directly swing the sword, cutting through your image of the Buddha. Sekiso talks of the principle when he says, "He has no country." The principle is absolute emptiness. What is your expedient to make it your own?

Kassan and Sekiso say they each express one piece. Master Bansho commented, "Where is the person with two faces on one die?" How can you bring both pieces together, because in reality they're not two separate things?

There are numerous paths to enter the way of Zen. There are as many paths as there are practitioners. Even Bodhidharma talked about entering by method or entering by principle. Kassan is talking about entering by method, Sekiso, entering by principle. Either way, drop off attachments to your own thoughts, ideas, judgments, and opinions. Whether it's by expedient or principle, it doesn't matter. We don't even need to call it anything at all. Wherever you are, enter Zen from there! Wherever you are, always take heed. Become a whole person—even half a person will suffice for now! Don't let this understanding die out.

CASE 69

Nansen's Cats and Cows

PREFACE TO THE ASSEMBLY

He hates to incur the disgrace of becoming a Buddha or becoming an Ancestor. Affirmatively, he places those having horns and bearing fur in a superior position. Therefore, the true light does not blaze, and the great wisdom is like a fool's. Furthermore, he takes advantage in being deaf and pretends to be illiterate. I wonder who this is?

MAIN CASE

Attention! Nansen addressed the assembly, saying, "All Buddhas of the Three Times don't know of *it*; but cats and cows know of *it*."

APPRECIATORY VERSE

Limping, limping. Palsied, palsied.
Frayed, frayed. Unkempt, unkempt.
The hundred aren't appropriated. Even one is not worthwhile.
Wordless, wordless. He himself knows the calm of the fields.
Potent, potent. Who's to say in his guts he's a fool?
Throughout the Dharma realm, all becomes his food.
With drooping nose, he's content to be full.

The preface to this case says that one should not want to disgrace himself by becoming a Buddha or Ancestor. It is better not to blaze brightly, but just to be very simple, like a cat or a cow. Dogen had his first *kensho* experience when he heard the words of this main case being spoken by his first teacher, Master Eisai. Dogen asked, "If we are all intrinsically enlightened, why did the Buddhas and Ancestors have to struggle so hard in their practice?" This is the question that sent Dogen to Master Tendo Nyojo in China.

There are a number of interpretations to the present koan. The most obvious one would be that we should somehow be like cats and cows. They are very natural and contented. Cows are contented chewing their cud, but many of them are herded to the slaughterhouse where they end up in a hamburger. Cats earn their daily meals by lying around all day and purring when you pet them.

If we dig a bit deeper, we recall that not knowing is the most intimate thing (see Case 20). Then the Buddhas of the Three Times that don't know it are most intimate. The cats and cows that know it are projecting their cat and cow perspective onto reality.

Referring to the source of knowledge, Nansen said, "Clearly, if you speak of it, then horns will grow on your head." In other words, you'll become a cow if you speak of it. I might add, "And fur will grow on your body." You'll become a cat too.

Later, hearing the words of Nansen, a monk asked Master Chosha, "Why don't the Buddhas of the past, present, and future know of it?" Chosha said, "Before entering Deer Park, they still had realized a little." Before entering Deer Park where the Buddha lectured, the Buddhas knew a little and when they left they didn't know anything. Listening to Shakyamuni Buddha, they dropped all concepts. The cats and cows that left Deer Park are like half-baked fellows. They didn't understand a thing and stuck to their old way of knowing.

There is a third interpretation of this case. All Buddhas of the three times are sitting on a heavenly seat on a solitary peak. In Case 66, Kyuho said, "After all, it is not precious." Cats and cows that have to come down the mountain are precious. Cats and cows are in the world. They face the slashing of the butcher's knife and the aggression of the neighbor's dog.

The verse says, "Limping, limping. Palsied, palsied. Frayed, frayed. Unkempt, unkempt." This refers to Yakusan who when challenged by one of his students said, "I am limping and palsied, ungainly in a hundred ways, clumsy in a thousand. Yet I go on this way." Near the end of his life, Master Joshu said, "Originally I intended to practice to help save others; who would have suspected that instead I would become an idiot?"

We practice because somehow we feel incomplete and are not totally satisfied with our life. In our mind, we're trying to gain something, or accomplish something. Then if we accomplish something, we have to let that go or it becomes another attachment. Yakusan is clumsy and Joshu is an idiot. Which is the true person of Zen? Where does that source of knowledge not reach? Why do cows and cats know it? The verse says, "Throughout the Dharma realm all becomes his food." Having no preferences, you can eat everything and be enlightened by everything. You can liberate everyone, even other cats and cows.

CASE 70

Shinzan Questions the Nature of Life

PREFACE TO THE ASSEMBLY

One who hears of the elephant's crossing the river is still affected by the current. One who hears that the nature of life is unborn is still held back by life. If one argues about bamboo shoots and braided bamboo twine in terms of before and after samadhi, the sword will be long gone. Then indeed, one has notched the boat. If one kicks out the wheel of activity, how can one in particular proceed down the one road? Please try to let me discuss it, and let's see.

MAIN CASE

Attention! Priest Shinzan questioned Priest Shuzan, saying, "Knowing clearly that life has the nature of being unborn, why is one held back by life?" Shuzan said, "The bamboo shoot eventually becomes a bamboo. Right now, can you use it as a bamboo sheath, instead?" Shinzan replied, "You will be enlightened on your own later on." Shuzan said, "I am just like this. What's your meaning, Joza?" Shinzan remarked, "This is the administrator's quarters. That is the cook's quarters." At that, Shuzan bowed low.

APPRECIATORY VERSE

Vastly clear, attachments left behind.
Elevated calm, unfettered.
Peaceful home, rare the person who arrives.
Minor ability, the level is discerned.
Capacious body and mind go beyond right and wrong.
Right and wrong gone beyond.
Alone, he stands everywhere, leaving no tracks.

Both Shuzan (this is not the Shuzan of Case 65) and Shinzan were disciples of Rakan Keichen (Master Jizo) in the tenth century and Dharma brothers of Hogen whom we've met in several cases. Shuzan is also known as Ryusai Shoshu and Shinzan is Seikei Koshin. Shinzan's question refers to a sutra in which Manjushri, the bodhisattva of wisdom, asked, "Is there anyone who knows clearly that the nature of life is unborn and yet is held back by life?" A young girl who was present answered, "One who sees clearly yet whose strength is not adequate is held back by life." If you have an insight but you haven't fully integrated it in your life, you are held back.

The preface says, "If you argue about before and after samadhi in terms of bamboo shoots and braided bamboo, the sword will be long gone. Then indeed one has notched the boat." That image refers to a warrior who dropped his sword in the lake and marked the spot by notching the side of the boat where his sword fell off, so that he could find the sword again later. When he got back to shore, someone asked, "Where did you lose your sword?" The foolish warrior replied, "Right here! I notched it!"

Shuzan says something similar: that the bamboo shoot eventually becomes a bamboo. Bamboo rope is made from the sheath, the covering of mature bamboo. But bamboo shoots are tender and have no strength. They can't be used for rope. The bamboo shoot eventually becomes bamboo, but right now, can you use it as bamboo rope? The bamboo shoot represents an awakening, or an insight, but initially it is too immature to be used well.

No matter how much we may try, like an alcoholic, we often fall back into bad habits even though we might have seen clearly. That's one of the problems of our practice, quite frankly. We don't know how to take care of these bad habits.

Students have idealized images of Buddhas and bodhisattvas as totally free of all of the limitations of life. But as Bernie Glassman, my elder Dharma brother, once said, after enlightenment, you don't automatically become a better basketball player. What makes you think everything else is going to be perfect, according to your current image of what's perfect? You are still conditioned by your environment and your upbringing due to this so-called incomplete development in your practice. Just as you would have to practice to develop your basketball skills, you have to continue practicing to dissolve your bad habits.

Shinzan tells us essentially, "You will be enlightened on your own later on." Shinzan doesn't approve of Shuzan's statement. What is it that Shuzan doesn't get? He makes sense, doesn't he? We get sucked in by the power of words. What is strength and what is weakness? What is right and what is wrong? What's large and what's small?

Later on, Shuzan was asked by a monk, "How does one get out of the Three Realms?" The Three Realms are form, formlessness, and desire. Shuzan said, "When the Three Realms become one, then you escape it." When you realize that the bamboo shoot is the bamboo sheath, you're no longer held by invisible chains.

Shinzan says in this case, "This is the administrator's quarters. That is the cook's quarters." This is the bamboo shoot, that's the bamboo sheath. What's wrong with that? Dogs bark and cats meow. What's wrong with that? Mountains are high, and valleys are low. Where is the fault? You're just as you are, what is holding you back?

Kobun Chino, a modern Soto master, told a story of dropping to the floor weeping in uncontrollable grief when as a child he received the news of his father's passing. And then, when he rose to his feet, both he and the world seemed irrevocably changed. "I think of bowing that way," he said. "You go down, and when you come back up again, you're a different person. The world has changed." When we bow, we just totally put ourselves into it. And then there's no separation between you and the Three Realms, between you and life, and between you and death.

Master Bansho commented on this case, "When you perceive the strange as not strange, the strangeness will dissolve by itself." All of our attachments and deluded ways of being are what's familiar to us. When we let go of that, it becomes strange. When we see that the strange is not strange, the strangeness will dissolve by itself. Don't reject anything, then each barrier dissolves by itself. "Alone, she stands everywhere, leaving no tracks." As long as we appreciate who we are, then the bamboo shoot is the bamboo shoot and the bamboo sheath is the bamboo sheath. The administrator's quarters are where the administrator lives, and the cook's quarters are where the cook lives—and each place is splendid indeed.

CASE 71

Suigan's Eyebrows

PREFACE TO THE ASSEMBLY

To sip blood and to blow it at others stains one's own mouth. To buy drinks for others all one's life is to pay their debts. To sell paper for three years is to lack enough for demon money. Bansho preached for the sake of everyone. Is there any balancing up here?

MAIN CASE

Attention! At the end of the summer training period, Suigan addressed the assembly, saying, "All summer long, Dharma brothers, I have instructed for your sakes. Look, have I any eyebrows left?" Hofuku said, "A man who is a thief has a timid heart." Chokei said, "Growing." Ummon said, *"Kan."*

APPRECIATORY VERSE

The heart of the thief, guts that excel all others;
clearly, universally, a confrontation with brethren.
Hofuku's and Ummon's pendulous noses betray their lips.
Zuibi's and Chokei's luxurious eyebrows reflect in their eyes.
Bumpkin Zen monks: When will it ever end?
You're superficially saying, "Cut off intention and expression
    altogether."
Burying yourselves, withholding your energy, swallowing your speech.
Distressing past Ancestor, facing the wall, carrying a board.

This case occurs in several collections and it's considered to be quite important. All four of these men were successors of Master Seppo. At the time of this case, Suigan was serving as head monk for the training period. Hofuku, Chokei, and Ummon were his older brothers in the Dharma.

It's said that if you preach the false Dharma, your eyebrows will fall out. And so Suigan says, "All summer long, Dharma brothers, I have instructed for your sakes. Look, have I any eyebrows left?" Talking to his older Dharma brothers after a summer of teaching, Suigan wants to know if what he said was okay. Is he humbly asking for their feedback or is he arrogantly challenging them? Regardless, all three of his Dharma brothers bite the hook that he throws out.

Their teacher Seppo says, "A good thief is not recognized by ghosts and spirits." A good teacher of Zen employs all kinds of skillful means to liberate his or her students. Sometimes they have to be covert and trick the student when he or she is being stubborn. If Suigan were a good thief, he could pick our pockets and we wouldn't even know it. Hofuku says, "A man who is a thief has a timid heart." Suigan is coming out of the shadows and exposing himself, showing himself for what he is, a thief who steals everything away, even ideas and concepts. But he has a timid heart, because he's still asking if he's done a good job of stealing. Is Hofuku criticizing Suigan? What's he really saying?

Chokei says, "Growing." In other words, "Your eyebrows have grown." Rather than falling out, they're actually growing longer and bushier—a mark of wisdom. But we can look at this comment from another way, too. "Your eyebrows were okay the way they were, but now they've grown. You've added something extra." Is Chokei criticizing Suigan or praising him?

Ummon's expression is very well-known in Zen circles. *Kan* means "barrier" or "gate." This is the *kan* of *Mumonkan* ("Gateless Gate" or "Barrierless Barrier.") It is a popular character for Zen calligraphies. *Kan* transcends approval and disapproval. What is this barrier? Koans such as this give each one of us an opportunity to see our need for approval, our lack of trust in ourselves, our lack of confidence that we can practice without rewards. To see this koan, you have to penetrate Ummon's *kan*.

The preface presents some strong images referring to Suigan's statement, "I'm preaching for the sake of others." It says, "To sip blood and to blow it at others stains one's own mouth."—to regurgitate the teachings for the sake of others is just fouling your own mouth. "To buy others drinks all one's life is to pay their debts." You can't really clarify this great matter for the sake of somebody else—and yet you do what you can to help others clarify it, without spoiling it for them. The last line is, "To sell paper for three years is to lack enough for demon money." Demon money is the paper money offered at Chinese funerals to help the dead on their way to the next world—so they can pay off the demons that block their path. But if we give it all away, how are we going to help others, when the time comes? Or if you barter it all away, you won't be able to pay the ferryman to take you across the river to the next world.

Years ago, at the Zen Center of Los Angeles, when Maezumi Roshi first told me to give talks in the zendo, I was like Suigan, and I asked him what he thought about my talk. He never once gave me a clear answer. I never got any detailed feedback. The most he said was, "It was okay." One sesshin he had me give a talk on a particular koan case. After the talk he said, "It was okay," and then the very next day, he gave a talk on the same koan case! He painted large portions of the canvas that I didn't even touch. So, how should I take it? I could imagine, "Well, he was embarrassing me in front of everybody. I missed some of the key points of the koan." Or I could be open to what he was saying and just take it as a learning experience. I won't deny that I had both reactions. I was the "thief with the timid heart."

The verse to this koan says, "Burying yourselves, withholding your energy, swallowing your speech." If you pull back your energy, then you're not doing any training, but if you say too much, then you're spoiling the child. If you don't honor the child as much as you do the parent, then the family will decline in a generation. It's important that Suigan gave these talks for the sake of everybody. Each one of his Dharma brothers had something to say, to further illuminate and share their understanding. That's what we have to see. If the students don't become independent, then the teacher has failed. Yet the student must also get rid of arrogance and self-serving attitudes. There has to be a letting go, a surrender. As long as we hold onto our own images of who we are, we're stuck. Let go of it all. Dig deep and let go.

Ummon once told his assembly, "Why are you all aimlessly coming here looking for something? I only know how to eat and shit. What use is there in explaining anything else?" Where are you looking? *Kan!*

CASE 72

Chuyu's Monkey

PREFACE TO THE ASSEMBLY

To be distant from the river, to fight with one's brains—hiding one's self and concealing the soldiers. When you meet face to face, you both hold the real spear and the true sword. That is the reason for this praiseworthy complete functioning and great activity of accomplished Zen students. Go from looseness to tautness. Let's spit it out and see.

MAIN CASE

Attention! Kyozan asked Chuyu, "What is the meaning of Buddha Nature?" Chuyu replied, "For your sake, I'll tell you a simile: There is a room with six windows and in the middle is a monkey. A person outside calls, 'Monkey! Monkey!' and the monkey responds. In like manner, when all of the six windows are called, they all respond." Kyozan asked, "What about when the monkey sleeps?" Chuyu got down from his meditation cushion and grabbed him, saying, "Monkey! Monkey! You and I have just met."

APPRECIATORY VERSE

Sleeping cold in the snowy hut, the year-end passes.
The utterly quiet vine-covered gate stays closed at night.
The withered orchard sees the changes.
Spring breezes blow ashes from the flute.

Chuyu, who lived in the eighth century, is Kyozan's Dharma uncle. Kyozan appears in a number of cases in this collection and Chuyu is relatively unknown. Chuyu's simile is a way of pointing to reality. We have a Zen expression: "What we say about the moon isn't the moon itself. It's the finger pointing at the moon." The point of all koans is to point directly to our true selves, but even within a simile, there is a significant teaching.

The great physicist Albert Einstein said that as far as the laws of physics refer to reality, they are not complete, and as far as they are complete, they don't refer to reality. We can describe things up to a point, but that's just a description. If we have a complete system, it doesn't reflect reality. Commenting on this case, Bansho said, "Although a simile is temporarily appropriate, it's not ultimately appropriate."

Here, Chuyu says that there's a room with six windows. We each have six windows on the world: eyes, ears, nose, tongue, body, and mind. Chuyu says, in the middle of the room—which we can take to mean our body—there's a monkey. What's that monkey doing? It is looking at bright, shiny objects all of the time, just as we get caught up looking at our bright, shiny ideas. What is this monkey?

When you call, "Monkey! Monkey!" the monkey hears. When the monkey moves its tongue, there are sounds. When the sun shines, the monkey sees. What is this monkey?

The monkey wants to be in charge. It controls you, at least what it thinks you are. It wants you to be safe, well fed with compliments, adulation. But the monkey has a limited perspective, it doesn't see the whole picture. Yet nonetheless the monkey draws conclusions based on its limited perspective, and then it controls your life according to those conclusions.

Many times, I've mentioned our unspoken truths. They may be hidden from you, but the monkey depends on them. The monkey is quite intimate with these unspoken truths. We have certain images that we try to protect and the monkey will protect them. What is this monkey?

Kyozan takes the simile further: "What about when the monkey is asleep?" We can take this in a number of different ways. It could mean, "What about when the monkey relinquishes control?" or "What about when we really are asleep?" or "What about when all of these six windows and the objects of the senses and the subject are all forgotten? Then what?"

When your monkey is asleep and you pinch your finger in the door, do you wake the monkey and say, "Hey! Monkey! Is it okay if I get my finger out of this door? It hurts like hell!" I don't imagine you do. You don't wait for the monkey to tell you your finger hurts and you should therefore move it.

What about when you hear the sounds of the birds? Do you ask the monkey, "What is that?" What's the role of the monkey there? It's amazing! We can function very nicely when the monkey's asleep. When you hear, you just hear—even when the monkey is asleep. When you see, you just see—even when the monkey is asleep. Who are you when you're so totally absorbed in whatever it is that you're engaged in that you forget the self? Then what's the function of the monkey?

Even when the monkey is asleep it can still function naturally and intuitively from the heart. When the six windows are forgotten, the true monkey appears everywhere and is enlightened by the ten thousand things.

Chuyu got down from his meditation cushion and grabbed Kyozan, saying, "Monkey! Monkey! You and I have just met." Chuyu is cutting through Kyozan's conceptual understanding and wants him to respond directly. Monkey! Monkey! Now I know who you are! How about you: Do you know who *you* are?

CASE 73

Sozan's Requited Filial Piety

PREFACE TO THE ASSEMBLY

Depend on grasses and become attached to trees and you'll become a ghost. Hang onto indignity or hold a grudge and you'll be cursed by a devil's spell. When you call in such people, burn paper money and offer a horse. When you dismiss them, purify the water and write down a charm. How can the home be made peaceful?

MAIN CASE

Attention! A monk asked Sozan, "When mourning clothes aren't worn, what then?" Sozan replied, "Today I have requited my filial piety." The monk asked, "After requiting filial piety, then what?" Sozan said, "I would love to get stumbling drunk."

APPRECIATORY VERSE

The house of unbroken honor admits no neighbors.
Many years of sweeping the gates, not letting in dust.
Turning from full brightness, the moon hangs low, a crescent.
As winter solstice passes, *yin* rises to the east-northeast.
Requite filial piety anew, and meet with the spring.
Drunken steps, crazy songs: so what if my cap falls off?
Tousled hair, weaving walk, who cares?
Tranquil, replete: a person who is stumbling drunk.

Sozan was a disciple and the closest successor of Tozan, as I've mentioned before, and together they're the founders of the Soto School in China. Sozan became a monk at the age of nineteen. In China and Japan, when a man becomes a monk he's said to have "left home" and is thereafter known as a home-leaver. So, as a home-leaver, what is a monk's obligation to filial piety? What's his duty as a child?

In this koan, Sozan is talking about fulfilling his obligation to his Dharma parent, not his biological parent, as such—although it could also be taken in that way. The monk said, "When mourning clothes aren't worn, what then?"—How long do we mourn the loss of our teacher? When do we no longer wear mourning clothes? How can we be free of our attachment to our teacher? How do we requite our filial piety? How can we fulfill our obligations to our teacher? I'm emphasizing that side of it, but it's the same thing dealing with our biological parents.

Once when I was on a trip to Japan, I was hosted by Maezumi Roshi's family, including Baian Hakujun, his father and teacher in the Soto lineage. Roshi had a number of brothers who were also Zen priests, and they treated me very well. Upon returning, I asked Roshi how I could repay their hospitality, and he replied, "Sit well." That's a clue to how to repay your filial obligations to your teacher.

Here Sozan replies, "Today I have requited my filial piety." Today, I've fulfilled my obligations as a Dharma heir. What's he really saying? "I am complete as I am right now. What more needs to be done? I light incense, bow to my Ancestors, yet I am complete and independent as I am." Being independent, he depends upon no one for approval. Can we all say that we're independent? There's an easy way to find out. If there's anybody who gets under your skin, you're not independent. I still miss Maezumi Roshi—but being independent doesn't mean having no feelings nor does it mean that we are not interdependent. Everything we do affects others and everything they do affects us.

There are some Buddhist teachers who teach their students to think loving thoughts about everyone. I think it's wonderful to think loving thoughts— but it is not effective if one's loving thoughts are an act of pretense. If you have a moldy cake and you put wonderful frosting on top and take a bite, it's still going to be vile, though the frosting might taste good. So those loving thoughts have to come from your whole being, not just from a kind of facade or mask that you put on. Our training is not about *pretending* to be a good Zen student. This practice is about digging down, and bringing to light all of your follies, bringing them to the surface, really looking at them and allowing them to be, and then transforming them. But to force some kind of a loving behavior on top of it, that will hide all these things from us. Your whole being has to be lovingness, but unless you totally appreciate yourself, it won't happen. That's independence.

After requiting filial piety, then what? Now that you're totally independent, what are you going to do? "I'd love to get stumbling drunk." Bansho commented, "All things are beautiful with wine." Every day is a good day, when you're stumbling drunk. Is that what Sozan is really saying?

Every Japanese Zen master I've ever met loves to drink. So, what about the fifth grave precept: Do not be intoxicated. Sozan, commenting on this precept elsewhere, said, "Do not be intoxicated by the wine of delusion." When you drink, you get stumbling drunk. You could say that's delusion. Does Sozan mean he really gets stumbling drunk? What's it like when you're stumbling drunk? You don't care what anybody thinks or says about you or anything. So do we take it as a metaphor, or should we literally go out and get drunk?

A monk once asked Sozan, "How can illusion be truth?" Sozan replied, "Illusion is fundamentally truth." The monk said, "Well, when illusion is faced, what is revealed?" Sozan said, "Illusion is revealed." The monk said, "In that case, then from start to finish one cannot escape illusion." And Sozan said, "If you pursue illusive forms, you cannot attain them." Don't deny that folly is truth. That's what's so, that's what's going on. But if you face it, it's revealed as what it is: folly. But if you try to pursue it as truth, then you'll never attain it.

In the end, what kind of wine is Sozan talking about? Let's drink to freedom, independence, not being bound, not holding ourselves down; let's drink to acting naturally, without analyzing, without judging. Let's all get stumbling drunk on Sozan's wine!

CASE 74

Hogen's Substance and Name

Wealth has ten thousand virtues. Traceless, there's not a speck of dust. Keeping apart from all appearances, it conforms with all dharmas. Stepping from the top of a hundred-foot pole, the body fills the ten directions of the world. Tell me: Where does it come from?

MAIN CASE
Attention! A monk asked Hogen, "I've heard it said in a sutra that all dharmas arise from a non-dwelling base. What is this non-dwelling base?" Hogen replied, "Form arises before substance. Name occurs before naming."

APPRECIATORY VERSE
Eliminating footprints, stopping communications.
White clouds are rootless: What color is the pure wind?
Scattering heaven, it has no mind; holding earth, it has power.
It clarifies the deep source of a thousand ages;
makes molds for the ten-thousand shapes.
The way of countries and the way of dust.
Understand this and Samantabhadra is everywhere!
The gate of the tower: open it, and all people are Maitreya.

In the Vimalakirti Sutra, Manjushri, the bodhisattva of wisdom, asked Vimalakirti, "What is the source of the body?" Vimalakirti said, "Craving is the source." Manjushri then asked, "What's the source of craving?" Vimalakirti said, "Baseless discrimination is the source of craving." Manjushri said, "What's the source of baseless discrimination?" Vimalakirti said, "Inverted thinking is the source of discrimination." Then Manjushri asked, "What's the source of inverted thinking?" Vimalakirti said, "Non-abiding is the source." And Manjushri said, "What's the source of non-abiding?" Vimalakirti said, "Non-abiding has no source. Manjushri, all things arise from this non-abiding root."

Vimalakirti could have just said that the root of the body is non-abiding. He could have said non-abiding is the source of craving, of false discrimination, of erroneous discrimination, the basis of all our attachments. This non-abiding is the same thing as non-dwelling in this case. All dharmas arise from a non-dwelling base.

The monk in this case asks, "What is this non-dwelling base from which all things arise?" He's trying to grab onto something that's fixed in order to feel secure and safe, but everything arises from a non-dwelling base which by its very nature is ungraspable. Sometimes we call that non-dwelling base "emptiness." But Zen emptiness is not nihilism or denying everything. The non-dwelling base is always changing because it is empty of any fixed thing and is impermanent.

Hogen, the master in this case, lived at the end of the ninth and the beginning of the tenth century in China. One of his most famous teachings was that "not knowing is most intimate" (see Case 20). Not knowing is a great way to practice life. Not knowing is the same thing as non-dwelling, as the non-abiding basis.

If you see a pattern of behavior that happens over and over and over again, that causes you more and more difficulty, that's the basis of suffering. Don't say non-dwelling basis! That's just some kind of delusive knowledge you're holding onto—and the basis of that knowledge is non-dwelling.

We can use difficulties in life as opportunities for awakening, bringing forth our finest human qualities: compassion, humor, wisdom, and fearlessness. When our life gets difficult, we feel overwhelmed. It's good just to slow down, and really look into it. What's going on? Is it true that nobody in the history of the universe has suffered as much as I'm suffering right now?

How can an inner shift take place? We have to question our "self-evident" truths and "fundamental" knowledge, and arouse our willingness to approach life in a new way. Our problems may not disappear, but they will become workable, because we see them in a new light. We can recognize these difficulties, and that recognition can bring greater awareness. By honoring this not-knowing instead of fighting it and trying to make it into something fixed, we discover new possibilities in the midst of our problems. We feel safer when we think we have all the answers. But this most intimate not-knowing is not safe; it's a continual journey into the unknown.

When Hogen replies, "Form arises before substance. Name occurs before naming," *that* is the non-dwelling basis. When you get up at night to go to the kitchen or the bathroom and you bump into a chair, do you care whether it was the chair or the table? I don't think so. You just say, "Damn! That hurt!" What about the hurt? Did it arise because you hit the chair? Why do you feel pain instead of pleasure? Why do you name it "pain" or name it "pleasure"?

Once there was a monk who was on a pilgrimage and lay down to sleep in a field. After dark he woke up with a terrible thirst, and he groped around and found a vessel with rainwater in it. He greedily gulped it down and was satisfied, and then he contentedly fell back asleep. When the morning light broke, he saw that he was sleeping in a charnel ground and saw that he had been drinking out of a piece of broken skull—and it still had some flesh clinging to it. Thereupon he started to vomit, violently. As soon as he named it, he got sick.

Everything arises from a non-dwelling base and everything returns to a non-dwelling base. Whether you believe it or not, there's not a square inch of firm ground upon which to stand. As long as you act as if there is a fixed base, you will tangle yourself in vines. When you see eye to eye with Hogen, then you will understand that Samantabhadra, the bodhisattva of benevolence, is everywhere and that all people are Maitreya, the future Buddha.

CASE 75

Zuigan's Permanent Principle

PREFACE TO THE ASSEMBLY

Even though you try to call it thus, it quickly changes. At the place where knowledge fails to reach, it should not be talked about. Here: Is there something to penetrate?

MAIN CASE

Attention! Zuigan asked Ganto, "What is the original, permanent principle?" Ganto replied, "Moving." Zuigan asked, "How about when it moves?" Ganto said, "You don't see the original, permanent principle." Zuigan was flabbergasted. Ganto remarked, "When you agree, you are not liberated from the senses and their dust; when you don't agree, you sink into life and death forever."

APPRECIATORY VERSE

Perfect jewel without flaw: a great gemstone needs no polish.
Where the person of the Way is praiseworthy, she has no sharp edges.
When the path of agreement is forgotten, senses and dust are empty.
Liberated body without dependence. Alive and frisky!

In this koan Master Ganto vividly points out that if we hold onto the notion that there's no fixed thing, an "original, permanent principle," we're stuck there too! Zuigan was Ganto's student in ninth-century China.

When we sit and quiet our minds, and we look at what's going on without prejudice, without preconceptions, it's amazing how many fixed ideas we have about reality. We call sitting with non-judgmental awareness *shikantaza* or just sitting. In shikantaza we may be trying to stop and observe our mind, but if we observe with our conditioned mind, we're just filtering everything through our prejudices. We just have to dig deeper! How are we conditioned? What are our expectations? We're all conditioned by the way we're raised, the country we're raised in, and the values of everybody around us. But we can keep looking. How can we really be free from prejudices? Look, look!

The verse says that a praiseworthy person of the Way has no sharp edges. If you have sharp edges, then you get snagged on everything! I recall a cartoon about a caveman who was trying to craft the first wheel. He had a cart, and on his first attempt the wheels were square, rather than circular. In the caption, he said, "Damn! It still doesn't work!" When we have sharp edges, we just don't roll freely! It's the same with a wheel. It doesn't roll freely. Having sharp edges doesn't necessarily mean being aggressive or assertive. We can have sharp edges even when we're being passive. As long as we're protecting some kind of an image of how we think things should be, or how we want things to be, there will be sharp edges. Your fixed point of view does not roll freely.

There's a Zen poem that says, "Make your mind as flexible as water: now square, now round." It's up to the shape of the bowl. In this case, Ganto says to Zuigan, "When you agree, you're not liberated from the senses and their dusts. When you don't agree, you sink into life and death forever." I might say it like this: when you agree, wholeheartedly agree but don't stick to that agreement; when you deny, wholeheartedly deny, but don't be fixed on that denial.

What Master Dogen wrote about samadhi, meditative absorption, is relevant here, "With right samadhi, no matter what level of calm is reached, there is awareness. There is full mindfulness and clear comprehension. This samadhi is the samadhi which can give rise to wisdom. One cannot get lost in it. Practitioners should understand this well." When you are deep in your concentration, there is still awareness. You don't go off into some kind of a trance. When your mind is really quiet, and your concentration is deepening, that's the best time to really see. What are those fixed principles upon which I base my activities, my actions, my responses, my thoughts, my ideas, my opinions, my judgments? Where are my edges? Look!

The Sixth Ancestor said that samadhi is the substance of wisdom, and wisdom itself is the functioning of samadhi. Wisdom and samadhi go hand in hand. Without really focusing and concentrating your mind, wisdom won't arise, and if you don't maintain it well, wisdom won't function. So it comes down to our practice in many ways. Practice sitting on the cushion, quieting your mind, and not thinking about all kinds of things.

But what are we dependent on? And what keeps you from being "alive and frisky"? Each one of us has to look and see for ourselves.

I recall an old Zen verse:

> How many times have I changed my firmly determined mind?
> Mind, mind—how unreliable!

So how about "no mind"? Can you rely on that? Each one of us has to keep looking and see what it is that's snagging on all of the edges of our life. Just keep working on it, alive and frisky.

CASE 76

Shuzan's Three Phrases

PREFACE TO THE ASSEMBLY

One phrase clarifies three phrases. Three phrases clarify one phrase. Three and one do not interact. Clear and obvious is the path of the utmost. Tell me: Which phrase is first?

MAIN CASE

Attention! Shuzan addressed the assembly, saying, "When you are awakened by the first phrase, you become a teacher of Buddhas and Ancestors. When you are awakened by the second phrase, you become a teacher of men and devas. When you are awakened by the third phrase, you can't even save yourself." A monk asked, "Osho, by which phrase were you awakened?" Shuzan replied, "After the moon sets in the third watch, one penetrates through the city."

APPRECIATORY VERSE

Withered skulls of Buddhas and Ancestors skewered on one stick.
The water clock's drop after drop moves the pointer minutely.
Essential activity of devas and men.
Firing a thousand pounds by catapult.
Thunderheads glistening and glowing swiftly shoot down lightning.
You over here! See the transformations.
When meeting the lowly, be noble. When meeting the noble, be lowly.
Leaving the finding of the jewel to Mosho, the ultimate Way stretches
　　endlessly.
Letting the butcher's knife sort freely in the dead ox, there's implicit trust
　　each moment.

We previously met this Shuzan in Case 65.

The three phrases mentioned in this case were first enumerated by Hyakujo in the early ninth century. He said, "The teachings all have three successive phrases. First, one should be taught to produce a good mind. Second, the good mind is forgotten. Third, only the final good is realized." Then he explains further. "The immediate mirror awareness is your own Buddha Nature; it's good in the beginning." In other words, to see your true self, it's good in the beginning. "To not keep dwelling in the immediate mirroring awareness is good in the middle." In other words, after you've seen into your True Nature, then let it go. "To not keep making an understanding of not-dwelling is the final good." In other words, don't dwell in not-dwelling.

When you first hear Shuzan's explanation of the three phrases, you might think that it's backwards. He says, "When you are awakened by the first phrase, you become a teacher of Buddhas and Ancestors. When you are awakened by the second phrase, you become a teacher of men and devas. When you are awakened by the third phrase, you can't even save yourself." Isn't it better to be a teacher to Buddhas and Ancestors than to be unable to save yourself?

Let's look more closely at this. If you realize that your True Nature is the same as Buddha Nature, then you're the teacher of Buddhas and patriarchs. If you let go of that, you are the teacher of men and devas. Devas are minor gods—not great gods, just minor ones. But then, if you don't dwell in non-dwelling, you can't even save yourself. Why is that? What self are you saving? If you totally forget the self, who are you saving? Just be free.

As recorded in Case 43 of the *Gateless Gate*, Shuzan held up his staff and said, "If you call this a staff, you are committed to the name. If you do not call it a staff, you're opposing the fact. Tell me: What do you call it?" These words of Shuzan contain all three phrases. How do you see them?

In the present case, the monk asks Shuzan, "By which phrase were you awakened?" Shuzan says, "After the moon sets in the third watch, one penetrates through the city." When the moon sets, everything is dark. When it is dark, one can move freely through the city without being seen. When you realize the state of oneness, you don't illuminate duality or dichotomy— thus it is said to be after the moon sets. When you are not stuck to ideas of right and wrong, you can easily penetrate through the city. In the morning she passes through London and in the evening she enters Los Angeles.

There is nothing holding her down. Now, how would you express it?

The lines of the verse correspond to the phrases in the koan. "Withered skulls of Buddhas and Ancestors skewered on one stick." That's the first phrase. When you meet the Buddha on the road, kill him! When you meet the Ancestors on the road, kill them! If you want to be a teacher of Buddhas and Ancestors, let go of the idea of Buddhas and Ancestors. Pierce them all the way through with one skewer. Then you're free.

"The water clock's drop after drop moves the pointer minutely. Essential activity of devas and men. Firing a thousand pounds by catapult." A water clock has a water reservoir with a little hole in it, and the drops come down at a fixed rate and hit a little lever on a gear which causes a pointer to turn and keep the time: moving the pointer minutely. That's being attentive minute after minute. The activity of firing a thousand pounds by catapult is beyond ordinary skill, but being enlightened by the ten-thousand dharmas, you have that kind of power. It's seductive here, why not rest for a while? That's the second phrase.

"Thunderheads glistening and glowing swiftly shoot down lightning. You over here! See the transformations." Sometimes, shooting down lightning, sometimes glistening and glowing, but not attached to anything. This represents the third phrase, but how it manifests is in the next line. "When meeting the lowly, be noble. When meeting the noble, be lowly." Because in your heart you know fundamentally everyone is equal, there's no resentment and no delight in being high or low.

Shuzan's last comment, "After the moon sets in the third watch, one penetrates through the city" contains all the three phrases. If you can see that clearly, you will know by which phrase he was awakened. Now tell me: By which phrase are you awakened?

CASE 77

Kyozan Holds His Own

PREFACE TO THE ASSEMBLY

It's like a man who tries to draw emptiness. No sooner does he use the writing brush then he goes wrong. How is it possible to bring forth the pattern or make a model? How is it possible? I have already revealed the stopper. If there are rules, then cite the rules. If there are none, then give an example.

MAIN CASE

Attention! A monk asked Kyozan, "Osho! Don't you know characters?" Kyozan said, "I hold my own." At that, the monk circled him once clockwise, and said, "What character is this?" Kyozan drew the character of a cross on the ground. Then the monk circled him counterclockwise and said, "What character is this?" Kyozan modified the cross so that it was a swastika. The monk drew a circle in the air and raised his hands palms up to give the appearance of an *ashura* supporting the sun and the moon and said, "What character is this?" Kyozan drew a circle around the swastika, and the monk gave the appearance of a fierce temple guardian. Kyozan remarked, "Just so! Just so! Keep it and maintain it well."

APPRECIATORY VERSE

The void inside the ring of the Way is never filled;
the character for the seal of emptiness has never been revealed.
Marvelously orbiting the wheel of heaven and axis of earth,
mysteriously stringing together military warp and literary woof.
Releasing, opening, kneading, gathering;
standing alone, going anywhere.

Activity sends forth the mysterious gist, and sparks lightning in the
   blue heaven;
the eye enfolds the purple rays, and sees stars in the bright of day.

Master Kyozan, who appears in this collection many times (see appendix)
was called "little Shakyamuni" because he had many ways of guiding people.
Shakyamuni was said to have offered ten thousand different skillful means to
bring about awakening. Kyozan lived in the ninth century, and was the successor of Isan, and as I said before, together they formed the Igyo School of
Zen. That school is known for using mystical symbols in its teaching. These
symbols are said to have been passed down through the Sixth Ancestor. In
fact, they've been passed down from teacher to student until today. My own
teacher passed some to me.

Master Tangen had said to Kyozan, "Previously the National Teacher
Echu received the transmission of a total of ninety-seven symbolic circles
from the Sixth Ancestor. He in turn passed these to me, and he said, 'Thirty
years after I have died, a novice monk will come from the south who will
greatly revive this teaching. When this time comes, pass the teaching on to
him, and don't let it end.' I realize that it is you! You must uphold and preserve it." He passed the secret text to Kyozan, and after receiving and examining the text, Kyozan burned it.

One day, Tangen said to Kyozan, "The symbols that I gave you are
extremely rare and esoteric and precious." Kyozan said, "After examining
them, I burned them." Tangen said, "This Dharma gate of ours cannot be
understood by most people. Only the Buddha, Ancestors, and all the Old
Ones can fully understand it. How can you burn it?" Kyozan said, "After
examining it, I fully comprehended its meaning. There was no use keeping
the text." Tangen said, "Even so, when transmitting this from disciple to disciple, people of future times won't believe it." Kyozan said, "If you would
like another copy, that won't be a problem. I'll make another copy and give
it to you. Then it won't be lost." Tangen said, "Please do." Kyozan repro-
duced it without a single omission or error.

Each of these symbols has a meaning, but although they are interesting, you
cannot hold onto these conceptual explanations to penetrate this koan.
Nonetheless, the circle is the body of the Buddha (though it is also sometimes

represented as a cross). This empty circle also represents the dwelling place of the body of the Buddha. The fourteenth Indian Ancestor, Nagarjuna, is said to have concealed his body on the teaching seat and manifested a circular form of the full moon. Though he was sitting before them, all the monks saw was the circular form. Kanadeva, the Indian Ancestor who succeeded Nagarjuna said, "This is the Venerable One showing us the form of Buddha Nature by manifesting it." That is the shape of formless samadhi.

The swastika is an ancient Buddhist symbol. If you look at swastikas, you'll see there are two kinds of them: one of them looks like it's rotating clockwise, and the other looks like it's rotating counterclockwise. The swastika is a symbol which denotes wealth or well-being. Its meaning was perverted in Nazi Germany in the last century. Even today, on Japanese maps a swastika indicates the location of a Buddhist temple. The swastika also denotes working for others with expedient means arising from true wisdom. Realize that the Buddha and sentient beings are not different and then put that wisdom into practice.

When the monk drew a circle in the air and raised his hands palms up to give the appearance of an ashura supporting the sun and the moon, Kyozan enclosed the swastika in a circle. This circle contains everything, including the Buddha and awakened activity. It is so large that it even contains itself. Everything is in balance and harmony. Ashuras are "fighting spirits" and represent the world of desires. What kind of state is it that is in harmony and yet supported by desires?

The last symbol from this case, the appearance of a fierce temple guardian, is particularly interesting. The name of that guardian is Rucika. Among the thousand Buddhas of the Eon of Virtue, Rucika was to be the last to attain buddhahood. When he heard that news, he cried and said, "Why am I so unfortunate to be the last one?" But then he started laughing and said, "I will get all the merit, the skills and techniques, of the prior 999 Buddhas." He would have the advantage of everyone else's experience. When Einstein was asked why he was so brilliant, he said that he stood on the shoulders of giants—all of those who came before him.

Rucika is now represented as a thunderbolt-bearing deity who protects the Dharma. When the monk posed as Rucika, his meaning expressed what all the Buddhas attend to, which is to keep and maintain the Dharma well. So Kyozan says, "Just so! Just so! Keep and maintain it well."

All of these symbols represent the Great Matter which is the right transmission of the Buddha's wisdom from generation to generation. Master Sekito says, "The Dharma transmitted by the Ancestors up to me is not the matter of samadhi, or effort, but of the attaining of the wisdom of Buddha. To have the Great Matter without having Buddha's wisdom is like a blind person holding a mirror."

The empty circle represents the dwelling place of the body of the Buddha, the swastika denotes working for others with expedient means arising from true wisdom. Realize that the Buddha and sentient beings are not different and then put that wisdom into practice. The problem is that we dwell in our thoughts, ideas, symbols, and images. We don't realize that we dwell in the land of the Buddha: that's the land of the unborn and the undying, that manifests as being born and dying. This is not a symbol, but your life as it is.

CASE 78

Ummon's Farm Rice-Cake

PREFACE TO THE ASSEMBLY

When you seek the cost all over heaven, you'll be paid the price all over the earth. To seek after a hundred schemes is just a shame. Isn't there someone who knows to advance and retreat, and who recognizes the duality?

MAIN CASE

Attention! A monk asked Master Ummon, "What is speech that transcends the Buddhas and goes beyond the Ancestors?" Ummon replied, "Farm rice-cake."

APPRECIATORY VERSE

"Farm rice-cake" is speech transcending Buddhas and Ancestors.
In this phrase there's no flavor. How can you penetrate it?
Zen monks, who one day know satisfaction,
will see no shame on Ummon's face.

You can buy rice-cakes at the supermarket. Although now they make them with all kinds of flavors, the original rice-cake, called "farm rice-cake" in this case, had no flavor—which is in itself a marvelous flavor. A Zen verse says "nothing exceeds the flavor of pure water." Farm rice-cake is made by the farmer's wife to nourish the farmer and his workers as they toil in the fields. It is plain, utilitarian, and flavorless—like pure water.

Master Ummon was born in 864 and died when he was eighty-five years old. He appears many times in this collection as well as in the *Gateless Gate* and *Blue Cliff Record*. In total, Ummon appears more than any other master. He began to teach independently when he was forty-seven years old and taught for almost forty years.

This particular case, like many cases in this collection, is a segment of a much longer conversation: Ummon spoke to the assembly of monks, "Even if a single word instantaneously puts the ten thousand differences in the same groove, including the minutest particles, it is still an expression of teaching. What then is a patch-robe monk to say? If you argue about the words of the Ancestors and the Buddhas, the unique way of Zen will be destroyed. Is there any one here who can put it right? If you can speak, come forward." Then a monk asked, "What is speech that transcends the Buddhas and goes beyond the Ancestors?" Ummon said, "Farm rice-cake."

The longer version of this koan continues with the monk asking, "What connection is there between farm rice-cake and the speech that transcends the Buddhas and Ancestors?" And then Ummon said, "Exactly! What's the connection! What are you calling Buddhas and what are you calling Ancestors?"

To assist the monk further Ummon explained, "Right now is anything the matter? If you really don't have any clue, then for a time go into yourself and investigate thoroughly on your own. In the twenty-four hours of the day, when you are wearing a robe, eating, defecating, and urinating, even including the flies in the latrine, is there still any speech that transcends Buddhas and Ancestors?"

Ummon's "farm rice-cake" was picked up by Master Dogen six hundred years later: "All Buddhas are realization. Thus, all things are realization. That includes a rice-cake, and a painting of a rice-cake…. Know that a painted rice-cake is your face before your parents were born." If you really understand what a rice-cake is and what a painted rice-cake is, you understand who you are.

Dogen also says, "Ummon's rice-cake is a statement that goes beyond Buddhas and surpasses the Ancestors, an activity that enters Buddhas and enters demons…. When you understand this meaning with your body and mind you will thoroughly master the ability to turn things, and to be turned by things."

Instinctively we are attracted to Buddhas and repulsed by demons. As long as you think you can hide your demons somewhere else, they will torment you from their hidden place. You had better bring out your demons and paint them nicely, using everything that you know—all of your tools and ingredients. Then you can simultaneously play with Buddhas and demons while they play with you. When you realize the essence of that farm rice-cake, the essence of the ten thousand things will be revealed.

CASE 79

Chosha Advances a Step

The wife in the Ba family of Kincha Danto was a special spirit. She pounded millet cakes in a jar of emerald: Who would be so boisterous? If you don't get into a wave that astonishes people, it would be hard to meet with a fish that satisfies you. How about this phrase: Step out with a great stride.

MAIN CASE

Attention! Master Chosha told a monk to go and ask the hermit E Osho, "What about before you saw Nansen?" The monk did so and E was silent for a while. The monk asked, "How about after seeing him? Then what?" E said, "Nothing special." The monk returned and told this to Chosha, and Chosha said, "There is a man on top of a hundred-foot pole. Though he has a degree of understanding, it's not yet the real thing. From the top of the hundred-foot pole he should advance a step, and the ten directions of the world will be his entire body." The monk asked, "How do you advance a step?" Chosha replied, "The mountains of Ro province; the waters of Rei province." The monk said, "I don't understand." Chosha remarked, "The four oceans and the five lakes are within the king's control."

APPRECIATORY VERSE

The jeweled man's dream is broken by one cock's crow.
Look around at life, and everything is equal.
The wind and thunder carry news, awakening hibernating creatures.
Wordless peach and plum. Under them, people's footpaths naturally form.
When the season comes, work to till the soil.
Who's afraid in spring paddies to sink in mud to the knees?

Here Master Chosha is encouraging us to take a step forward, from wherever we may be. Each one of us is stranded on a hundred-foot pole. We may have climbed up for the view or we may have fallen to it from another perch. No matter where we are in our Zen practice or our life we're always standing on top of a hundred-foot pole. But we must not rest there. We must step forward into the unknown void in order to experience the boundless life.

Chosha was a successor of Master Nansen and a Dharma brother of Master Joshu. He gained a reputation as being a vigorous teacher. Chosha said to the famous Kyozan when Chosha was a young stubborn monk, "Everyone is looking at the full moon and enjoying it." Kyozan replied, "Everyone is completely endowed with this, but they are unable to make use of it." Chosha said, "I invite you to use it now." Kyozan said, "How would you use it?" Chosha knocked Kyozan down with a shove and jumped on his chest. Kyozan said, "Whoa! Just like a tiger!" Thus he came to be known as Tiger Cen, which is an abbreviation of one of his Dharma names.

The other main character in this case, Hermit E, is also a disciple of Nansen, and there's nothing recorded about him other than this one case. He was supposed to have been recognized by Nansen in secret, but evidently Chosha wasn't impressed with him.

Once Chosha told his assembly, "The whole universe in the ten directions is the light of one's self." In that kind of talk, Chosha is encouraging each one of us to see the light that illuminates the reality of all things. Without it, we're like ghosts walking around, rattling our chains. It's like being in a dream from which we cannot awaken. To awaken, we need to have trust to let go. That's what this koan is about.

Once a student came to the Indian Ancestor Upagupta asking to be ordained as a disciple. Upagupta said, "In order to be ordained you must believe in my words, and never disobey my instructions." The man agreed and Upagupta conjured a precipitous cliff and made the man climb up a tree on the edge. Then Upagupta instructed him to release his foothold. The man did so. Upagupta instructed him to let go of one hand, and the man did that. Upagupta instructed him to let go of the other hand, and the man exclaimed, "If I let go of this hand, I'll fall over the cliff and die." Upagupta said, "You had promised to follow my instructions. How can you disobey me?" At that moment, the man took the plunge, and he let go of his hand and fell. He no longer saw the tree or the cliff, and suddenly he realized the Buddha Way.

We can believe all we want. We can make up all kinds of ideas in our heads about what it is to let go, to be free, to be unencumbered, but no matter how much we think about it, that's not it. We can't satisfy our hunger by looking at a menu. What is it that keeps us from taking that step into the unknown void?

A monk once asked Chosha, "Who is it who becomes a Buddha?" Chosha said, "It's *you* that becomes a Buddha!" The monk didn't know what to say, so Chosha said, "Do you understand?" The monk said, "No." What is there to understand? Chosha tried to give him an analogy, "If someone trips on the ground and falls down, and then they use the ground to get up again, does the ground complain?"

Every evening we chant the bodhisattva vow, "Sentient beings are numberless. I vow to save them." If you are the ground and one of them trips and falls on you, and gets back up by pushing off on you, do you complain? The vow means *all* sentient beings! It doesn't mean, "Not that person, because he's a jerk." It's the same thing with stepping off the top of the hundred-foot pole. "I can let go of this, and I can let go of the other thing, but you want me to let go of *that?* Oh no! If I let go of that, then who will I be?" Precisely!

How can you live your life freely? You can ascend the mountain, but you have to descend it to be free. Hermit E left Nansen and stayed on his lofty peak. From his short dialogue with the monk, Chosha felt that he was still holding onto something.

I heard that Philip Kapleau told one of his students who was acting with apparent humility, "Don't be so humble! You're not that good!" If you're nothing special, why do you have to say you're nothing special? Both before and after awakening are hundred-foot poles. The ground is always shifting; there's no place to rest.

In Case 38 of the *Gateless Gate*, Master Goso said of our practice, "It's like a buffalo passing through a window. Its head, horns, body, and four legs have all passed through. Why is it that the tail cannot?" There's something that can't quite pass through. Some people have incredible abilities, but somehow there's always something sticky there. There's always something that sticks. In each stage of our practice, it's something different.

Our habit-ridden consciousness holds us in one place, if we don't see it and let it go. We need to watch it very carefully without judging. You can see how quickly you fall into old patterns of behavior. It's almost like trying to separate yourself from your shadow. And it gets more and more subtle. Before realizing it, our old patterns pop up. So how can we step forward from the top of that hundred-foot pole? That hundred-foot pole can be any precipice, any difficulty. And when you do step forward, where are you? Are you on top of another hundred-foot pole?

The monk in this case says, "How do you advance a step?" and Chosha replies, "The mountains of Ro province; the waters of Rei province." In other words, manifest your body in the ten directions.

But the monk says, "I don't understand." Chosha remarks, "The four oceans and the five lakes are within the king's control." Who is that king? Who is it who becomes a Buddha? The whole universe in the ten directions is your whole body. Fishes and foxes frolic everywhere.

The verse says, "Who's afraid in spring paddies to sink in mud to the knees?" If you don't sink into the mud in the spring, how will you enjoy a bowl of rice in the summer? We have to enter those places that scare us, and we must do so over and over again.

The Great Way is not something to believe in. It's something you have to realize for yourself. As long as you want to hold onto this limited view of who you are, you'll never do it. All kinds of discomforts come up during zazen and the rest of your life, but as long as you have the faith and determination you can encounter them with your eyes open. Just keep going forward step by step from the top of the hundred-foot pole.

CASE 80

Ryuge Passes the Chin Rest

A great sound is rarely heard; a great vessel matures slowly. In the hurly-burly of a hundred chatterings, he plays the fool, patiently letting time pass for thousands of years. Tell me: What kind of person is this?

MAIN CASE

Attention! Ryuge asked Suibi, "What is the meaning of the Patriarch's coming from the west?" Suibi said, "Go and get the chin rest for me." Ryuge brought the chin rest for Suibi, and Suibi then treated him to a blow. Ryuge remarked, "Hit me if you wish, but there's still no meaning to the Patriarch's coming from the west." Later Ryuge asked Rinzai, "What's the meaning of the Patriarch's coming from the west?" Rinzai said, "Go get the cushion for me." Ryuge brought the cushion to Rinzai, and Rinzai treated him to a blow. Ryuge remarked, "Hit me if you wish, but there's still no meaning to the Patriarch's coming from the west." Later still, when Ryuge was living in a temple, a monk said, "Osho, in former times you asked Suibi and Rinzai about the meaning of the coming of the Patriarch. Did they both clarify it or not?" Ryuge replied, "They clarified it alright—but there's still no meaning to the Patriarch's coming from the west."

APPRECIATORY VERSE

Cushion and chin rest confront Ryuge.
Having the chance, why aren't you an adept?
He doesn't think to clarify it by making quick conclusions.
He's afraid of their loss of position, and having to go to heaven's edge.
How can you hang a sword in the vast sky?

Instead, the Milky Way floats a raft.
In the unsprouted grasses, he hides the huge elephant.
In the bottomless basket, he puts the living snake.
Today, everywhere, rivers and lakes—what obstacle is there?
In all great and small harbors are boats and carts.

Master Ryuge lived in the ninth and tenth centuries in China, and was a successor of Master Tozan. This same koan appears in the *Blue Cliff Record* as Case 20, except there the last part is missing, though the parts about Ryuge being hit with the chin rest and cushion are identical. It's generally considered in the *Blue Cliff Record* that Ryuge is not well accomplished, that he's kind of green. Any monk would know that as soon as he gave the chin rest to his teacher he's going to get hit—so why not hit the teacher first? That's what Obaku did in Case 2 of the *Gateless Gate*. Obaku asked his teacher Hyakujo a question, and Hyakujo said, "Come here. I'll tell you." As he came close, Obaku hit Hyakujo and Hyakujo laughed. "I thought that I was a red-bearded barbarian, but here I see a barbarian with a red beard." Masters Wanshi and Bansho, the compilers of the *Book of Equanimity*, hold Ryuge in high regard.

Let's appreciate some of the subtleties of this case. In a capping phrase to this case as it appears in the *Blue Cliff Record*, Master Engo comments, "While he was given a fine horse, he did not know how to ride. Alas." In contrast, the preface here says, "In the hurly-burly of a hundred chatterings, he plays the fool, patiently letting time pass for thousands of years." Ryuge was patient. Patience is one of the six *paramitas*, the perfections which are aspects of the enlightened person. (These are usually listed as patience, generosity, morality, effort, concentration, and wisdom.) Thus the interpretation here is that Ryuge knew perfectly well what he was doing, and was expressing "no meaning."

When Ryuge was traveling around China, he visited various teachers. When he was at Suibi's place, he complained, "I, your student, have been here for more than a month. Every day the master enters the hall to speak, but we have not received any instruction about even one Dharma." Suibi replied, "So what?" Ryuge left Suibi at that time and went to see Master Tokusan. He said, "From afar I've heard of Tokusan's one phrase Buddhadharma, but up to now I have not heard the master say one phrase about Buddha-dharma. What is this?" Tokusan said to him, "So what?"

Then Ryuge went to Tozan and asked the same question. Tozan didn't say, "So what?" but rather, "Are you accusing me of something?" Ryuge liked that answer better. He stayed with Tozan, and he eventually had a deep awakening with Tozan, and became his successor.

It's hard to know all the conditions that give rise to a particular result, so when somebody asks, "Why?" or, "What's the meaning of...," there is a tendency to rationalize and simplify. The trap is that as soon as we try to figure out why, we are distancing ourselves from now. For example, a man who can't develop a loving relationship with a woman might wonder why, and after years of therapy and introspection, he discovers that he blames his mother. She's the "why"—she was too controlling, she was too critical, she smothered me, and so on. When you have a "why" where does it get you? It only allows you to pass the responsibility for your own misery to someone else, to something else.

If you want to know the "meaning" of anything in Zen, start looking at your own misery, your own pain. Start *experiencing* your own suffering. You have to look into the dark places in your own personality that you have been carefully avoiding for your entire life. Shine light there. Even the smallest light from the tip of glowing incense will dispel a thousand years of darkness. By starting to shine even a feeble light into those dark places, they will become visible. Once you start this process, the clarity begins to take shape. By bringing your hurt, blockages, and rigidity to light, they will naturally dissipate on their own.

But what about Ryuge's "no meaning"? Maezumi Roshi once said that this Ryuge's "no meaning" is the same as Joshu's "*Mu.*" *Mu* is a presentation of your true self. This "no meaning" is not the same as the no meaning of a nihilist, who believes that all traditional values and beliefs are unfounded, and that all existence is consequently senseless and useless, and thus denies intrinsic meaning and value in life. Ryuge's "no meaning" is the meaning of life. If you really understand that "no meaning," it probes the depths of the earth and the heights of the heavens. It liberates humans, and it liberates animals, fighting spirits, hungry ghosts, and gods. This "no meaning" is why Bodhi-dharma came from the West. This "no meaning" is why you have a spouse who's impossible to relate to. This "no meaning" is why you go to the mountains instead of the seashore. This "no meaning" is why you are ambitious yet your child drops out of college. When you understand this "no meaning," as the poem "Faith in Mind" says, "All self-centered striving ceases. Doubts and irresolutions vanish and life and true faith are possible." Or, as Master Hakuin put it in the "Song of Zazen," "To regard the thought of no-thought as thought, whether singing or dancing, we are the voice of the Dharma." When we see the meaning of no-meaning as meaning, whether singing or dancing, we are the voice of truth and this very place is the lotus land of purity, this very body is the body of Buddha.

The verse to this case says: "In the unsprouted grasses, he hides the huge elephant." How would you hide an elephant in the short grass? Perhaps Ryuge has tremendous patience and insight, but hides it all well. "In the bottomless basket, he puts the living snake." Don't be fooled by appearances. One thing that I always admired about Maezumi Roshi was that he would come into a room and naturally find his place in it, without pomp, without adulation. The atmosphere of the room was enough for him to sense how to naturally fit in. Thus the verse is praising Ryuge. He had many elephants and many snakes in a bottomless basket, but nobody saw them.

CASE 81

Gensha Comes to the Province

PREFACE TO THE ASSEMBLY

With movement, the shadow manifests. With awareness, dust arises. Raised up, it's clear. Thrown down, it's intimate. When true men of the Way meet, how do they converse?

MAIN CASE

Attention! Master Gensha arrived at Hoden Province and was received with many kinds of entertainment. The next day he asked Venerable Shoto, "Where did all of yesterday's festivities go?" and Shoto lifted a corner of his robe. Gensha remarked, "There's no relation between them at all."

APPRECIATORY VERSE

Hiding the boat in the darkened valley.
Thrusting the pole into the clear source.
Dragons and fish don't know yet that water makes their lives.
A broken stick doesn't impede them.
A little stirring up goes on.
Master Gensha, Venerable Shoto.
Box and lid, two arrows colliding.
Poking stick, covering grass.
When hiding, the old turtle nests in the lotus.
When sporting, the colorful carp fiddles with duckweed.

Gensha lived in China at the end of the ninth and the beginning of the tenth centuries, and was a disciple of Master Seppo. Master Dogen was critical of some ancient teachers, but he had nothing but high praise for Gensha. Let us appreciate him.

Before he became a monk, Gensha was a fisherman, as was his father. Once when they were out fishing together, they had an accident and his father fell into the sea. Gensha tried to save him but couldn't. After his father drowned, in his remorse and despair, Gensha decided to become a monk and to practice Zen. Compared to other novice monks, he was at an advanced age—in his thirties!—and perhaps his life experience helped him understand his practice and the meaning of life and death.

Many years later on a pilgrimage, Gensha painfully stubbed his toe on a rock, and cried out in pain. He had an enlightenment experience as he thought to himself, "If everything is empty, where does this pain come from?" Then he went back to see Seppo, who said, "Did you go on your pilgrimage just to cut your foot and have a hard time?" Gensha said, "Please don't kid me!" Seppo was pleased, and said, "What you have just said should be spoken by everyone, but they lack your sincerity. Why don't you continue to visit other masters?" Gensha said, "Bodhidharma did not come to China, and the Second Patriarch did not go to India." Gensha learned that if we set ourselves in opposition to pain, as if it were something else, it only makes us hard and bitter. Yet if we open up to pain, we find not a demon, but our true self. If we imagine the pain is something else other than who we are, we'll never really know ourselves.

A layman named Kyo came to see Master Gensha, wanting to know how he could put his energies into his practice of Zen. Master Gensha called out to him and said, "Kyo!" And Kyo said, "Yes, Master?" Gensha said, "Do you hear the sound of the bubbling brook outside the window?" He said, "Yes I do." Gensha said, "Enter Zen from there." Sometime later another student asked Master Gensha, "What if at that time there had not been a bubbling brook? What would you have said to that student?" Gensha called out the student's name, "Chu!" "Yes?" "Enter Zen from there!"

Wherever you are, enter Zen from there. In the winter, it's cold; enter Zen from there. In the summer, it's hot; enter Zen from there. When you're feeling desperate, enter Zen from there. When you're feeling angry, enter Zen from there. When you're feeling rejected and sad, enter Zen from there. When you're feeling confused, enter Zen from there. If your mind is wandering in all kinds of fantasies, enter Zen from there. Pain in your legs? Enter

Zen from there. Hopelessness? Enter Zen from there. It's hard to realize because it's so close.

When Venerable Shoto lifts a corner of his robe in response to Gensha's inquiry about the past, he is revealing it couldn't be closer. Remember yesterday's festivities? It couldn't be closer. What about yesterday's sorrow? Where is the pain of your lonely adolescence? It couldn't be closer. What about all of your conditioning? It couldn't be closer. What about your inherent spontaneity and freedom? It couldn't be closer. Even in the black mountain cave of demons, complete freedom is working. It couldn't be closer.

So why would Gensha say, "There is no relation at all"? A duck quacks, and a dog barks. What's the relation there? The sky is blue. The grass is green. What's the relation? Yesterday's yesterday; today is today. What are you talking about? It couldn't be closer. You lift the corner of your robe. It's right here. What are you talking about? I don't see the dancing girls and the sword swallower and the horn blowers. Firewood is firewood and ash is ash. Dogen said, "Firewood does not become ash. Each is complete on their own." What is the relation?

If Shoto is indicating that yesterday's festivities are right here, then Gensha is taking the other side, that yesterday and today are totally different. But maybe Shoto's not saying that. Maybe he's saying, by lifting the corner of this robe, "I'm here. That's there. So what?" Why is there no relation at all? When the Buddha was enlightened, he said, "I, the stars, the sun, the moon, the great earth, and all beings everywhere are simultaneously enlightened." If that's so, then where can he be? Everywhere you look is the body of our beloved Shakyamuni. Everything you hear is the sound of our beloved Shakyamuni. What's the relation? Where can you hide?

If you're everything, what kind of relation can there be? If you can find it, what relation is there? If it cannot be found, what relation is there? Gensha says, "There's no relation between them at all."—there's no separation, no difference. I've just given you two opposite interpretations of Gensha in this koan: Which is the true one?

True and not true—what's the relation? What is the relation of no relation at all?

CASE 82

Ummon's Sounds and Shapes

PREFACE TO THE ASSEMBLY

When sounds and colors are not let go, this is to be conditioned by the environment. Seeking by sound and seeing by shape, one will not see the Tathagatha. Aren't you pursuing a way to return home?

MAIN CASE

Attention! Master Ummon addressed the assembly, saying, "Hearing a sound, realize the Way. Seeing a shape, enlighten the mind. Avalokiteshvara Bodhisattva brought money to buy a farm rice-cake. But, released from her hands, it became a bean-jam cake."

APPRECIATORY VERSE

Leaving the gate, spurring up the horse; sweep away the comet.
The smoke and dust of ten thousand lands clears by itself.
In the twelve sense-fields, trivial influences are forgotten.
The three thousand worlds are illuminated with pure bright light.

We've met Master Ummon before in several cases (see appendix). Here he says, "Hearing a sound, realize the Way." Does the Way have any sound? "Seeing a shape, enlighten the mind." Does the mind have any form? The preface says that if you don't let go of sounds and colors, then you're just conditioned by your environment, and if you search by way of sounds and colors, you'll never find the Tathagatha.

Ummon's statement in this case comes from the Diamond Sutra: Buddha said to one of his disciples, "Subhuti, what do you think? May the Tathagata be perceived by the thirty-two marks of the great man?" Subhuti said, "Yes, certainly the Tathagata can be perceived by them." Then Buddha said, "Subhuti, if the Tathagata may be perceived by such marks, any great imperial ruler is the same as the Tathagata." Then Subhuti said, "World-Honored One, as I understand the Buddha's words, the Tathagata may not be perceived by the thirty-two marks." Thereupon, Buddha spoke this verse:

> Whoever sees me by form,
> whoever seeks me in sound,
> twisted are his footsteps upon the Way,
> for he cannot perceive the Tathagata.

Yet Ummon says, "Hearing a sound, realize the Way. Seeing a shape, enlighten the mind." Which is it? Should we see a shape or not? There are two recurring stories in Zen literature about being enlightened by seeing a form or hearing a sound. We encountered them in the commentary on Case 38 in this collection: Master Reiun Shigon was enlightened when he saw a peach blossom falling off the tree and Master Kyogen was enlightened upon hearing the sound of a little pebble striking bamboo.

Maezumi Roshi used to say constantly bumping up against each other in residence at the Zen Center was like stones buffeted in the river. The water churns them up and they bump against each other and become polished, gradually losing their sharp edges, becoming completely smooth. This is what Ummon was talking about: seeing shapes so clearly they become no-shape. But this grinding away of ego-centered imperfection doesn't feel very good at the time!

The last part of this case is unusual. "Avalokiteshvara Bodhisattva brought money to buy a farm rice-cake. But, released from her hands, it became bean-jam cake." A farm rice-cake is probably the most bland rice-cake that you can imagine, and here it becomes a flavorful bean-jam cake. One ancient teacher commented on this case: "Ummon enters samadhi in the east and arises from it in the west. He enters samadhi in the male body and arises in the female body." Can you do that? Show me! Avalokiteshvara bought a rice-cake and opened her hand to reveal a bean-jam cake. This is not a magic trick, not conjuring—it's freedom.

When is a rice-cake a bean-jam cake? When is suffering and misery the functioning of freedom?

The verse says, "The three thousand worlds are illuminated with pure bright light." That light of the three thousand worlds shines through reflections and echoes. If we don't attach to reflections and echoes, the light is released. Each one of us is that pure bright light. How can we let it shine freely? Master Hyakujo said, "Far beyond the senses, the pure light shines by itself." It does not depend on shapes and sounds. But if your twelve sense-fields, the six senses and the six sense consciousnesses, extend throughout the whole universe, what then? I thought it was a farm rice-cake but it's a bean-jam cake! Swallow it down and digest it fully.

CASE 83

Dogo's Nursing

The whole body is ill; Vimalakirti is hard to cure. This grass is the medicine and Manjushri uses it well. Isn't it wonderful to encounter and grasp a man facing the ultimate, and obtain this place of peaceful ease?

MAIN CASE
Attention! Isan asked Dogo, "Where have you been?" Dogo said, "I've been nursing." Isan said, "How many people were sick?" Dogo replied, "Some are sick, some are not." Isan pursued, "Isn't it you who's not sick?" Dogo responded, "Sickness and nonsickness have nothing at all to do with *it*. Speak quickly! Speak quickly!" Isan remarked, "Even being able to say it misses entirely."

APPRECIATORY VERSE
Marvelous medicines never touched his lips.
A divine doctor never had to take his pulse.
Seeming to exist, he's not nothing.
Being utterly empty, he's not something.
Unextinguished, he's born; undestroyed, he lives eternally.
He even goes utterly before the ancient Buddhas and walks alone among
    the empty kalpas.
Being quiet—heaven covers, earth supports.
Being active—the crow flies, the rabbit runs.

What is sickness? What is nonsickness? What does it mean to be sick? What is it to be well?

As illustrated in the preface to this case, whenever we talk about sickness in Zen, Vimalakirti comes up. We've met Vimalakirti in Case 48. Vimalakirti said he was sick because all sentient beings are sick. There are all kinds of sickness: sickness caused by anger, fear, mistrust; sickness caused by love and hate, and war and peace. All share the same root cause: the sickness caused by attachment to duality.

There's also the sickness of constantly worrying about what you eat and being constantly angry at the food industries. If you are constantly anxious about what you take into your body, you're turning it all to poison. Better to set the mind at rest, beyond sickness and nonsickness. When you set the mind at rest, the body is at rest. There's no separation. Don't get me wrong: of course I try to exercise and eat right—but that's not the only key to being truly healthy.

In the Vimalakirti Sutra, Manjushri Bodhisattva said, "Householder, of what sort is your sickness?" Vimalakirti said, "It is immaterial and invisible." Manjushri said, "Is it physical, or mental?" Vimalakirti said, "It is not physical, since the body is insubstantial in itself. It's not mental, since the nature of mind is like illusion."

Isan and Dogo both studied with Hyakujo. Dogo succeeded the Dharma from Yakusan Igen, who is in our Soto lineage. They lived in the eighth and ninth centuries. Isan asks, "How many people were sick?" Dogo answers him ambiguously in this koan: "Some are sick, some are not sick." There are those who are sick while being healthy, and those who are healthy while being sick. In our own minds, we create all kinds of distress and discomfort for ourselves because of our self-grasping ignorance. But Vimalakirti says that the mind is an illusion, and we create suffering and sickness. That kind of sickness is in many ways worse than having a serious illness, because we're miserable even though our body and mind are perfectly fine.

"Some are sick, some are not sick." Vimalakirti says we're all sick. Who are the ones who are not sick? Thus Isan asks, "Isn't it you who's not sick?" Not sick yet sick: What kind of state is that? But, Isan is challenging him too, implying, "Aren't you stuck on one side?" Aren't you like the fellow who carries a board over one shoulder and can only see one side of the street because the board is obscuring the view? But Dogo retorts, "Don't go calling me a

board-carrying fellow. Sickness and nonsickness have nothing to do with it."
These categories are useful, but they are fabrications. Isan says, "No matter
what I say, it wouldn't reach it." The two of them are challenging each other.
Ultimately, whatever you say about it doesn't reach it. But since you have to
say something, tell me: What would you say?

The verse says, "Being active—the crow flies, the rabbit runs." The crow
represents the sun, and the rabbit represents the moon. The crow flies across
the sky, rising in the morning, sinking in the evening. The moon waxes and
wanes; it is always changing. Isan says, "Even being able to say it misses
entirely." Is he sick or is he not sick? He looks healthy, but seems sick. Or
does he seem sick but look healthy? Which is it? Healthy or sick? Speak
quickly! Is it nothing, or something, or not nothing, or not something, or
both nothing and something, or neither nothing nor something, or none of
the above?

It's hard to put your finger on it.

CASE 84

Gutei's One Finger

PREFACE TO THE ASSEMBLY

One hearing, a thousand awakenings; one understanding, a thousand consequences. A superior person with one realization takes care of everything; mediocre and inferior ones, though they hear a great deal, mostly don't have faith. Let's try to show the most accurate, simple point and see.

MAIN CASE

Attention! Gutei Osho, whenever he was questioned, simply raised one finger.

APPRECIATORY VERSE

Old Gutei's fingertip Zen.
For thirty years, inexhaustible.
Truly a man of the Way has limitless stratagems,
but common people can't see it in front of them.
What is gained is so utterly simple,
yet expedients become endless in number.
Thousands of lands and seas swallowed up by a hair-tip.
Boundless dragons falling into whose hands?
Ninko's holding the fishing pole is appreciated.
I too raise one finger and say, "See?"

This case not only appears in the *Book of Equanimity* but is also in the *Gateless Gate* and the *Blue Cliff Record*—the three major collections of koans. Gutei learned his one-finger Zen in the ninth century from his teacher Tenryu. In the *Gateless Gate*, Master Mumon elaborates the story further: "One time, Gutei had a young attendant. When a visitor asked, 'What is the Zen your master's teaching?' the boy also stuck up a finger. Hearing of this, Gutei cut off the boy's finger, and as the boy ran out screaming in pain, Gutei called to him. When the boy turned his head, Gutei stuck up his finger. And the boy was enlightened."

This longer story appears only in the *Gateless Gate*, yet people seem to cling to that story about the boy attendant because they think they understand it. Also people want to judge Gutei, either because of his great compassion or his great cruelty. But the essence of this koan is still the first line. "Gutei Osho, whenever he was questioned, simply raised one finger."

That's all there is to this koan. What's the essential truth of Zen? He just raised one finger. Why did Bodhidharma come from the west? Raised one finger. Does a dog have Buddha Nature? Raised one finger. What is your original face? Raised one finger. What is that one finger? It's not the finger pointing at the moon, it's the moon itself. The morning star that brought Buddha to enlightenment, the sun, the great earth, and all beings everywhere. It's enlightenment. It's delusion. It's effort. It's sloth. It's humility. It's pride. It's compassion and greed. And whatever you say it is, it's not that.

Don't think that that finger represents something. That finger penetrates the depths of the ocean, and beyond the Milky Way. It penetrates to your best-kept secrets, and yet it hides nothing. It reveals Tenryu's guts, and Gutei's guts, and the boy-attendant's guts, and your guts! So tell me: How do you present that one finger?

Some Zen masters criticize Gutei because of his lack of diversity and his crudeness. No matter what you brought to Gutei, he raised one finger. Some say he had no imagination. Gutei doesn't need it—just one finger!

The verse says, "Ninko's holding the fishing pole is appreciated." Ninko made a huge fishing pole—which he baited with fifty calves and cast into the sea every morning for a year without fail. Finally, an enormous fish took the bait and Ninko managed to bring him in. Due to Ninko's consistent effort, everyone in the land had a meal of fresh fish. This line is eulogizing Gutei. He waited until he got a catch, without figuring how long it would take. He would just keep throwing out the same line, the same bait, over and over and over and over again. He caught a big fish! His attendant was enlightened, and now our bellies are full.

Gutei's one finger was never exhausted, never boring, always there, always available. That one finger appears on countless hands, and so his expedient means become endless in number. All you need to do is see it, appreciate it, and maintain it.

Late in his life, Gutei said, "I used Tenryu's one-finger Zen my entire life and never exhausted it." Then he died. Where is Gutei's finger now?

CASE 85

The National Teacher's Seamless Tomb

Having the hammer which crushes empty space, and having the means even to split apart a mountain, then one reaches the seamless and faultless place. Who is he who is thus?

MAIN CASE

Attention! Emperor Shikuso asked National Teacher Chu, "One hundred years after you die, what would you wish?" The National Teacher said, "Build me a seamless tomb." The Emperor replied, "I beg you, what style of tomb would that be?" The National Teacher remained silent for a while, and then asked, "Do you understand?" The Emperor said, "I don't understand." The National Teacher said, "I have a Dharma disciple by the name of Tangen, who knows all about it." Later on, the Emperor requested the meaning of it from Tangen, who replied:

> South of Sho and north of Tan,
> yellow gold within fills the whole country.
> A ferry boat under the shadowless tree.
> In the crystal palace, there is no one who knows.

APPRECIATORY VERSE

Alone boundlessly, boundlessly. Whole perfectly, perfectly.
The power of sight fails to reach its craggy heights.
The moon falls, the abyss is empty, night's darkness deepens.
Clouds depart, the mountain is slim, autumn's features flourish.
the Eight Principles correctly positioned,

The five elements' energy harmonized.
The body from the first is within. Do you see?
Manyo's father and son seem as if they know.
India's Buddha and Ancestors cannot do a thing with it.

National Teacher Chu, who served as the official teacher to the emperor of China, was the disciple of the Sixth Ancestor. He lived for one hundred years, from 675 to 775. He must have been close to a hundred years of age, and was probably very tired and maybe even lame when Emperor Shikuso asked him what he wants a hundred years after he dies. But even so, the National Teacher continued to teach.

National Teacher Chu advised his monks, "Don't think of good or evil."— and that's how to build a seamless tomb. If there is even a hair's breadth of difference, then heaven and earth are infinitely split apart.

When I was working as an oceanographer, we would put instrumented buoys out in the ocean to monitor the environment. There were two main hazards that would cause the buoys to break free and drift: harsh weather, when huge waves would rip out the moorings, and sharks. They like to bite mooring lines.

Sometimes the mooring line would be several miles long. It was always a pity when a shark nipped the line and set the buoy adrift with all of its expensive instruments. One clever oceanographer discovered that sharks would not disturb the lines if they were seamless. To an oceanographer, a seamless mooring line would have no gradations or variations. If you had to stitch two pieces of line together, you'd have to make it look like one line, with no joints. To a shark, a seamless mooring line looks like nothing, or at least nothing worth biting. They only attend to discontinuities or gaps in the fabric of the line.

If you're steady, consistent, and uniform in your practice, you become seamless and invulnerable to shark attacks! There are no indications of unevenness, no gaps, no inside, and no outside.

The National Teacher is silent when the Emperor asks him, "What manner of tomb is that?" What kind of silence is this? If you mimic the National Teacher, are you creating a seamless tomb or just a poor replica? Don't think that silence is it. Some Zen students think that if they just sit still enough, then they'll become Buddha. If you're attached to sitting like a stone Buddha, you should be out in the garden with the other stone Buddhas. You'll make a nice ornament! To become a living Buddha, you have to smooth out all the rough edges: your judgments, opinions, projections, images, and deluded thoughts. Without totally revealing your hidden pain and insecurities, your zazen will be more about hiding those secrets than about being free. It takes courage to tread on that hairy edge of the unknown, to look under the bed and in the closet, and to see those demons face to face. You need to maintain the mind of not-knowing.

The Diamond Sutra says, "If you view all things that appear as never having appeared, then you will realize your true self." Each moment is fresh. It's seamless. There is no baggage from the past, and no projections to the future.

Let's appreciate Tangen's poetic answer line by line. "South of Sho and north of Tan." This phrase denotes all of China, which to the Chinese was like saying all the world. We might say, "South of the Arctic, north of the Antarctic." "Yellow gold within fills the whole country." Yellow gold is not just in Fort Knox. It is the golden Buddha. Everywhere you look and for every person you encounter, you see Buddha's golden skin. Even the wind whispers his name! "A ferry boat under the shadowless tree."—This boat will take everyone without exception and their baggage to the other shore, from delusion to enlightenment. It waits in full daylight, right here, under the shadowless tree where everyone can see it, "In the crystal palace, there is no one who knows." Crystal is transparent, hiding nothing. Let us be like that. When we let go of our ego-grasping mind, there's no one who knows. Everything is revealed, yet there's no one home to explain it. Explanations do not reach it anyway. It's perfectly clear as it is. If you fully appreciate and actualize Tangen's verse, the seamless tomb is already built.

To be truly seamless there must be no gap! Maintain the mind of not-knowing, of nongrasping. As soon as we hold onto something, there's a seam. That seam rends the entire edifice, and a parade of a thousand unruly sharks, disguised as delusive thoughts, enters and starts doing all their mischief.

CASE 86

Rinzai's Great Enlightenment

Even with a copper head, iron forehead, deva eyes, dragon eyeballs, falcon beak, shark jaw, bear heart, and leopard liver—under the diamond sword no plans are accepted, and no measurement is possible. Why does it have to be thus?

MAIN CASE

Attention! Rinzai asked Master Obaku, "What is the ultimate meaning of Buddhism?" In response, Obaku hit him. This happened three times, so he left Obaku and went to see Master Daigu. Daigu asked, "Where do you come from?" Rinzai replied, "I came from Obaku." Daigu asked, "What did Obaku have to say?" Rinzai said, "I asked, 'What is the ultimate meaning of Buddhism?' three times, and three times I tasted his stick. I don't know if I was at fault or not." Daigu exclaimed, "Obaku is such an old grandmother to be so very kind to you, but still you come and ask if you are at fault or not." At these words, Rinzai attained great enlightenment.

APPRECIATORY VERSE

Fledgling phoenix, a thousand-league horse—
a true wind traverses the bamboo flute
and life's activities function freely.
When coming suddenly, lightning strikes swiftly.
Where deluded clouds part, the sun shines alone.
Stroking the tiger's whiskers, don't you see?
He is indeed a great and powerful man.

This story of Rinzai's awakening is very well-known. This koan is actually a short excerpt from the event as recorded in the *Transmission of the Lamp*:

From the beginning of his residence with Obaku, Rinzai's performance of his duties was exemplary. At that time, Bokushu served as the head monk. Bokushu asked Rinzai, "How long have you been practicing here?" Rinzai said, "Three years." Bokushu said, "Have you gone for an interview with Master or not?" Rinzai said, "I haven't done so. I don't know what to ask him." Three years of study! Master Bansho commented that this record surely must be incorrect. How could Obaku allow a student to remain for three years without asking a question?

With utmost compassion, Bokushu told Rinzai what to ask! Bokushu said, "Why not ask him, 'What is the essential meaning of Buddhism?'" Rinzai very dutifully went to see Obaku, and before he could finish his question Obaku hit him a sharp blow. Bokushu asked him what happened. Rinzai said, "Before I could get the words out, he hit me! I don't understand!" Bokushu said, "Go ask him again!" Rinzai asked Obaku again, and Obaku hit him again. Then Rinzai asked a third time, and Obaku hit him a third time. Rinzai related this experience to Bokushu, saying, "You urged me to go ask about the Dharma, but all I got was a beating. Because of evil karmic hindrances, I am not able to comprehend the essential mystery, so today I am going to leave here." Bokushu said, "If you are going to leave, you must say goodbye to the Master."

Rinzai bowed and went off, and then Bokushu went to Obaku and said, "That monk who asked you the questions: although he is young he is extraordinary. If he comes to say goodbye to you, please give him appropriate instruction. Later he will become a great tree under which everyone on earth will find refreshing shade." The next day, when Rinzai came to say goodbye to Master Obaku, Obaku said, "You don't need to go somewhere else, but just go over to the Goan Monastery, and practice with Daigu. He will explain to you."

When Rinzai reached Master Daigu, Daigu said, "Where have you come from?" Rinzai said, "From Obaku." Daigu said, "What did Obaku say?" Rinzai said, "Three times I asked him about the essential doctrine, and three times I got hit. I do not know where my fault was." Daigu said, "Obaku is so kind! He exerted himself to the utmost for you. Why do you still speak of fault and no fault?" whereupon Rinzai suddenly had a great awakening and said, "There's not much to Obaku's Buddhadharma!" Daigu grabbed him and said, "You little bed-wetter! You just said you don't understand, and now you say there's not much to Obaku's Buddhadharma?" And Rinzai hit Daigu three times. Daigu pushed him away, and said, "Your teacher's Obaku. It has nothing to do with me. Go away!"

So, Rinzai returned to Obaku, who saw him coming and said, "This fellow who's coming and going, how can he ever stop?" Rinzai replied, "Only through grandmotherly concern." He was praising his teacher: "I'm only stopping because of your grandmotherly kindness." Rinzai then bowed and stood in front of Obaku. Obaku said, "Who has gone and returned?" Perhaps you've been asked a similar question. Rinzai said, "Yesterday I received the Master's compassionate instruction. Today I went and practiced at Daigu's." Obaku said, "What did Daigu say?" Rinzai then recounted his meeting with Daigu, and Obaku said, "This old fellow Daigu talks too much! Next time I see him I will give him a swat!" Rinzai said, "Why wait until later? Here's a swat now!" and he hit Obaku. Obaku yelled and said, "This crazy fellow has come here and grabbed the tiger's whiskers!" Then Rinzai shouted, "*Katsu!*" And Obaku then yelled to his attendant, "Take this crazy man out of here!"

Rinzai's lineage is one of the two surviving lineages of Zen. Rinzai's enlightenment is important to understand. It's important that we realize what he realized. Letting go of all concepts of enlightenment, just be present to the moment.

The very first sentence from the *Transmission of the Lamp* says, "From the beginning of his residence at Obaku, Rinzai's performance of his duties was exemplary." The Buddha said, "If you students exert meticulous effort, nothing will be difficult to accomplish." And I add that if one who practices becomes lax, it will be impossible to accomplish anything.

When you're sitting zazen, that's like rubbing two sticks together to make a fire. As you keep rubbing, it starts to get warm and maybe a little uncomfortable. But if you stop there, you've missed the best part! When your practice gets difficult, that's the best part. Keep going! Master Dogen said, "Be precise, not careless. Proceed forward; do not regress." Rinzai's meticulous effort in his duties at the monastery prepared his body and mind for his encounters with his teachers.

In our Zen practice, we're not like beasts of burden or assembly-line workers, just doing the same thing over and over and over again. We have to infuse life, vitality, and energy into everything that we do by being present. Whether it's painting the wall, cleaning the kitchen, or pulling the weeds, it's the most wonderful weed pulling I've ever done. I want to do that over and over and over and over again, with each breath. Many times we talk about our unspoken truths, the conditioning that we aren't even aware of. How can we expand our awareness so that we see it functioning? It took Daigu's comments for Rinzai to see Obaku's intent. How do you see it directly?

CASE 87

Sozan's With or Without

PREFACE TO THE ASSEMBLY

Though one tries to close the gate, it opens with a push. Though a boat seems to want to sink, a push of the pole rights it at once. Entering the deep valley, there is no way to return. Stretching to heaven, a great mountain reveals a gateway. Tell me: Where can you go?

MAIN CASE

Attention! Sozan arrived at Isan's and asked, "I've heard that you say, 'To be with or without words is like a vine dependent on a tree. When suddenly the tree falls, the vine withers.' Where do the words return to?" Isan laughed aloud, "Ahhaahhaa!" Sozan said, "I've come four thousand *li* selling cushions. Osho, how can you play around with me?" Isan called his attendant and told him to get some money, and give it to this monk. Then he prophesized, "Later on, there will be a one-eyed dragon who will enlighten you." Later Sozan arrived at Myosho's place and told him this story, and Myosho observed, "I would say that Isan was right from head to tail, but he did not meet up with the one who knows." Sozan again asked, "When a tree falls and a vine withers, where do the words return to?" Myosho said, "Once again, you make Isan laugh!" At these words, Sozan had a realization, and exclaimed, "From the first, Isan's laughter had a sword!"

APPRECIATORY VERSE

A vine withers, a trees falls, and Isan is asked.
The great laugh—*Ahhaahhaa!*—is not to be made light of.
Clearly see that within the laugh there is a sword.

When words and thoughts are without a path,
schemes are extinguished.

The Sozan Kyonin in this case is recorded as a Dharma heir of Tozan, but he should not be confused with Sozan Hunjaku, who founded the Soto School with Tozan. This old monk Sozan was apparently quite a character! He seems to have been a rather contradictory fellow. He traveled around a lot, and his search for enlightenment took him to many teachers. The dates of his birth and death are not recorded, but from his contemporaries, we know that he lived in the ninth century in China.

He was said to have been very short of stature, and apparently was also ugly and often sickly. The other monks contemptuously called him Uncle Dwarf. Yet he was cleverer than his fellow monks and often bested them in Dharma combat. He was not well loved by his peers. It was said that his innate power in displaying the innermost mystery was that of a person who could chew the iron tip of an arrow. He was very tenacious. When the other monks were stumped in their studies, they would say, "You only have to ask Uncle Dwarf."

Some accounts of Sozan are not so flattering. When he was at Tozan's monastery, and he knew that Tozan was about to transmit the Dharma to Sozan Hunjaku, Uncle Dwarf sneaked under the Master's rope chair and lay down on his stomach. Tozan was not aware of it. At midnight, Tozan had the secret Dharma transmission ceremony for Sozan, and Uncle Dwarf was hiding in the room the whole time. When the transmission was complete, Sozan Hunjaku bowed twice and hurried out. Uncle Dwarf stuck his head out from under the chair, and he cried out, "Tozan's Zen is in the palm of my hand!" Tozan was astonished and said, "Stealing the Dharma by using the dirtiest of means will avail you nothing." Thereafter, according to some accounts, Tozan's rebuke caused Uncle Dwarf to vomit whenever he wanted to talk about the Dharma. And yet, after many years, and in spite of his trickery, Uncle Dwarf eventually was approved by Tozan.

Some students are high maintenance, and some are low maintenance; Uncle Dwarf was definitely a high-maintenance monk. He was the burr under the saddle of many of his teachers, yet he should be praised. Sozan made an arduous journey in order to question Isan. Bansho warns that when walking next door to see the neighbors we should have the same resolve as Sozan. Even though he was a high-maintenance and difficult rascal, Uncle Dwarf's mind always was on realizing the truth. Where is your mind when you go to visit the neighbors?

Sozan arrived at Isan's and asked, "I've heard that you say, 'to be with or without words is like a vine dependent on a tree. When suddenly the tree falls, the vine withers.' Where do the words return to?" Isan gave a great belly laugh, *"Ahhaahhaa!"* To be with or without words, still you're clinging to words. When everything you rely on, when everything you depend on falls away, then what? When your health, your means of financial support, your friends, and your family fall away, then what? When you've lost everything you hold dear, to where do you return? It's quite an important, serious question. Yet Isan just gives Sozan a hearty belly laugh! You can well imagine Sozan's reaction.

Sozan had made a great effort to arrive at Isan's. He walked four thousand *li*, about a thousand miles, on foot. He had sewn and sold cushions to sustain himself along the way. He made this great pilgrimage because he had this question burning in his gut. And then Isan laughs!

Isan wasn't laughing at Sozan—he was just laughing! Then Isan sent him to old one-eyed Myosho. Myosho basically tells him, "Isan expressed it right, but you just didn't get it." Yet Sozan persists, he asks his question again to Myosho. And Myosho says, "Once again, you make Isan laugh!" Then Sozan realizes it: "From the first, Isan's laughter had a sword!" Finally, Sozan saw not only the intent of Isan's laughter, but the content of Isan's laughter, the spirit of Isan's laughter. That laugh was the very expression of what everything returns to when everything falls away.

CASE 88

The Shurangama's Unseen

PREFACE TO THE ASSEMBLY

To have seeing and unseeing is to light a torch at midday. To have no seeing and no unseeing, is to pour out black ink at midnight. If you believe that seeing and hearing are like the phantom's shadow, you will know that sounds and colors are like flowers in the sky. Tell me: Is there any sutra teaching at all that we Zen students may talk about?

MAIN CASE

Attention! In the Shurangama Sutra, Buddha says, "When I am unseeing, why don't I see the unseen place? If you say that you see the unseen, that is not the unseen feature. If you don't see my unseen ground, then naturally it's not a thing. Why isn't it that you are not?"

APPRECIATORY VERSE

The great ocean utterly dried;
vast space completely filled;
Zen monks with long noses;
old Buddhas with short tongues.
The silken thread passes nine curves;
the jeweled loom barely rotates once.
Instantly meeting together, who recognizes *him*?
Finally, you'll believe this man who's unaccompanied.

The words of this koan don't seem to make much sense at first, they don't appear to be logical. But you should know that our usual concepts of logic do not necessarily reveal the true meaning of a koan. Let's look a little closer.

The Shurangama Sutra is also called the Brilliant Buddha's Crown, and has been exceptionally important in Chinese Buddhism for centuries. For centuries, Chinese Buddhist masters have written commentaries on this text. One major reason for its popularity is that it mentions fifty deviant mental states associated with the five skandhas of form, sensation, perceptions, conceptions, and consciousness. For each state, a description is given of the mental phenomena experienced by the practitioner, the causes of the phenomena, and the difficulties which arise from attachment to and misinterpretation of the phenomena. So, in essence, what's presented in this sutra is the classification of spiritual experience and the causal factors involved in the experience of phenomena. Although the fifty states presented are by no means exhaustive, the approach taken has the potential of offering a framework for understanding spiritual experience.

It's a controversial text, in part because it only appears in the Chinese canon and thus is considered "apocryphal," but also because it gives very clear and graphic presentations of *wrong* practice, *wrong* views, and the *wrong* use of spiritual power, as well as listing deceptions of deviant spiritual teachers. At one time, the text was even actively suppressed by certain authorities. Nonetheless one of the main themes of this work is that, in themselves, the teachings of the Buddha and knowledge of the Dharma are worthless; they only become valuable when accompanied by practice and insight. The text says, "A distinction is made between the mind characterized by discriminating consciousness and true mind. True mind is found everywhere."

Take the main case, and replace "not seeing" with "not knowing": "When I maintain the mind of not-knowing, why don't I know the not-knowing place?" If you know it then it's not not-knowing! "When I don't know, why don't you know my not-knowing?" If you say that you know the not-knowing, then it's not the not-knowing. "If you don't know my not-knowing ground, then naturally it's not a thing." If it were a thing then it would have properties that you could know. "Why isn't it that you are not not-knowing?" If the two negatives make a positive, this line could read: "Why is it that you are not-knowing?" or from the original "Why is it that you are?" If you are not a thing, what are you and how can you even exist? That is the fundamental question. When you penetrate the koan, "Who am I?", you will know the answer.

We can temporarily rephrase the first part of the main case as, "If seeing were a thing, then you could also see my seeing. And if we objectify not-seeing, then when I don't see, why don't you see my not-seeing?" Now you might get a sense of what this phrase means.

Since seeing is not a thing, how could it not be you? How come it's not true seeing? In the Heart Sutra, we chant, "No eye, no ear, no nose, no tongue, no body, no mind." This implies no seeing, no hearing, and so on. As soon as we label these things, then there's a separation. The labels are not it. What this koan is essentially asking is, if you realize that state of seeing as not-seeing, what is that? Is that your true self? How can you say that it's not your true self? Or, to put back the double negative, "Why isn't it that you are not?"

This phrase has its logic, based upon the experience of emptiness. In a way, the language is a bit stultified, but when you sit with it, each phrase will be revealed.

How do we know what is real and what is not real? According to our Buddhist understanding, everything is impermanent, empty. When you work on a koan, when you try to penetrate into a koan, use all of your understanding to unravel it. Test your understanding against what you know about reality. If you're making it into something fixed, you know right off that that doesn't conform with reality as we Zen Buddhists understand it. So, since your seeing and your not-seeing is not a thing, how could it not be you? Nothing is other than you. This text is saying: "You're not a thing, but then if you're not a thing, what are you?"

The preface to this case says, "To have seeing and unseeing is to light a torch at midday. To have no seeing, no unseeing, is to pour out black ink at midnight." Thus when you clearly see that not-seeing and that seeing, then your true self becomes revealed.

I can imagine that as you try to grasp this teaching, your brain may start to hurt! But truly, if you clearly see that you are not a thing, what is suffering and how does it appear? What does pain become?

The verse says, "The silken thread passes nine curves." This refers to Confucius being challenged by an emperor to thread a jeweled bead that, instead of having a straight hole through it, had a hole that was curved nine times. Confucius tied the thread to an ant, and he put honey in the bead. The ant crawled through and pulled the thread with it through the bead. That's how Confucius solved this koan.

"The jeweled loom barely rotates once." When a shuttle passes through a loom, the pattern begins to appear. When it only rotates once, a pattern is not yet formed. That's the mind of not-knowing: no pattern yet formed. Solving these difficult challenges, threading a nine-curved bead, no pattern is formed.

The Shurangama Sutra also tells us that conceptual knowledge and opinions are the root of ignorance. When conceptual knowledge and points of view are forgotten, wherever you are is nirvana. When we maintain the mind of not-knowing, nirvana is everywhere.

Although this may seem to be twisted logic, just like Confucius you can find your way through. It just depends upon your deep understanding of seeing and not-seeing.

CASE 89

Tozan's No Grass

Move and your body is buried ten thousand feet deep. Don't move, and right there a sprout grows. You'll be fine, if you quickly sweep away both of these and cast out the in-between. Furthermore, buy straw sandals and go on a pilgrimage to realize it.

MAIN CASE
Attention! Master Tozan addressed the assembly, saying, "It's the beginning of autumn and at summer's end, my brothers, some of you will go east, and some west. But straightaway go to a place where there is no grass for ten thousand *li*." After a pause he added, "But for such a place where there is no grass for ten thousand *li*, how can you go there?" Later Master Sekiso said, "Go out the gate, and there's grass." And Master Taiyo later said, "Don't go out the gate, and there's grass everywhere."

APPRECIATORY VERSE
Grass all over.
You, inside and outside the gate, see for yourself!
In a thicket of briars it's easy to place your feet.
In darkness, outside drawn blinds, it's hard to turn your body around.
See! See! How many!
For a time, be as an old tree with wintry skeletal branches;
be about to pursue the spring breezes, about to enter the burned-
out fields.

For Americans grass makes up a beautiful lawn, but to the Chinese and Japanese grass is a weed. In the rock gardens of Japan, blades of grass are immediately removed; it's just the gravel and rocks and trees and moss that remain. No grass means no weeds, no delusions, and no attachments. "No grass for ten thousand *li*," means no grass anywhere (there are about three *li* to a mile). So, in this case, if you go outside the monastery gate, there's grass, and if you don't go outside the gate, there's grass. What are you going to do?

Master Sekiso and Master Taiyo comment on this case although they weren't present for the original event. They weren't even in Tozan's assembly. The compiler of this case collected their comments later. Sekiso commented later the same year and Taiyo made his remark a hundred years later still.

During the time that Tozan was teaching, in the middle of the ninth century, the imperial government was persecuting Buddhists, but Tozan was so well-known that nobody bothered him. Sekiso, on the other hand, hid as a layperson among a commune of potters. He made pots for three years instead of teaching Zen. At the end of that terrible persecution, in 847, one of the monks who was at Tozan's summer retreat met with Sekiso. Sekiso asked him what Tozan taught and the monk told him. Then Sekiso replied, "Go out the gate, and immediately there's grass." The monk went back to Tozan and told him about this, and Tozan proclaimed, "That is a saying of a teacher of fifteen hundred monks." Actually, upon hearing Sekiso's statement, many monks implored Sekiso to become a monk again. He did so and eventually he became the abbot of Stone Frost Monastery, which attracted fifteen hundred monks. Tozan's statement proved prophetic.

A hundred years later, Taiyo said, "Don't go out the gate, and there's grass everywhere." For a hundred years Zen monks had been repeating, "go out the gate and immediately there's grass." Then Taiyo says, "There's grass inside the gate too." Now, what are we repeating a thousand years later?

As mentioned in Case 44, Taiyo was a Soto Ancestor who entrusted his lineage to the Rinzai teacher, Fuzan Hoen. The Soto lineage would have ended if it hadn't been for this. After Taiyo died, Fuzan protected Taiyo's Dharma, and transmitted it to Tosu Gisei. Tosu Gisei is a testament that the Soto and Rinzai Schools do indeed complement each other. There's a kind of carping that goes on between Rinzai and Soto adherents, even today in Japan—but at its base this kind of squabbling is foolish. My teacher Maezumi

Roshi tried to bring both schools together, particularly since he was empowered by masters from both the Soto and the Rinzai Schools.

The point of this koan is to see one's true self and remain undisturbed inside and outside. To be undisturbed outside means seeing the True Nature of phenomena without adding anything extra; to be undisturbed inside means seeing the True Nature of one's self without sprouting delusions. In the *Gateless Gate* Master Baso said that mind is Buddha. It's our everyday mind, the mind with which we wake up, the mind with which we urinate, the mind with which we eat our breakfast, the mind with which we walk, the mind with which we practice zazen, and the mind with which we work—this very mind is Buddha. Yet when we try to describe it, it eludes us. As soon as we describe it, grass springs up everywhere.

I recall a cartoon in which there were two scientists standing in front of a chalkboard with mathematical symbols and equations all over it. At the end of the equations one of the scientists had written, "Then a miracle occurs!"—and followed that with his solution. The other scientist commented, "I think you need to refine your analysis a little." Yet when you enter the zendo, walk to your seat, sit down on a cushion, and start to practice zazen, a miracle does occur! A miracle occurs when you're walking. A miracle occurs when you're sitting down. A miracle occurs when you're focusing on your breathing. When this miracle occurs, true self reveals its face. There's no linear, logical way you can explain it to anyone unless they have had a common experience.

Yet thoughts arise continually like grass and we miss this miracle. When thoughts arise rapidly in a sequence, it gives rise to ideas. It's like a crowd of people. Each person in the crowd is moving around individually, but the effect gives rise to the appearance of the phenomenon you call a crowd. But whenever you look closely at a crowd, all you see is individuals, with spaces between them. If we look closely at our mind, we see there are gaps between the thoughts. Who are you when there are gaps between the thoughts?

In the *Blue Cliff Record* Master Tozan said, "When you're hot, be hot; when you're cold, be cold." What self is there, other than that? Going outside the gate, I meet myself everywhere. Inside the gate, I meet myself everywhere.

The modern Rinzai master Soyen Shaku said, "Don't think that your body is your body; it's the body of all beings. Don't think that your mind is your mind; it's the mind of all beings." We act as if we had lasting, independent, and separate selves. And it's our constant preoccupation to foster and protect it. It's an ingrained, unconscious habit that most of us are unlikely to question or explain. Yet all of our suffering is associated with this preoccupation. All loss, all gain, all pleasure, and all pain arise because we identify so closely with this vague feeling of the self that we have. We take it for granted.

The verse to this case says, "In darkness, outside drawn blinds, it's hard to turn your body around." Since it is difficult to see, you have to be exceedingly careful. Wherever you turn, grass springs up. Truly, though, there's no firm ground upon which to stand. As soon as you make it firm, that's a grass. How can you turn your body without creating weeds?

CASE 90

Kyozan Respectfully Declares It

PREFACE TO THE ASSEMBLY

To say, "I alone am sober," is indeed to be stumbling drunk. Kyozan speaks of a dream as if he were awake. Bansho talks thus, and all of you listen thus. Tell me: Is this waking or is it dreaming?

MAIN CASE

Attention! Kyozan had a dream in which he went to Maitreya's place and sat in the second seat. The Venerable One said, "Today it is time for the one in the second seat to speak." At that Kyozan stood up, struck the sounding post, and said, "The Dharma of the Mahayana is beyond all words. I respectfully declare it."

APPRECIATORY VERSE

In a dream, wearing robes and meeting the elders,
a forest of saints stretches away to his right.
To be appointed and not give way, strike the sounding post.
Speak the Dharma without fear—a roaring lion,
a heart peaceful as the ocean,
a liver capacious as a peck or a bushel.
From a mermaid's eye, tears flow,
a clam's guts make a pearl.
Sleep-talking—who knows my activity leaks away?
Those with splendid eyebrows should laugh at family skeletons
    so presented.
Separate from the propositions, transcending the hundred negations,
Master Baso and his disciples stopped using medicine for illness.

We've met Kyozan many times in this collection (see appendix).

In this koan, Kyozan talks about a dream. There is a famous dream story from the Daoist literature: "One day, about sunset, Chuang-zi dozed off and dreamed he had turned into a butterfly. He flapped his wings, and sure enough, he was a butterfly. What a joyful feeling as he fluttered about. He completely forgot that he was Chuang-zi. Soon, though, he realized that the proud butterfly was really Chuang-zi who dreamed he was a butterfly. Or was it a butterfly who dreamed he was Chuang-zi? Maybe Chuang-zi was a butterfly, or maybe the butterfly was Chuang-zi."

What is it to be dreaming and what is the state of being awake? What's delusion, and what's enlightenment? In his last Dharma words, Maezumi Roshi said, "The Dharma of thusness has been intimately conveyed from Buddhas and Ancestors. Is has nothing to do with being complete or incomplete, nor does it concern enlightenment upon enlightenment, or delusion within delusion." Delusion within delusion is like a dream within a dream. Master Dogen talks about it as quite a high state of accomplishment that has unlimited merit.

Everything seems to have a real existence, but when we look at it, we realize, as the Diamond Sutra says, "This fleeting world is like a phantom, like a dream." Yet our dreams can seem very real indeed. Everything we see, think, and feel, in our self-grasping ignorance, is a dream. But if everything we experience is a dream, what then is real? To say everything is real is delusion, to say nothing is real misses it. We exist—but not in the way we think.

Padmasambhava, the great eighth-century Tibetan sage said, "When there is no distinction between dream and the waking state, then perfect meditation is realized." Maezumi Roshi used to say, "Practice your koan even when you're sleeping." Because your self is no self, it can arise according to whatever the conditions are, whether you are dreaming or awake. When your dreaming state and your awakened state are not distinguished, perfect meditation is realized.

In his dream, Kyozan stood up and he struck the sounding post, saying, "The Dharma of the Mahayana is beyond all words. I respectfully declare it." Ironic, isn't it? He's telling you in words that it's beyond all words. Tell me: How do you understand this?

Master Ryuge said, "When deluded, you're like a monarch in the dream. When enlightened, you are like a peasant awakening from sleep." If you could govern your dreams, you could be whatever you want to be. So, why not be royalty? Who wants to be a peasant in their fantasies? Yet the Bible says (Matthew 5:3), "Blessed are the poor in spirit: for theirs is the Kingdom of Heaven." But, what's a peasant other than having little, having nothing, carrying nothing around, and being free from encumbrances? Sounds like a description of enlightenment. Going beyond all words, how would you declare it?

CASE 91

Nansen's Peony

PREFACE TO THE ASSEMBLY

Kyozan uses a dream state to reveal the real. Nansen points to the awakening place to make the unreal. If you know that awakening and dreaming are fundamentally nothing, you'll finally believe that real and unreal transcend duality. Tell me: With what kind of eye is this person endowed?

MAIN CASE

Attention! Riko Taifu on one occasion asked Master Nansen, "Dharma Master Jo is exceedingly wonderful. He said, 'Heaven and earth have the same root. The ten thousand things are one body.'" Nansen, pointing to the peony in the garden, said, "Taifu, people nowadays see these flowers as if in a dream."

APPRECIATORY VERSE

Subject and object penetratingly illuminate the root of nature.
Busily appearing and vanishing, its gate is seen.
Letting the mind sport outside the kalpa, what question could there be?
Fixing the eyes before you, wisdom is subtly present.
When the tiger growls, the lonely wind stirs around the rocks;
when the dragon howls, moving clouds over the caves are dark.
Nansen breaks up the dream of those people
who lack knowledge of the magnificent Maitreya.

This koan was classified by Master Hakuin in the eighteenth century as a *nanto* koan, a koan particularly difficult to penetrate. Of course, how much we see depends on each one of us. This same case appears in the *Blue Cliff*

Record, Case 40. It's a wonderful koan. In fact, it says so right in the koan itself: "Dharma Master Jo is exceedingly wonderful. He said, 'Heaven and earth have the same root.'" I add that joy and sorrow have the same root. Tell me: How is this so?

You can learn about Dharma Master Jo in Case 92. In order to see this koan, you need to reveal the ten thousand things as one body. You need to know what is this root of joy and sorrow, heaven and earth, of right and wrong, and enlightenment and delusion.

In the "Song of Enlightenment," Yoka Daishi says, "Neither try to eliminate delusion, nor search for what is real. Ignorance, just as it is, is Buddha Nature. This worldly body itself which appears and disappears like a phantom in this world is nothing other than the reality of life. When you wake up to the reality of life, there's not any particular thing which you can point to and say, 'This is it!'" When you wake up, you still can't name it. To say this is real and that's unreal is to fall into delusion.

Master Nansen says, "People nowadays see these flowers as if in a dream." Do you think that your dreams are only fantasy and that your awakened state is real? In Case 90, Kyozan, in a dream, was trying to make reality. Here, Nansen, pointing to the awakened state, is saying it's unreal. Even awake, you can't put your finger on it. As the preface says, "If you know that awakening and dreaming are fundamentally nothing, you'll finally believe that real and unreal transcend duality."

In the fascicle of the *Shobogenzo* called "Uji" (Being-Time), Master Dogen wrote, "Each instant covers the entire world." How can you cover real and unreal in one instant? We think that our dreams are unreal and our wakened state is real, but fundamentally, they're both empty, without inherent existence. Being empty, how can you transcend real and unreal?

Hold a flower in your hand. It's quite amazing. Don't think, don't analyze, don't judge, don't evaluate, don't rationalize! What is it? Is it real or is it unreal? Are you awake or are you dreaming?

If you hear the word *flower*, it brings up an image. If you see a flower, and think *flower*, it brings up an image. Is what you see a flower or is it not a flower?

One day Master Kisei told his monks, "Sometimes mind surpasses words. Sometimes words surpass the mind. Sometimes mind and words surpass themselves. Sometimes they do not surpass themselves." In Western philosophy, our logic is based upon the binary system. It's right or it's wrong. It's a one or a zero. But in Zen we understand there are other possibilities. In reality, our mind doesn't work like a computer's binary code. Nonetheless we want to put everything in a box: It's either real or else it's not real! We forget there are other logics: It can be both real and not real. It can be neither real nor not real.

If you think that everything, as it is, is enlightened nature, that's a dream. At first, we begin the study of Zen, then we have some insight, then we manifest that understanding in our life. But that's all a dream. Or perhaps you don't study Zen, perhaps you never have any insight, perhaps you manifest no wisdom in your life—that's a dream too. Both enlightenment and delusion are dreams that originate from the same root. What is the one root? But even if you can answer, that root is in a dream too.

But what is this dream that Nansen's talking about? Consider the hazy moon that is covered by wispy clouds. It appears and disappears. Is it real or is it a phantom?

In *The Record of Transmitting the Light*, Master Keizan wrote this poem:

> Though clear waters range to the vast blue autumn sky,
> yet how can they compare to the hazy moon on a spring night?
> Most people want to have pure clarity,
> but sweep as you will, you cannot empty the mind.

What a pity! Try to sweep the mind clear and you leave a trace. How magnificent, the hazy moon on a spring night! It is a wonderful dream!

CASE 92

Ummon's One Treasure

Gaining the great samadhi of supernatural play, understanding the *dharani* of sentient beings' speech and words; Bokushu's pulling forth the spinning drills of the Shin Dynasty; Seppo's fiddling around with the poison snake of South Mountain—don't you recognize these men?

MAIN CASE
Attention! Great Master Ummon said, "Between Heaven and Earth, within the universe, there is one treasure, secretly dwelling in a mountainous shape. Holding forth a torch, facing into the Buddha hall, bring the triple gates above the torch."

APPRECIATORY VERSE
Gathering in reverberations, disliking embellishments—
upon returning, where is your life?
Ranka the woodcutter wonders at having no road;
Koko the apothecary surprisingly had a house.
At night, the river's golden ripples float the Judas Tree's silhouette.
Autumn wind's snowy mist embraces the reed flowers.
Winter fish, resting on the bottom, don't nibble bait.
Amusements ended, a pure song turns the boat around.

The first sentence Ummon speaks in this case was written by Dharma Master Jo in the fifth century. He was a scholar and disciple of the great Kumarajiva who translated the sutras into Chinese. He also appears in Case 91. Jo was sentenced to death for disobeying an imperial order. He asked for a seven-day stay of execution and finished his treatise during that time. He also wrote, "This treasure is empty inside and outside, alone and still, invisible. Its function is a dark mystery."

This treasure is secretly dwelling in a mountainous shape, which is but your own body. We say it's *secretly* dwelling because if you try to look directly at it, you can't see it. And its function is a dark mystery; you cannot fathom how it functions. Can fire burn fire? Can teeth bite themselves? This one treasure does not recognize the one treasure.

This dark mystery is beyond words. It is like trying to explain to another person how to walk. If he or she has never had the experience of walking, how would you explain it? You can't. Do you tell your leg to lift, and then it lifts up? No! You just know how to do it after years of practice. Can you explain how your liver works to somebody else? How about your kidneys? What about sitting zazen and following your breath? Your whole body has to learn. The thought that you grab onto and chase into the realm of fantasy: Can you feel that with your whole body? If you can't, pay closer attention!

There once was a man who lived near a military base which, every morning at precisely six o'clock, would fire off a cannon. The man became so acclimated to it that he slept right through the noise. Then one morning the gun malfunctioned and didn't fire—and at precisely six o'clock the man jerked awake saying, "What was that?"

When everything is functioning smoothly, you don't notice it. You don't notice how your heart functions or how your kidney functions unless they're in distress of some kind. You think you notice how this one treasure functions when you're attached to your view of right and wrong—but then it becomes something other than the one treasure. Then it is not the one treasure.

Master Dogen said, "When the right time comes, the one treasure can be grasped. It is suspended in emptiness, hidden in the lining of clothes, found under the chin of dragons and in the headdresses of courtly ladies." You know that Bodhidharma sat for nine years facing the wall. The treasure hung on the wall for nine years, but he didn't dare look right at it. If you want to see it, come here and I'll give you a big whack, and then you'll know what it is!

In this case, Ummon recites from Dharma Master Jo's treatise, and then adds his own comment: "Carry a torch and face into the Buddha hall." This line seems clear; but then he adds, "Bring the triple gates above the torch."

There are three gates that you walk under as you go into a monastery. Note that Ummon doesn't say, "Bring the torch under the triple gates." If you can bring the triple gates over the torch then you can also take Mount Everest out of your shirt pocket. Quick: Show me!

Bansho comments on Ummon, "Genuine teachers of the Way never limit students to the sphere of reality!" In other words, "Don't get caught in thinking things have to be real!" Don't get tied up with the real, but also, don't get tied up with the unreal. Transcend them both at once!

The one treasure cannot be directly grasped, yet it manifests everywhere. Wherever you look, you see it, and yet when you try to clarify it, it's gone. Master Joshu said, "I do not abide in clarity." Master Ummon expressed it. How about you?

CASE 93

Roso's Not Understanding

PREFACE TO THE ASSEMBLY

Jade thrown at magpies and gold held in the mouths of old rats: its worth is unrecognized and its use is unknown. Isn't there someone who suddenly perceives the jewel in the clothes?

MAIN CASE

Attention! Roso asked Master Nansen, "A man doesn't know the wish-fulfilling *mani* jewel. It is set down intimately in the Tathagata's storehouse. What is this storehouse?" Nansen said, "It is the give-and-take of you and me." Roso said, "What about no give-and-take?" Nansen said, "That's also the storehouse." Roso asked, "What about the jewel?" Nansen called his name and Roso answered. Then Nansen said, "Leave. You don't understand what I'm saying."

APPRECIATORY VERSE

Separating right and wrong, illuminating gain and loss;
responding to this in one's heart, pointing to this in one's palms.
Give-and-take and no give-and-take are both the storehouse.
King O awarded it for those who had competence,
Emperor Ko obtained it from Mosho.
Turning the hub utilizing one's abilities.
We clear-eyed students mustn't be negligent.

The Lankavatara Sutra, written in about 300 A.D., describes the "storehouse consciousness" and that is the storehouse referred to in this case. The Lankavatara Sutra teaches that there are in fact eight consciousnesses.

The first six consciousnesses are the ones we are familiar with: eye consciousness, which perceives shapes; ear consciousness, which perceives sounds; and likewise nose consciousness perceives smells; tongue consciousness, which perceives tastes; body consciousness perceives tangibles; and mental consciousness perceives thoughts. The seventh consciousness is a higher form of mental consciousness which receives and disposes of the data from the lower consciousnesses. It's a discriminator that can either correctly interpret the data or lead to an error in judgment, because of the passions which blind it. This consciousness feeds information back and forth to the lower consciousnesses, thereby directing perception.

The eighth consciousness is the storehouse consciousness. This storehouse consciousness is used to explain such phenomena as memory and experiential continuity. It is the receptacle of all the perceptions, thoughts, and habit energies that are in our consciousness. It's like a granary full of karmic seeds, all of which have the potential to grow into something else according to causes and conditions. They can lead to right or wrong views and right or wrong action. And furthermore, the storehouse consciousness contains everything that ever was or ever will be.

The karmic seed of enlightenment is already in the storehouse consciousness; it just needs the right causes and conditions to bring it forth. The possibility of continuing in deluded views is there too. But the storehouse is passive, and it remains inactive unless it's touched by some activity, by karma. All Buddhas arise from the storehouse, and the enlightened state can be awakened all of a sudden, but until the causes and conditions bring it out, it's inaccessible. All of your other consciousnesses can't penetrate the storehouse. This is a philosophical interpretation, but to really penetrate this koan, you need to reveal the intimate expression of the storehouse.

Ultimately, however, the functioning of the storehouse consciousness is a mystery—just as the works of God are said to be. Consider Ecclesiastes 8:17, "Then I behold all the work of God, that man cannot find out the work that is done under the sun: because however much man may toil in seeking he will not find it out. Even though a wise man claims to know, he shall not be able to find it."

In this koan Nansen says, "It is the giving and taking of you and me." Standing up is a mystery, sitting down's a mystery, hearing a sound is a mystery, uttering a sound in response is a mystery—yet that's what happens in the give-and-take.

The preface asks, "Isn't there someone who suddenly perceives the jewel in the clothes?" This refers to a story in the Lotus Sutra, where there were two friends who met. One was poor and the other was rich. They were drinking together, and the poor one passed out. While he was asleep the rich one took a jewel of great value and stitched it inside his clothing, so that he would find it and then he wouldn't be poor anymore. According to the legend, though, the man never found the jewel—so he continued to live as a poor person even though he had such treasure so close.

The Apostle Paul says in Romans 11:33, "Oh, the depth of the riches and wisdom and knowledge of God. How unsearchable are his judgments, and how inscrutable his ways!" We Buddhists can substitute the term *storehouse consciousness* for *God* in this phrase.

Roso asks, "How about when there's no give-and-take?" Nansen says, "That's also the storehouse." We can look at that "no give-and-take" in several ways. When we don't interact, what's that? That's the classic conundrum: If a tree falls in the woods and no one's around to hear it, is there a sound? When there's no give-and-take, is there a sound or not?

But that's not what Roso and Nansen are talking about. In the Heart Sutra, it says, "No eye, no ear, no nose, no tongue, no body, no mind. No color, sound, smell, taste, touch, phenomena." That's the absolute state, where you and others are so identified that everything disappears—no give and no take. When you're communicating with somebody and you're totally identified with him or her, there's no give-and-take. Just this.

How do you play the guitar without using your hands? How do you kick a soccer ball without using your feet? When you give and take, completely give and take—and then there's no give-and-take. The storehouse has all kinds of seeds: absolute seeds, relative seeds. Whatever you look for is there.

Roso says, "What about the jewel?" Here he's basically saying, "You can't know the storehouse, so how are you going to know what's inside of it?" More importantly, how can you limit it to calling and answering? Nansen calls Roso and Roso answers. Then Nansen scolds him, "Leave. You don't understand what I'm saying." If Roso hadn't answered, what would Nansen have done?

The verse says, "Emperor Ko obtained it from Mosho." Emperor Ko lost his jewel, and he couldn't find it. He sent one of his advisors, whose name was Knowledge, to find it. Knowledge couldn't find it. He sent one whose name was Free From Stupidity. Free From Stupidity couldn't find it. He had another advisor whose name was Eating Shame, and he couldn't find it. Finally, he sent Mosho, whose name means "Subtle Form" or "No Form"—and Mosho found it.

Those who are greedy can't reach it. Those who are totally satisfied don't need it. Still, they all are continuously revealing it.

CASE 94

Tozan's Illness

The inferior don't criticize the superior; the mean don't move the noble. Although one has self-control and follows others, one cannot burden the heavy by means of the light. When the four elements are maladjusted, how does one attend and nurture?

MAIN CASE

Attention! Tozan was ill. A monk asked, "Osho, you're sick. Is there someone not sick?" Tozan answered, "Yes, there is." The monk asked, "Does the one who is not sick look after you?" Tozan replied, "This old monk is able to look after others!" The monk asked, "Osho, how about when you look after others?" Tozan said, "Then the having of sickness is not seen."

APPRECIATORY VERSE

Sloughing off a stinking skin-bag, churning a red heap of flesh.
Before you the nose is straight, right now the skull is dried.
The old doctor doesn't see previous ailments;
the little one's seen, but it's difficult to approach.
When the field's water drains, autumn's wet recedes;
when the white clouds dissipate, the old mountain is chilled.
Stop and eradicate; don't deceive and cheat.
Using nonaccomplishment inexhaustively, he gains the rank.
Exalted tree-top: you're not in the same class.

In this koan, old master Tozan is very sick, and the monk who comes to visit is somewhat rude. Could you imagine visiting your dying teacher and saying, "You're sick. Is there someone not sick?" If he looked up from his sickbed and said, "Get out of here!" wouldn't that be an appropriate answer? But Tozan indulges this monk.

The Heart Sutra says that form is emptiness. Can you see the emptiness of sickness when you're sick? Can you see the emptiness of health when you're healthy?

Some friends own a dachshund whose hindquarters are totally paralyzed. This dog walks using his front legs and drags his body behind him. They put handicapped ramps throughout their house although he is actually pretty good at climbing stairs. My friend says the dog doesn't even know that he's paralyzed. He doesn't know the one who's ill. He doesn't know the one who's not ill, either. This dog just moves with his front legs, and drags his body behind him. He's a very happy dog. I'm sure he'd wag his tail if he could.

The monk asks, "Does the one who's not sick look after you?" Tozan says "This old monk is able to look after others." Doesn't this seem a little backward? Wouldn't you expect the one who is not ill to look after the one who is ill? When you're sick, how do you take care of the one who's not sick? When you're depressed, how do you take care of the one who's not depressed? Don't let your samadhi leak out! Don't let your samadhi be a broken vessel.

In Case 98, Tozan is asked about practice and says, "As to that, I always take heed." Always pay attention. That's how you can look after the one who's not sick. Attention! Embrace the one that's depressed. Embrace the one that's ill.

The monk asks Tozan, "How about when you look after others?" Tozan replies, "Then the having of sickness is not seen." You don't see the one who has any illness. What happens when you take care of the one who's not ill, not stressed, or not depressed? Illness vanishes; stress vanishes; depression vanishes. So where do they go? Don't worry, if you want, you can pull them back at any moment! When you're ready for self-pity, you have plenty of thoughts you can use to pull it up.

As you know, the Buddha started his quest because he wanted to eliminate the suffering of sickness, old age, and death. Yet Bansho commented that the ancients, about to die, frolicked in the realm of old age, sickness, and death. Is that what Tozan is doing here?

When we fear old age, sickness, and death, we're bound at the mercy of temporary circumstances. Our life becomes obsessed with denying our condition, or with trying to change the unchangeable. What a pity!

There is always the thought that things shouldn't be the way they are. If we get rid of *should be, could be, would be,* and of *could have been, should have been,* and *would have been*—what's left? Get rid of your ideas of life and death, and what's left? Of course, we have very strong evolutionary forces that preserve life, but let's do our best to make this life a life that understands the one who does not get old, who does not get sick, and who does not die as well as the one who gets old, gets sick, and dies. This understanding is not something that we can hold onto and write down.

When Tozan was ready to die, he composed a poem for the assembly, shaved his head, sat erect, and died—then everybody started crying and wailing so much that he opened his eyes and scolded them for not giving a dead man any peace! He roused himself to prepare a meal for them, which he called a "Stupidity Meal" to the chagrin of his students. He extended his life for seven more days—then bade them farewell again. He was frolicking and he still had more to teach.

The verse to this koan says, "When the field's water drains, autumn's wet recedes; when the white clouds dissipate, the old mountain is chilled." The best way to understand it is when you're sick, be sick. When you're well, be well. "Stop and eradicate; don't deceive and cheat." If you really want to experience the one who's not sick, you have to see the root of the sickness. Don't just treat the symptoms.

CASE 95

Rinzai's One Stroke

PREFACE TO THE ASSEMBLY

When Buddha comes, hit him. When a demon comes, hit him. With the principle, thirty blows. Without the principle, thirty blows. Do you mistakenly regard this as due to some kind of bitterness, or his not distinguishing good and right? Try to see if you can say.

MAIN CASE

Attention! Master Rinzai asked the administrator monk, "Where have you been?" The monk said, "I have come back from selling brown rice in the province." Rinzai asked, "Is it all sold?" The monk replied, "It is all sold." Rinzai, drawing a line with his staff, said, "Did you sell this?" Thereupon the monk shouted. At that, Rinzai hit him. Next the head cook, the *tenzo*, came and Rinzai told him about the previous incident. The head cook remarked, "The Administrator Monk did not understand your intent, Osho." Rinzai retorted, "How about you?" The tenzo bowed low. Rinzai hit him, too.

APPRECIATORY VERSE

Rinzai's total activity—excellent quality.
His staff-tip has the eye to distinguish autumn fur.
Sweeping away fox and hare, his style is precipitous.
Lightning and fire scorch, transforming fish and dragons.
Life-giving sword, death-giving sword.
Leaning against heaven, illuminating the snow,
more sharply than the hair-blown sword,
evenly performing the decree, distinguishing delicate flavors:
Who meets this painful spot utterly?

It might seem to you that Rinzai is being mean, but he is actually being kind. In the Mahayana tradition, the appropriate response always depends upon circumstances. When Rinzai asked the administrator monk, "Where have you been?" consider the situation: Rinzai is the abbot of the monastery and the administrator monk is one of his senior students. Every time a Zen master asks a question of his students in that environment, there's always a hidden thorn in the mud. You should know that the master is rarely only talking about coming and going.

The range of subjects of pretty much all koans in one way or another is fairly circumscribed: it is emptiness, or enlightenment, or stages of enlightenment, letting go, realizing your true self, manifesting your Buddha Nature, seeing diversity in unity, seeing unity in diversity, transcending unity and diversity, and maybe a few other variations.

The monk here doesn't take the first bait, so Rinzai throws out a second line. Is he asking about selling rice when he says, "Is it all sold?" Did you sell every bit of it, including your self? Did you see that all form is empty, including inside and outside? Did you drop away body and mind? But even that second arrow didn't go very deep. The monk had all of his defenses up. He said, "Yeah, I sold it."

Still Rinzai doesn't give up. He throws out more bait: He holds up his staff, draws a line, and says, "Did you sell *this*?" *This* is priceless. You may have sold the rice, but you can't put a price on *this*.

Then the monk realizes he's in the middle of a Dharma encounter and probably thinks to himself, "Oh, you mean *that* rice! I guess I had better shout," and so he shouts—and Rinzai hits him. The head cook wants to show Rinzai that he understood, so he bows, he doesn't shout—and Rinzai hits him too! Was he at fault? What was Rinzai demonstrating by hitting him?

Rinzai really cared about his monks. He used his stick to put energy in the monk's body. In many of these cases, a blow from the stick and everything's forgotten! See Case 86 for how Rinzai responded to blows from his teacher.

In the preface to this case, it says, "When Buddha comes, hit him. When a demon comes, hit him." Don't be attached to either Buddha or demons.

The verse says, "More sharply than the hair-blown sword." That's a sword that's so sharp, that if the wind blows a hair against it, the hair is cut in two. A student once asked Rinzai, "What is a hair-blown sword?" and Rinzai said, "Dangerous! Dangerous!" In other words, "Watch out!"

The verse also asks: "Who meets this painful spot utterly?" That's the key point. Rinzai said, in talking about his total activity, "When it comes up in the hand, deal with it in the hand. When it comes up in the eye, deal with it in the eye. When it comes up in the ten directions, deal with it like a whirlwind." Depending upon the time, the place, the people involved, and the intensity of the situation you will know how to deal with it. We all practice because we haven't totally met that painful spot. What do we ever do totally? Isn't there always something we hold back, always something we hold onto that we keep in reserve? So, if you meet the painful spot utterly, what happens to you? Dangerous! Dangerous!

CASE 96

Kyuho's Disapproval

PREFACE TO THE ASSEMBLY

Ungo is not concerned with relics resulting from a man's having faithfully observed the precepts. Kyuho did not like to expire while sitting, or to pass away while standing. Gozu didn't need hundreds of birds to convey flowers in their beaks to honor him. Obaku did not envy a monk's crossing over water by floating on a hat. Tell me: Besides those feats, is there something superior?

MAIN CASE

Attention! While Kyuho was at Master Sekiso's monastery, he became Sekiso's attendant. When Sekiso passed away, the assembly wanted to appoint the head monk of the meditation hall as chief priest. Kyuho did not approve, and so said, "Wait until I question him. If he understands our late master's intent, I will serve him as I did our late master." Then he asked the head monk, "Our late master said, 'Go through, desist, cease. One thought is ten thousand years. Cold ashes and withered trees, and one strip of pure white silk.' Tell me: What state of affairs does this clarify?" The head monk said, "It clarifies the affair of a one-colored state." Kyuho said, "If that is so, you do not quite understand our late master's intent." The head monk said, "Don't you approve me? Prepare and bring incense to me." Kyuho did so and then, burning the incense, the head monk declared, "If I did not understand our late master's intent, I won't be able to expire while the incense is still burning." So saying, he sat down and died. Kyuho patted him on the back, saying, "It's not that you can't expire while sitting or pass away while standing. It's just that you haven't seen our late master's intent, even in your dreams."

Sekiso's primary point intimately transmitted to Kyuho.

Expire with the incense smoke and it's still hard to succeed the true
   lineage.

The crane nesting on the moon has a thousand-year dream;
the man dwelling in the snow is lost in one-colored merit.

When sitting cuts off the ten directions, you still bump your head.

Move one step closer, and you'll see a flying dragon.

Ostensibly this koan is about the role of supernatural powers in relation to the path—if we call the ability to die at will a supernatural power. As the preface makes clear, being able to die at will or have wild animals eat out of your hand, being able to read others' minds, or being able to walk on water is not the point of our practice. If you sit intensely, you might find that you can cultivate some of these powers or other ones. Use them as you would any other skill, for the benefit of all beings everywhere. Don't think you're special if you cultivate some of these powers. That was the head monk's fault. Having supernatural powers does not equate to understanding the intent of his late master.

When Master Rinzai was asked about having supernatural powers, he said, "Yes, I have them." "What are they?" He said, "When I'm hungry, I eat, and when I'm tired, I sleep." That's marvelous functioning!

The melodrama with the head monk is only a secondary point of this koan. The main point is to understand what Sekiso's intention really is. The head monk's accomplishments have merit, but he still hasn't seen into the late teacher's intent, even in a dream.

The late master had said, "Go through, desist, cease. One thought is ten thousand years. Cold ashes and withered trees, and one strip of pure white silk." One interpretation of "go through" is that he's saying to go through all of the rest of these states he mentions, but let's take it as a state in itself. How do you go through a gateless gate? You never waver and are steady and consistent. Maintain faith in yourself and in your practice. Maintain courage to face whatever comes up in your practice. Whatever obstacles come up, just go through. Master Hakuin said that a person, even though he may live in the mountains, can nonetheless taste for himself whether the waters of the great sea are salty or fresh—just by taking one step at a time until he reaches the shore of the ocean and then dips in his finger.

"Go through, desist, cease." Desist holding onto your ignorance. Desist your self-grasping ignorance. Desist the kind of thinking that gets you into trouble. Thinking is in itself fine, but grabbing onto thoughts and images of your self will bring you suffering.

Once you learn how to desist, how to let go of your ego-grasping mind, then cease thinking that you're something special because you let go of your ego-grasping mind! When we practice and have some realization, we may grab onto our experiences to make ourselves better than everybody else. Whatever you think you've accomplished, desist! If you can pass away before the incense burns, desist. If you've dropped away your self-grasping ignorance, then drop away that dropping away. Then it becomes still more subtle.

"One thought is ten thousand years." Whether large or small, yesterday or tomorrow, each creature does not fail to completely cover the entire ground. You can find infinity in a grain of sand or ten thousand years in one thought.

In Case 47 of the *Gateless Gate*, Master Mumon wrote this verse:

> The one instant, as it is, is an infinite number of kalpas.
> An infinite number of kalpas are the same as this one instant.
> If you see into this fact, the true self that is seeing has been seen
>   into.

The cattle ticks, in their life cycle, live on cattle and they mate, and then the offspring drop off the cattle and climb up on a blade of grass and wait until another cow comes by. When another cow comes by, they jump on that cow. In that way they maintain a vibrant gene pool. They sit on that blade of grass until they are stimulated by the scent of a cow. Scientists were interested in how long ticks would stay on that blade of grass waiting for a cow to come by. They took them to the lab. They were in a dormant state waiting for the cow to come by (scientists call it dormant, but we might say it is samadhi). After several months, the scientists stimulated it with the pheromones of a cow, and the ticks jumped.

What does time mean for that cattle tick? Whether it's ten minutes when that next cow comes, or a day, or a week, or a month, it is the same thing. That tick is not sitting there, thinking, "When is a damn cow going to come by? I've been waiting here for two days already!" Not one thought! Just pure awareness.

"Cold ash and withered trees." The head monk will surely become cold ash after he's cremated and the fires have cooled down. How can you become cold ash and still have hot blood pumping through your veins? If you drop away body and mind, that's called the state of cold ash. There's no fear of death and no yearning for it—because you've already dropped away all ego attachments.

"Withered tree": When Americans think of a withered tree, we think of something ugly and dead, but here the withered tree symbolizes maturity. In terms of our practice, it is not only having had experiences of awareness and seeing clearly and having dropped away attachments, like leaves from an old oak. There's something else about a withered tree: the sun can penetrate right through. It doesn't obscure or filter anything. It's just right there. That's a very accomplished state.

The last one of the late master's teachings is, "One strip of pure white silk"—this is what was used for calligraphy in China. Yasutani Roshi used to encourage his students to be like a clean sheet of white paper, clean uncluttered openness on which you can draw anything at all. Or we can imagine becoming like a mirror that reflects anything without getting stuck. It will reflect garbage, but it won't stink. One strip of pure white silk is free to be anything, according to what the situation is. The head monk was attached to that one-colored state. When it snows, everything's white, but when the sun comes out and the snow melts, the multicolored hidden bodies are exposed. Conditions change all of the time.

There's a Zen saying that might help you see this koan: "When your bow is broken and your last arrow spent, then shoot with your whole heart!" Let go of all your devices, supernatural and common, and be genuine. Then you will understand the late master's intent.

CASE 97

Emperor Ko's Cap

PREFACE TO THE ASSEMBLY

Bodhidharma had an audience with Emperor Wu, basically in order to transmit Mind. Enkan knew Daichu; he's provided with an unimpeded eye. By saying "Great peace under heaven and long life to the country's king," the emperor's dignity is not offended. By saying, "The sun and moon soften their light and the four seasons are harmonized," the king's rule is brightened up. When a worldly king and a Dharma king have an interview, what sort of matters should they discuss?

MAIN CASE

Attention! Emperor Doko addressed Master Koke, saying, "This humble person has obtained the capital's sole treasure. It is just that no one prizes it." Koke said, "Lend me Your Majesty's treasure, and I'll see." The Emperor pulled down on his hat strings with both hands, and Koke remarked, "Who could ever put a price on Your Majesty's treasure?"

APPRECIATORY VERSE

His Majesty's basic intent is told to one who already knows.
All under heaven have total devotion, a sunflower's heart.
The capital's priceless treasure's taken out;
it's not comparable to Cho's jade and En's gold.
The capital's treasure presented to Koke,
the primal light is hard to price.
The emperor's reign sets an example for ten thousand generations.
The Golden-Wheel King's brilliance lights the four lands under heaven.

This case is about an interview between an emperor, who has the power to grant continued physical life or kill with a command, and Master Koke, who has the ability to give and take spiritual life with a word. Koke (830–888) was a direct successor of Master Rinzai. We don't know much about him, but all of the present-day Rinzai lineages pass through him.

To penetrate this koan we must first grasp what the treasure really is. Why does nobody prize it? Then we must see how a person of the Dharma treats a person of unbridled power.

If this treasure were bright and sunny and shiny, it would attract all kinds of seekers. But, when the treasure is hidden, who will see it and value it? If I ask you, like Koke said, "Lend me your treasure, and I'll see," if you tug on your hat strings and say, "It's me, the Emperor!" then you're neglecting others. And if you say it's others, then you're neglecting me. And if you say it's me and others, then you're neglecting not me and not others! If you say it's me, others, me and others, and not me and not others, then all you've done is confuse the issue.

Koke doesn't agree with the emperor's understanding in this case yet still encourages him without patronizing him or alienating him. "Who could even put a price on Your Majesty's treasure?" If he named the price too low, he would insult the emperor. If he named the price too high, he would give false praise. Truly, it's priceless.

There is a children's story about a royal tiger who had to find a new minister of state because he had just eaten the chicken who was filling the post. Three animals applied for the job: a goat, a monkey, and a rabbit. First, the tiger faced the goat and exhaled loudly, "Ahhhhhhhh! Tell me: Is my breath foul or sweet?" The goat was gagging, could hardly stand the smell, but he knew that if he told the tiger it was foul, he might not like it. So he said, "Your breath is very sweet!" The tiger said, "How can I trust a liar like you to handle my affairs of state?" And the tiger ate the goat. Next it was the monkey's turn. The tiger exhaled, "Ahhhhhhhh! Tell me: Is my breath foul or sweet?" The monkey had learned from the goat, so he said, "Oh, it's foul indeed!" The tiger said, "How can I trust so rude a fellow as you to handle my affairs of state?" So the tiger ate him too! Then it was the rabbit's turn. The tiger asked the same question, but the rabbit didn't answer immediately, he just sat there with his nose twitching. Finally, the tiger said again. "Tell me: Is my breath sweet or foul?" The rabbit just kept twitching his nose. Finally, after the tiger asked a third time, the rabbit said, "Sir, I have this terrible cold, and I can't smell a thing!" And the tiger said, "You're a clever fellow. I think that you will be a fine minister of state!"

Koke and the rabbit are teaching us how to navigate through the treacherous waters between life and death. How do you relate to people without insulting or flattering them? Great vows of compassion come and go, but who can put it into practice?

A line of the verse says, "All under heaven have total devotion, a sunflower's heart." Emperor Doko had conquered many lands, and demanded total devotion from all of his subjects and Koke turned to him like a sunflower turns to the sun. Yet the sunflower still keeps its roots in the ground. The head follows the sun, but the base doesn't move.

"The capital's priceless treasure's taken out." When the emperor pulls his hat strings, this is like a king tapping his crown. I once witnessed the Black Crown ceremony, performed by the Sixteenth Karmapa, in which he manifested as Avalokiteshvara Bodhisattva. At the moment when he puts the crown over his head, he manifested his treasure. I and several hundred others watched as he picked his nose. He had this beautiful jeweled crown over his head and that is how he manifested the great compassionate Avalokiteshvara Bodhisattva! How would you manifest the great compassionate Avalokiteshvara Bodhisattva?

In another koan, a monk said to Master Hogen, "We know that the master has hidden a jewel in his robe. Today at the assembly, please show it to us." Hogen said, "There is an appropriate way to get it." Did Hogen bring it out or not? How would you bring it out and how much is it worth?

CASE 98

Tozan's Heed

PREFACE TO THE ASSEMBLY

Kyuho cut off his tongue and went along with Sekiso. Sozan cut off his head, and didn't go against Torei. Men of old with tongues of only three inches could thus be intimate. Well, where are these expedients for the sake of others?

MAIN CASE

Attention! A monk asked Tozan, "Among the three bodies, which one does not fall into any category?" Tozan replied, "As to this, I always take heed."

APPRECIATORY VERSE

Not entering the world, not conforming to externals.
There's a family secret in the kalpa jar and empty place.
White duck weed, faint breeze, autumn river's dusk.
Ancient bank, boat returning, a belt of mist.

"The three bodies" refers to the three bodies of the Buddha, which have been articulated in the various Buddhist writings: the dharmakaya, the samboghakaya, and the nirmanakaya.

Dharmakaya literally means "body of great order" or "body of the Dharma." That body is the True Nature of the Buddha, Buddha Nature itself. Essentially, it's ineffable. If you express it, that's not the dharmakaya. The dharmakaya is your true self. The second body is the *sambhogakaya*, "body of delight," which refers to bodies of the Buddhas in paradise. It's sometimes described as the ecstasy of enlightenment. The *nirmanakaya* is the "body of transformation." It is the earthly body in which Buddhas appear in order to teach and serve others. It is represented by the historical person who was Shakyamuni Buddha.

There's an analogy from medicine that illustrates the relationship between the three bodies. The dharmakaya is medical knowledge, the sambhogakaya is the education that a doctor receives through which he or she realizes the knowledge of the dharmakaya, and the nirmanakaya is the act of utilizing this training to heal people. More simply, the dharmakaya is wisdom, the sambhogakaya is the realization of wisdom, and the nirmanakaya is utilization of wisdom.

So: which body doesn't fall into any category? These categories are all just ways of talking about things. Ultimately there are no three bodies of the Buddha. They are not three things, but rather just three different views of the same reality. And yet each one of them is a complete representation of the unified whole.

To divide reality into three, and then to ask which one doesn't fall into any category, is grasping after straws to begin with. To even ask such a question, Master Bansho says, is like a cat pissing in your house. When your cat pisses in the house, what's the appropriate response? Tozan said, "As to this, I always take heed."

As I mentioned before, Sochu Roshi used to tell us to always question everything. When you walk down the street, constantly ask, "What is it?" You see a car drive by, "What is it?" A dog barks? "What is it?" You feel the brisk wind. "What is it?" Smell the flowers in spring? "What is it?" One time he did a calligraphy for me, and he wrote on it in English, "A B C D C B A." Then he asked, "What is it?" And I said, "It's letters." He said, "No! It's not letters. What is it?"

Tozan said, "I always take heed." What's that *always*? It doesn't mean that I take heed when I feel good. It doesn't mean I take heed when I have had enough sleep. It doesn't mean I take heed when I feel like it. It means *always!* It's incredible.

The preface says, "Kyuho cut off his tongue and went along with Sekiso; Sozan cut off his head, and didn't go against Torei." Kyuho was a student of Sekiso, and when asked about the meaning of his late teacher, he said, "I would rather bite off my tongue than violate my late teacher's warnings." Sozan, a successor of Tozan, when asked about Tozan's "take heed," said, "If you want my head, cut it off and take it." If he tells you, then that's not it.

Kyuho and Sozan are being very intimate, although you might imagine that they are simply being contrary. Truly, theirs is grandmotherly kindness! If they were to tell it to you outright, then whatever they said would just become an idea or a concept. You have to experience these three bodies yourself. Nobody can do it for you. Elsewhere Tozan said, "Don't seek it anywhere else, or it will run away from you."

Everything that we do, everything that we say, everything that we think has consequences—pay heed! When you act, take heed. When you speak, take heed. When you think, take heed. Don't seek it anywhere else.

CASE 99

Ummon's Bowl and Pail

PREFACE TO THE ASSEMBLY

For chess, there's a special kind of knowledge. For wine, there's a special kind of stomach. A clever rabbit has three holes. A sagacious fox makes ten thousand raids. Moreover, there's a stubborn person. Tell me: Who is he?

MAIN CASE

Attention! A monk asked Ummon, "What about speck-of-dust samadhi?" Ummon said, "Rice in the bowl, water in the pail."

APPRECIATORY VERSE

Rice in the bowl, water in the pail.
Opening the mouth, exposing the kidneys;
seeking one who knows—
Try to think about it, and you fall into the second or third levels;
face to face suddenly becomes ten thousand *li* apart.
Master Ummon is worth a little.
Gold-cutting empathy: Who'd be thus together with him?
Flexible and firm mind. Alone, he can be like this.

Samadhi means "to make firm" in Sanskrit, but the word is used to refer to deep states of concentration or meditative absorption. There are different kinds of samadhi. In his final words, Maezumi Roshi told us to "play freely in self-fulfilling and other-fulfilling samadhi." "Self-fulfilling" samadhi is translated from the Japanese *jijuyu* samadhi. In the fascicle of the *Shobogenzo* called "Bendowa" (The Wholehearted Way), Master Dogen wrote: "Jijuyu samadhi is the proper method and standard of transmission from Buddha to Buddha. To achieve this samadhi, you must enter the true gate of zazen, the best method of manifesting enlightenment. It's present in everyone, but unless there is practice, it cannot be manifested. Unless there is realization, it cannot be perceived. One or many, horizontal or vertical, cannot limit or describe it. Speak it, and it has already filled your mouth. Let it go, and it fills your hand. Buddhas exist within *jijuyu* samadhi without attachment. Sentient beings also exist therein, but do not realize how their consciousness and perceptions function. Through this samadhi we can find true reality and achieve perfect harmony. Just abandon discrimination."

Ji means "one's self," *ju* means "receives," and *yu* means "freedom." So *jijuyu* means "one's self receives freedom" or "one's own freedom." This samadhi of one's own freedom is true freedom that comes from practice. And to realize it, you must "enter through the true gate of zazen." Without practice, it can't be manifested. We can talk about it all we want, but still we have to practice. We have to practice letting go of all of our attachments to our thoughts, our ideas, and our judgments, and furthermore, attachments to our projections, our images, and our ideals.

Dogen goes on to say, "This is a power which you cannot grasp with your rational mind. It operates freely, according to the situation in a most natural way. At the same time, this power functions in our lives to clarify and settle activities and to benefit all living things." I might add that it functions to benefit insentient things too. It benefits the environment and the whole world. But in order for it to do that, we have to sit, develop samadhi, develop this power of concentration, and realize self-fulfilling samadhi. Only then can we "play freely in self-fulfilling and other-fulfilling samadhi."

Samadhi is not just intense mental energy. All kinds of people can develop intense mental energy, the ability to concentrate on what they're doing. An excellent musician requires wonderful, intense concentration while performing. After the concert, the musician's spouse might say, "You forgot to take out the garbage!" If they start to argue, where did the samadhi go?

The point is not merely to develop intense mental energy, because in this intense mental energy, often there are two things: the object of the concentration, and the one who's concentrating. In Zen practice, samadhi ideally goes beyond concentration, and the two melt away. There's not two. There's not even one!

But this takes time and patience. At first, the inner creature of the mind is more like a monkey than a lion. In the "Tenzo Kyokan" (Instructions to the Cook) Dogen wrote, "The mind and emotions are unmanageable, like monkeys swinging in a tree, grabbing at bright lights, jumping here and there after anything that glitters." After the mind has run out of all of its tricks, it becomes bored. If you become bored in your practice, then you're making progress. Just be bored! Boredom is only another thought. Most people, when they run into barriers in their lives and their practice, end up blaming themselves and thereby rejecting the very agent of their realization: their own lives.

The Flower Ornament Scripture speaks of "entering right samadhi on every speck of dust." That's where the monk got his question, "What about speck-of-dust samadhi?"

If everything is absolute in itself, every speck of dust reveals the whole universe. You can enter right samadhi on a flower, on a pebble, on a soaring hawk, on a child crying, on a pile of rubble, on a broken tile, on a leaf falling in the wind. When you rise from right samadhi, everything is more luminous, including yourself, because the boundaries between self and other have disappeared, if even briefly. Samadhi manifests as wisdom, and wisdom manifests as compassion.

When the monk asked Ummon, "What about speck-of-dust samadhi?" Ummon said, "Rice in the bowl, water in the pail." Ummon has boiled it down for us. It doesn't mean that in the bowl there's rice, and in the pail there's water. It does not mean to eat rice and to drink water; nor does it mean that rice is white and water is wet. Strip away all of your ideas. Strip away everything extra and "rice in the bowl" and "water in the pail" will be revealed as speck-of-dust samadhi.

CASE 100

Roya's Mountains and Rivers

One word can make the country prosper; one word can make the country perish. This medicine can both kill or can save lives. Seeing this, a person of virtue sees it as virtue and a person of wisdom sees it as wisdom. Tell me: Where is the profit or loss to be found?

MAIN CASE
Attention! A monk asked Kaku Osho of Roya, "If the original state is clean and pure, then why suddenly do rivers, mountains, and the great earth arise?" Kaku replied, "If the original state is clean and pure, then why suddenly do the mountains, rivers, and great earth arise!"

APPRECIATORY VERSE
Seeing existence, don't take it as existence.
Turning the hand up, turning the hand down,
the man in Mount Roya—
he does not fall behind Gautama.

The specifics of Kaku Osho are not known, but he lived sometime in the tenth century. When his father died, Kaku carried the casket back to their original home. As he was passing through Li province, he climbed up to the ancient Zen monastery of Yakusan to pay his respects. When he looked around, he felt as if he had lived there before and because of that he formally left home and became a monk. He studied with Fun'yo Zensho and eventually became his successor.

During one winter training period, Fun'yo Zensho stopped the night zazen because it was so bitter cold that everybody was having a difficult time. One day, when he was in his quarters trying to keep warm, an Indian monk arrived there flying on a cloud, and begged the master not to waste the time. He said, "Though this congregation is small, six of them are great vessels and their teachings will liberate many beings." So the very next day, Fun'yo continued the schedule. One of those six is the famed master in this case, Kaku Osho of Roya.

In this case, the monk asked, "If the original state is clean and pure, then why suddenly do rivers, mountains, and the great earth arise?" If the mind is pure in its original state, why does it suddenly produce mountains, rivers, earth, and all the phenomena which continuously arise, change, decay, and then begin again?

In response, Master Roya just repeated the question, but made it into a statement. "If original state is clean and pure, how does it suddenly produce rivers, mountains, and earth!" In Zen, we call this, "mounting the bandit's horse to pursue the bandit." In the mouth of the monk these words are a question. In Roya's mouth they are a lion's roar. The original state is pure! Mountains and rivers suddenly appear!

Do you understand? The problem is that when painful or uncomfortable situations or feelings arise, we think that they're not pure. The truth is that they're neither pure nor impure. But we interpret them in a way that fits into our world view. If it doesn't fit into our world view, then it's impure. The basic problem is that one's world view is impure, based on false assumptions. We would rather criticize someone else to maintain our world view than to open our heart and include them in it.

In Case 23 of the *Gateless Gate*, the Sixth Ancestor said, "Think neither good nor evil. At such a moment what is your true self?" The Sixth Ancestor's statement could also be taken as an exclamation and then that statement is identical with Roya's. When you think neither good nor evil, the original state is pure. That is your true self! Mountains and rivers suddenly appear!

Referring to the pure original state and emptiness, Yasutani Roshi said, "Pure undefiled state can form the ten thousand dharmas. This emptiness is the world of absolute equality. Form is the world of absolute differences. Please appreciate the effect of this word 'absolute.' Absolute means the whole

universe is nothing but equality. The whole universe is nothing but differentiation. Therefore, equality and difference are always of the same value, or
rather than of the same value, they are the same thing. When one says 'equality,' equality swallows up differences. It's not rejecting differences. And differences have no place to show their face. That's what's called 'absolute
equality.' Likewise, when one says 'difference,' differences completely swallow up equality. They're not ignoring equality. And equality has no place to
show its face. That's what's called 'absolute differences.' Thus, although the
language is the same, the words 'absolute equality' and 'absolute differences'
as they are used in the Buddhadharma have a completely different meaning
from the way they are ordinarily used." This is a conceptual explanation, but
it offers a new spin. Thoughts can be transmitted by other thoughts, but living reality cannot be transmitted by thoughts.

A student said to Bankei, "My wisdom is tightly confined within me, but
I am unable to make use of it! How can I use it?" Bankei said, "My friend,
come closer!" When the student came a few steps closer, Bankei said, "How
wonderfully well you're using it!" We use it all the time. If the original state
is clean and pure, then why suddenly do the mountains, rivers, and the great
earth arise?

If our wisdom is tightly bound inside of us, how do we use it?

APPENDIX
Masters Referenced in The Book of Equanimity

I. ANCIENT CHINESE AND JAPANESE ANCESTORS

Key: A number alone (with no letter following it) indicates that the master appears in the main case corresponding to the number. **V** following the number indicates the master appears in the verse, **P** in the preface, and **C** indicates that the master is mentioned in the commentary.

ROMANJI (JAPANESE)	PINYIN (CHINESE)	WADE-GILES (CHINESE)	CASES
Bankei Butchi			57C 100C
Bansho Gyoshu	Wansong Xingxiu	Wan-sung Hsing-hsiu	4C 5C 10C 28C 31C 64C 68C 70C 71P 72C 73C 80C 86C 87C 90P 92C 94C 98C
Baso Doitsu	Mazu Daoyi	Ma-tsu Tao-i	6 8C 9C 16C 23C 25C 36 89C 90V
Beiko (Keicho Beiyu)	Jingzhao Mihu	Ching-chao Mi-hu	62
Bokushu Domyo	Muzhou Daoming	Mu-chou Tao-ming	64V 86C 92V
Chizo (*see* Seido Chizo)	Zhizang		6
Chokei Eryo	Changqing Huileng	Ch'ang-ch'ing Hui-leng	24 64 71
Chosha Keishin	Changsha Jingcen	Ch'ang-sha Ching-ts'en	62C 69C 79
Chuyu Koon	Zhongyi Hongen	Chung-i Hung-en	72
Daibai Hajo	Damei Fachang	Ta-mei Fa-ch'ang	66C
Daigu (*see* Koan Daigu)			86
Daikan Eno	Dajian Huineng	Ta-chien Hui-neng	5C 7C 12C 30C 42C 45C 75C 77C 85C 100C
Daiman Konin	Daman Hongren	Ta-man Hung-jen	12C

Daizui Hoshin	Dasui Fazhen	Ta-sui Fa-chen	30
Dogen (see Eihei Dogen)			
Dogo Enchi	Daowu Yuanzhi	Tao-wu Yuan-chih	21 35C 54 68C 83
E	Hui		79
Eihei Dogen	Yongping Daoyuan	Yung-p'ing Tao-yuan	8C 9C 18C 27C 30C 38C 45C 47C 53C 58C 59C 62C 66C 67C 69C 75C 78C 81C 86C 90C 91C 92C 99C
Eisai			69C
Eka (see Taiso Eka)			45C
Engo Kokugon	Yuanwu Keqin	Yuan-wu K'e-ch'in	48C 80C
Enkan Seian	Yanguan Qi'an	Yen-kuan Ch'i-an	25
Eno (see Daikan Eno)			
Esshu Kempo	Yuezhou Qianfeng	Yueh-chou Chi'en-feng	40 61
Fifth Ancestor (see Daiman Konin)			
Fuke			24C
Fuketsu Ensho	Fengxue Yanzhao	Feng-hsueh Yen-chao	29 34 65C
Fun'yo Zensho	Fenyang Shanzhao	Fen-yang Shan-chao	100C
Fuzan Hoen	Fushan Fayuan	Fu-shan Fa-yuan	44C 89C
Ganto Zenkatsu	Yantou Quanhuo	Yen-t'ou Ch'uan-huo	22 43 50 55 75
Genju	Yancong	Yan-c'ung	41
Gensha Shibi	Xuansha Shibei	Hsuan-sha Shih-pei	12C 21 24 55C 56C 81
Genyo Zenshin	Yanyang Shanxin	Yen-yang Shan-hsin	57
Gokoku Shucho	Huguo Shoucheng	Hu-kuo Shou-cheng	28
Goso Hoen	Wuzu Fayan	Wu-tsu Fa-yen	79C
Gutei Chikan	Jinhua Juzhi	Chin-hua Chu-chih	10C 24C 84
Hakuin Ekaku			19C 37C 53C 66C 80C 91C 96C
Hofuku Juten	Baofu Congzhan	Pao-fu Ts'ung-chan	71
Hogen Bun' eki	Fayan Wenyi	Fa-yen Wen-i	17 20 27 47C 51 64 70C 74 97C
Hyakujo Ekai	Baizhang Huaihai	Pai-chang Huai-hai	6 8 21C 25C 30C 53C 76C 80C 82C 83C
Isan Daian	Guishan Da'an	Kuei-shan Ta-an	30C

Isan Reiyu	Guishan Lingyou	Kuei-shan Ling-yu	15 25C 32C 37 38C 60 62C 68C 77C 83 87
Jizo (*see* Rakan Keichin)			12 20 27C 45C 51C 64 70C
Jo (Dharma Master Jo)			91 92C
Joshu Jushin	Zhaozhou Congshen	Chao-chou Ts'ung-shen	9 10 17C 18 39 47 57 63 69C 79C 92C
Kai (*see* Hyakujo Ekai)			6
Kaku (*see* Roya Ekaku)			47C 51
Kanchi Sosan	Jianzhi Sengcan	Chien-Chih Seng-ts'an	17C 50C
Kanzan	Hanshan	Han-shan	3V
Kassan Zenne	Jiashan Shanhui	Chia-shan Shan-hui	35 68
Keizan Jokin			52C 62C 91C
Kempo (*see* Esshu Kempo)			40 61
Kisei (Sekken Kisei)	Shexian Guixing	She-hsien Kuei-hsing	91C
Koan Daigu	Gaoan Dayu	Kao-an Ta-yu	86
Koke Sonsha	Xinghua Cunjiang	Hsing-hua Ts'un-chiang	97
Konin (*see* Daiman Konin)			
Koshu Tenryu	Hangzhou Tianlong	Hang-chou T'ien-lung	84C
Koun Ejo			38C
Koyo Seibo	Xingyang Qingpou	Hsing-yang Ch'ing-p'ou	44
Kyogen Chikan	Xiangyan Zhixian	Hsiang-yen Chih-hsien	29C 38C
Kyozan Ejaku	Yangshan Huiji	Yang-shan Hui-chi	15 25C 26 32 37 60C 62 72 77 79C 90 91V
Kyuho Doken	Jiufeng Daoqian	Chiu-feng Tao-ch'ien	66 69C 96 98C
Mayoku Hotetsu	Mayu Baoche	Ma-yu Pao-ch'e	16
Mishi Haku	Shenshan Sengmi		56
Mumon Ekai	Wumen Huikai	Wu-men Hui-k'ai	8C 33C 50C 55C 84C 96C
Myosho Tokken	Mingzhao Deqian	Ming-chao Te-ch'ien	87
Nansen Fugan	Nanquan Puyuan	Nan-ch'uan P'u-yuan	9 10V 16 20C 23 39 49C 69 79 91 93
Nan'yo Echu	Nanyang Huizhong	Nan-yang Hui-chung	42 77C 85
National Teacher Echu or Chu (*see* Nan'yo Echu)			

Obaku Kiun	Huangbo Xiyun	Huang-po Hsi-yun	8C 53 80C 86
Rakan Keichin (Jizo)	Luohan Guichen	Lo-han Kuei-ch'en	12 20 64 96P
Rakuho Gen'an	Luopu Yuanan	Lo-p'u Yuan-an	35 41
Razan Dokan	Luoshan Daoxian	Lo-shan Tao-hsien	43
Reiun Shigon			38C 82C
Rikko Taifu			91
Rinzai Gigen	Linji Yixuan	Lin-chi I-hsuan	8C 13 24C 29C 35C 37C 38 46C 53C 65C 80 86 95 96C 97C
Rohi	Lu Pi	Lu-pi	29
Roso Houn	Luzu Baoyun	Lu-tsu Pao-yun	23 93
Roya Ekaku	Langye Huijue	Lang-yeh Hui-chueh	47C 51 100
Ryuge Kodon	Longya Judun	Lung-ya Chu-tun	48V 49V 80 90C
Ryusai Shoshu(Shuzan)	Longji Shaoxiu	Lung-chi Shao-hsiu	12 17 30 70
Ryutan Soshin	Longtan Chongxin	Lung-t'an Ch'ung-hsin	14C
Ryu Tetsuma	Liu Tiemo	Liu T'ieh-mo	60
Sansho Enen	San sheng Huiran	San-sheng Hui-jan	13 33
Seido Chizo	Xitang Zhizang	Hsi-t'ang Chih-tsang	6 46C
Seigen Gyoshi	Qingyuan Xingsi	Ch'ing-yuan Hsing-ssu	5 35C
Seikei Koshin (Shinzan)	Qingxi Hongjin	Ch'ing-hsi Hung-chin	70
Seirin Shiken	Qinglin Shiqian	Ch'ing-lin Shih-ch'ien	59
Sekiso Keisho	Shishuang Qingzhu	Shih-shuang Ch'ing-chu	43C 66C 68 89 96 98V 98C
Sekito Kisen	Shitou Xiqian	S hih-t' ou Hsi-ch'ien	5C 7C 77C
Sensu Tokujo (Boatman Monk)	Chuanzi Decheng	Ch'uan-tzu Te-ch'eng	35C 68C
Seppo Gison	Xuefeng Yicun	Hsueh-feng I-ts'un	21C 24 29C 30C 33 50 55 61C 62C 63V 64V 71C 81C 92C 92V
Setcho Juken	Xuedou Chongxian	Hsueh-tou Ch'ung-hsien	9C 26 34
Shifuku Nyoho	Zifu Rubao	Tsu-fu Ju-pao	25
Shinzan (Seikei Koshin)	Jinshan (Qingxi Hongjin)	(Ch'ing-hsi Hung-chin)	70
Shisho	Zizhao		64
Shokei Eki	Zhangjing Huaiyun	Chang-ching Huai-yun	16
Shoto	Xiaotang		81

Shuzan (see Ryusai Shoshu)			12 17 30 70
Shuzan Shonen	Shoushan Xingnian	Shou-shan Hsing-nien	17C 63C 65 76
Sixth Ancestor (see Daikan Eno)			
Sosan (see Kanchi Sosan)			
Sozan Honjaku	Caoshan Benji	Ts'ao-shan Pen-chi	52 67C 73 87C 98C
Sozan Kyonin	Shushan Kuangren	Shu-shan K'uang-jen	87
Suibi Mugaku	Cuiwei Wuxue	Ts'ui-wei Wu-hsueh	63C 80
Suigan Reisan	Cuiyan Lingcan	Ts'ui-yen Ling-ts'an	71
Taiso Eka	Dazu Huike	Ta-tsu Hui-k' o	45C
Taiyo Kyogen	Dayang Jingxuan	Ta-yang Ching-hsuan	44C 89
Takuan			30C
Tangen Oshin	Danyuan Yingzhen	Tan-yuan Ying-chen	77C 85
Tendo Nyojo	Tiantong Rujing	T'ien-t'ung Ju-ching	18C 46C 69C
Tenryu (see Koshu Tenryu)			
Third Ancestor (see Kanchi Sosan)			
Toku	De		52
Tokusan Emmitsu	Deshan Yuanmi	Te-shan Yuan-mi	46
Tokusan Senkan	Deshan Xuanjian	Te-shan Hsuan-chien	14 22 24C 48C 50C 55 80C
Tosan Shusho	Dongshan Shouchu	Tung-shan Shou-ch'u	51C
Toshi (see Tosu Daido)			63
Tosu Daido	Touzi Datong	T' ou-tzu Ta-t'ung	63
Tosu Gisei	Touzi Yiqing	T'ou-tzu I-ch'ing	44C 64P 89C
Tozan Ryokai	Dongshan Liangjie	Tung-shan Liang-chieh	22 28C 49 52C 54C 56 56C 59C 61C 73C 80C 87C 89 89C 94 98
Ummon Bun' en	Yunmen Wenyan	Yun-men Wen-yen	11 19 21 24 26 31 40 46C 51C 55C 61 67C 71 78 82 92 99
Ungan Donjo	Yunyan Tansheng	Yun-yen T'an-sheng	21 49 54 56C
Wanshi Shogaku	Hongzhi Zhengjue (Tiantong)	Hung-chih Cheng-chueh	7C 21C 62C 80C
Yakusan Igen	Yaoshan Weiyan	Yao-shan Wei-yen	7 21C 69C 83C 100C

| Yoka Genkaku | Yongjia Xuanjue | Yung-chia Hsuan-chueh | 91C |
| Zuigan Shigen | Ruiyan Shiyan | Jui-yen Shih-yen | 75 |

II. INDIAN ANCESTORS AND BODHISATTVAS

Key: A suffix of **C** means the master appears in the commentary. If there is no suffix to the number, the number refers to the main case.

Avalokiteshvara Bodhisattva	54C 82 97C
Bodhidharma	2 3C 20C 23C 45C 68C 92C
Devadatta	5P 56C
Funda	58C
Hannyatara	3
Indra	4 61
Kanadeva	77C
Kumarajiva	92C
Mahakashyapa	13C
Maitreya Buddha	90
Manjushri Bodhisattva	1 48 70C 74C 83C
Nagarjuna	77C
Padmasambhava	90C
Shakyamuni Buddha	1 4 7C 13C 15C 16C 17C 19C 22C 30C 38C 47C 48C 54C 56C 58C 67 81C 82C 84C 86C 88 94C 98C
Subhuti	82C
Upagupta	79C
Vimalakirti	36C 48 74C 83C

III. MODERN ANCESTORS AND TEACHERS

Note: All of these masters appear in the commentaries.

Baian Hakujun	34C 49C 73C
Bernie Glassman	70C
Chogyam Trungpa	62C
Eido Shimano	8C
Hakuun Yasutani	2C 13C 44C 49C 96C 100C
Kalu Rimpoche	51C
Kobun Chino	70C
Koshi Uchiyama	7C
Musu Koryu	49C
Philip Kapleau	79C
Shunryu Suzuki	36C 64C
Sixteenth Karmapa	97C
Sochu Suzuki	8C 26C 37C 45C 64C 98C
Soen Nakagawa	29C
Soyen Shaku	89C
Sueng Sahn	51C
Taizan Maezumi	1C 4C 8C 19C 23C 34C 38C 40C 45C 49C 50C 52C 61C 63C 64C 65C 66C 67C 71C 73C 80C 82C 89C 90C 99C

Suggested Further Reading

App, Urs. *Master Yunmen: From the Record of the Chan Master "Gate of the Clouds."* New York: Kodansha International, 1994.

Cleary, Thomas. *Book of Serenity.* New York: Lindisfarne Press, 1990.

——. *Sayings and Doings of Pai-Chang.* Los Angeles: Center Publications, 1978.

——. *Secrets of the "Blue Cliff Record": Zen Comments by Hakuin and Tenkei.* Boston: Shambhala, 2000.

Cook, Francis Dojun. *How to Raise an Ox: Zen Practice as Taught in Zen Master Dogen's "Shobogenzo".* Boston: Wisdom Publications, 2002.

——. *The Record of Transmitting the Light: Zen Master Keizan's "Denkoroku."* Boston: Wisdom Publications, 2003.

Einstein, Albert. *Ideas and Opinions.* New York: Crown Publishers, 1954.

Epstein, Mark. *Thoughts Without a Thinker: Psychotherapy from a Buddhist Perspective.* New York: Basic Books, 1995.

Ferguson, Andy. *Zen's Chinese Heritage: The Masters and Their Teachings.* Boston: Wisdom Publications, 2000.

Fischer-Schreiber, Ingrid, Franz-Karl Ehrhard, Kurt Friedrichs, and Michael S. Diener. *The Encyclopedia of Eastern Philosophy and Religion.* Boston: Shambhala, 1989.

Foster, Nelson, and Jack Shoemaker, eds. *The Roaring Stream: A New Zen Reader.* Hopewell, New Jersey: Ecco Press, 1996.

Glassman, Bernard. *Infinite Circle: Teachings in Zen.* Boston: Shambhala, 2002.

Haskel, Peter. *Bankei Zen: Translations from the Record of Bankei.* New York: Grove Weidenfeld, 1984.

Koestler, Arthur. *The Act of Creation*. London: Penguin Books, Ltd., 1989.

Loori, John Daido. *Two Arrows Meeting in Midair*. Boston: Tuttle Publishing, 1994.

Maezumi, Taizan. *Appreciate Your Life: Zen Teachings of Taizan Maezumi Roshi*. Boston: Shambhala, 2001.

Maezumi, Taizan, and Bernard Glassman. *Hazy Moon of Enlightenment: On Zen Practice III*. Los Angeles: Center Publications, 1978.

————. *On Zen Practice: Body, Breath, Mind*. Boston: Wisdom Publications, 2002.

Miura, Isshu, and Ruth Fuller Sasaki. *The Zen Koan: Its History and Use in Rinzai Zen*. New York: Harvest Books, 1984.

Nishijima, Gudo Wafu, and Chodo Cross. *Master Dogen's "Shobogenzo"* (4 vols). London: Windbell Publications Ltd., 1994.

Powell, William F. *The Record of Tung-Shan*. Honolulu: University of Hawaii Press, 1986.

Price, A.F., and Wong Mou-Lam. *The Diamond Sutra and the Sutra of Hui Neng*. Boston: Shambhala, 1990.

Schloegl, Irmgard. *The Record of Rinzai*. London: The Buddhist Society, 1975.

Sekida, Katsuki. *Two Zen Classics:"Mumonkan" and "Hekiganroku."* New York: Weatherhill, 1977.

Shibayama, Zenkei. *Zen Comments on the "Mumonkan."* New York: Harper & Row, 1974.

Tanahashi, Kazuaki. *Moon in a Dewdrop: Writings of Zen Master Dogen*. San Francisco: North Point Press, 1985.

Thurman, Robert A.F. *The Holy Teaching of Vimalakirti: A Mahayana Scripture*. University Park: Pennsylvania State University Press, 1976.

Trungpa, Chogyam. *Cutting through Spiritual Materialism*. Boston: Shambhala, 2002.

Uchiyama, Kosho. *Refining Your Life: From the Zen Kitchen to Enlightenment*. New York: Weatherhill, 1983.

Waddell, Norman. *Wild Ivy: The Spiritual Autobiography of Zen Master Hakuin.* Boston: Shambhala, 1999.

Watson, Burton. *The Zen Teachings of Lin-Chi: A Translation of the Lin-Chi Lu.* Boston: Shambhala, 1993.

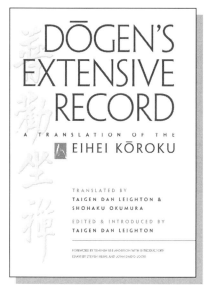

DŌGEN'S
EXTENSIVE
RECORD

A TRANSLATION OF THE
EIHEI KŌROKU

TRANSLATED BY
TAIGEN DAN LEIGHTON &
SHOHAKU OKUMURA

EDITED & INTRODUCED BY
TAIGEN DAN LEIGHTON

FOREWORD BY TENSHIN REB ANDERSON WITH INTRODUCTORY
ESSAYS BY STEVEN HEINE AND JOHN DAIDO LOORI

Dogen's Extensive Record
A Translation of the Eihei Koroku

Translated by Taigen Dan Leighton
and Shohaku Okumura
Edited and introduced by
Taigen Dan Leighton
Foreword by Tenshin Reb Andersen
with introductory essays by
Steven Heine and
John Daido Loori
752 pages, cloth with ribbon,
ISBN 0-86171-305-2, $65.00

"This massive work will be a valuable asset not just for students of the Zen teacher Dogen (1200–1253), but for all students of Zen and Buddhism in general. However celebrated his *Shobogenzo* might be, it presents only a partial Dogen. The *Extensive Record* covers Dogen's entire teaching career, especially the last ten years of his life, which he devoted wholeheartedly to training his successors. The translators, two Soto Zen teachers active in North America, have done an admirable job of rendering Dogen's thirteenth-century Chinese into modern English. The text is remarkably easy to read while also remaining faithful to Dogen's idiom. It is well annotated with footnotes, but not in an overly obtrusive manner. Lengthy indexes allow readers to find dates, names, Japanese pronunciations of Chinese names, and so forth. A detailed bibliography of Chinese, Japanese, and Western-language materials will assist readers who wish to consult other sources in their study of Dogen in particular or Buddhism in general. Three separate introductions provide so much supplemental information that no reader of this volume will be forced to turn elsewhere to make sense of it. In short, Leighton and Okumura's translation of *Dogen's Extensive Record* is a valuable contribution to the growing body of Zen literature available in English. It allows Western readers to discover a new side of Dogen, the side he presented to his own students on a daily basis. It will reward careful study."
—William M. Bodiford, in *Buddhadharma: The Practitioner's Quarterly*

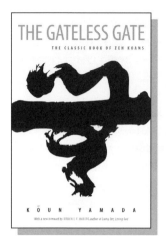

The Gateless Gate
The Classic Book of Zen Koans
Koun Yamada
Foreword by Ruben L.F. Habito
336 pages, ISBN 0-86171-382-6, $16.95

"Koun Yamada Roshi's insightful and profound commentaries on the *Gateless Gate* will help Zen students of all abilities to appreciate the significance of koans, not as riddles, but as touchstones of reality."
—Gerry Shishin Wick Roshi, author of *The Book of Equanimity*

*Includes: An in-depth Introduction to the History of Zen Practice * Lineage charts * Japanese-to-Chinese and Chinese-to-Japanese conversion charts for personal names, place names, and names of writings * Plus, front- and back-matter from ancient and modern figures: Mumon, Shuan, Kubota Ji'un, Taizan Maezumi, Hugo Enomiya-Lasalle, and Yamada Roshi's son, Masamichi Yamada.*

The Art of Just Sitting
Writings on the Zen Practice of Shikantaza, Second Edition
Edited by John Daido Loori
256 pages, ISBN 0-86171-394-X, $16.95

This unparalleled volume offers essential guidance—from the most influential Buddhist masters, and from many of modern Zen's preeminent teachers – on one of Zen's two most central practices. This new edition contains three new translations by renowned scholar-practitioners.

"The single most comprehensive treasury on the subject in English. This book will prove indispensable. A rare treasure."—John Daishin Buksbazen, author of *Zen meditation in Plain English*

On Zen Practice
Body, Breath, and Mind
Edited by Taizan Maezumi and
Bernie Glassman
Foreword by Robert Aitken
208 pages, ISBN 0-86171-315-X, $14.95

This updated landmark volume makes available for the first time in decades the teachings that were formative to a whole
generation of American Zen teachers and
students. Conceived as the essential Zen
primer, *OZP* addresses every aspect of prac-
tice: beginning practice, chanting, *sesshin*, *shikantaza*, working with Mu, the
nature of koans, and more.

The contributors to *On Zen Practice* are regarded as some of modern
Zen's foremost teachers, and are largely responsible for Zen's steady
growth in America. This newly refined volume is an unmatched teaching and reference tool for today's Zen practitioner.

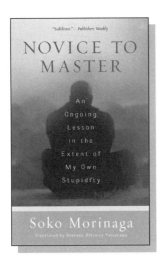

Novice to Master
An Ongoing Lesson
in the Extent of My Own Stupidity
Soko Morinaga
Translated by Belenda Attaway Yamakawa
160 pages, ISBN 0-86171-393-1, $11.95

"Anyone who reads this charming memoir
can only wish they had the opportunity to
meet this modest yet wise man. It provides
rich insight into the protocol of training for
the life of a Zen abbot, but is, in many ways,
universal—a headstrong young man is forced
to conform to a wiser force and shed his arro-
gance to achieve a higher state of knowledge and serenity. *Novice to Master* serves up the most subtle form of enlightenment."—*New York Resident*

"A spiritual autobiography by an accomplished master of Zen, and also
a compelling story of coming of age in post-war Japan. One can't help but
be drawn to the genuine tone of Morinaga's voice and his sense of
humor."—*Shambhala Sun*

—